MW01177878

Lancia integrale

The Complete Story

Other titles in the Crowood AutoClassic Series

AC Cobra	Brian Laban
Alfa Romeo Spider	John Tipler
Alfa Romeo Sports Coupés	Graham Robson
Aston Martin DB4, DB5 and DB6	Jonathan Wood
Aston Martin and Lagonda V-Engined Cars	David G Styles
Audi quattro	Laurence Meredith
Audi TT	James Ruppert
Austin-Healey 100 & 3000 Series	Graham Robson
BMW 3 Series	James Taylor
BMW 5 Series	James Taylor
BMW 7 Series	Graham Robson
BMW M-Series	Alan Henry
BMW: The Classic Cars of the 1960s and 70s	Laurence Meredith
BMW Z Series	Mick Walker
Bubblecars and Microcars	Malcolm Bobbitt
Citroën 2CV	Matt White
Citroën DS	Jon Pressnell
Datsun Z Series	David G Styles
Ferrari Dino	Anthony Curtis
Ford RS Escorts	Graham Robson
Jaguar E-Type	Jonathan Wood
Jaguar Mk 1 and 2	James Taylor
Jaguar XJ Series	Graham Robson
Jaguar XJ-S	Graham Robson
Jaguar XK Series	Jeremy Boyce
Jowett Javelin and Jupiter	Edmund Nankivell and Geoff McAuley
Lamborghini Countach	Peter Dron
Lancia Sporting Coupés	Brian Long
Land Rover – Series One to Freelander	Graham Robson
Lotus and Caterham Seven: Racers for the Road	John Tipler
Lotus Elan	Mike Taylor
Lotus Elise	John Tipler
Lotus Esprit	Jeremy Walton
Mercedes-Benz Saloons: The Classic Models of the 1960s and 1970s	Laurence Meredith
MGA	David G Styles
MGB	Brian Laban
MG T-Series	Graham Robson
Mini	James Ruppert
Porsche 911	David Vivian
Porsche 924, 928, 944 and 968	David Vivian
Range Rover – The First Generation	James Taylor and Nick Dimbleby
Rolls-Royce Silver Cloud	Graham Robson
Rolls-Royce Silver Shadow	Graham Robson
Rover P5 & P5B	James Taylor
Rover SD1	Karen Pender
Saab 99 and 900	Lance Cole
Sunbeam Alpine and Tiger	Graham Robson
Triumph 2000 and 2.5PI	Graham Robson
Triumph Spitfire & GT6	James Taylor
Triumph TRs	Graham Robson
TVR	John Tipler
VW Beetle	Robert Davies
Volvo 1800	David G Styles

Lancia integrale

The Complete Story

Peter Collins and Paul Baker

The Crowood Press

First published in 2003 by
The Crowood Press Ltd
Ramsbury, Marlborough
Wiltshire SN8 2HR

www.crowood.com

British Library Cataloguing-in-Publication Data
A catalogue record for this book is available from the British Library.

ISBN 1 86126 543 3

Designed and typeset by Focus Publishing, 11a St Botolph's Road,
Sevenoaks, Kent TN13 3AJ

Printed and bound in Great Britain by The Bath Press

Contents

Foreword

It's a cliché, I know, but Italians really do have a passion about their motor-sport. As a teenager I began to discover this in the 1960s when Ford tried, successfully, to beat Ferrari at Le Mans. The combination of Enzo Ferrari's attitude in turning down the blue oval's purchase overtures and the air of romantic craziness that seemed to surround Italian racing cars both worked their charm and soon had me trapped in a world of fascination and, quite frequently, frustration over Italian cars.

That was then, this is now, but this particular world has never ceased to amuse, delight and irritate to varying degrees, which is why I was finally persuaded to hammer away at my keyboard for considerably longer than my normal periodical efforts.

It is often small things that make you realise why you took certain turnings in life and this book involved many. Two stand out.

Entering a restaurant one evening in Turin with Giorgio Pianta, before we had even managed to sit down, there were cries of 'Eh, Pianta, buona'sera!' from a nearby table. After a brief but warm and animated discussion, Giorgio explained that this was an ex Abarth colleague. Perhaps nothing unusual in that, but it happens frequently. There is still a personal pride and passion behind all the men and women involved in this story that I never experience in other countries.

The second was being with Ing. Sergio Limone at the Automotoretro show, also in Turin, and seeing his eyes light up at the sight of an obscure Lancia Appia Monterosa. Sergio is one of the most accomplished competition car engineers in the world, but he has a heart, so I make no excuses pointing out that the Integrale was born out of a passion for extraordinary engineering and heritage.

Without the help of these two I would still be floundering but the same goes for Paul Baker who persuaded me to write this book and then put a huge amount of effort and time into making sure my task was made as easy as possible.

For the first time it is possible to see the creation of the unique Agnelli cabriolet and I am indebted to Ing. Rodolfo Gaffino for allowing me to use them. Neither would it be possible to write any rallying story without the comprehensive reports that were, and still are, provided by Martin Holmes.

The enthusiasm and help of Louisa Bracco and Enrico Masala in Turin was a constant inspiration. I only hope I have done a good enough job to repay their kindness and help. Perhaps the best thing I can say here is 'Viva Lancia!'.

I cannot finish without thanking Jacqui and my daughter Victoria without whom I would be missing some vital text and pictures. There were many others, John Whalley for instance, whose time I wasted on many occasions.

Many thanks to you all, to those I've mentioned and those I haven't, I hope you enjoy the result.

The last Evoluzione cars, built in the Maggiora factory at Chivasso, have probably done more to publicise the integrale than any of the other models.

www.tnlmotorsport.co.uk
A20 HFL

Preface

When I was asked to write a preface for this new book on the life of the Lancia Delta that started off being a four-wheel drive and grew to be an 'Integrale' my feelings changed immediately and I found myself back in the enthusiasm of that period.

In 1986 the FISA decided, after the dramatic accident to Toivonen to drastically change the technical regulations for rallies starting from 1987. The cars became Group A with a considerable reduction in power compared to Group B. The competitions department of Fiat, still referred to by most as Abarth, asked Fiat to build 5000 Delta berlinas with integral traction and turbocharged engine for homologation. This became known as the HF4WD.

The trials began in Autumn 1986 at the Fiat track La Mandria. Compared to the Delta S4 my first impression was that it was like 'going out for a drive'! It was 25 seconds a lap slower.

We started the season with a victory at Monte Carlo and I forgot all about my initial lack of enthusiasm and we all bounced back up.

In 1986 Fiat had bought Alfa Romeo and I was moved to their competitions department in mid 1987, but I was back with the Delta in 1991 as I was asked to oversee all of Fiat Autos sporting section. I was very pleased to go back to rallying as the Delta had now become very strong with many wins. I concluded the season achieving the fifth win in the World Championship.In December Fiat decided to retire the official rally team, just when we had introduced the Delta of a wider dimension which we nicknamed the 'Deltona'. Our main sponsor Martini decided to continue and we won an incredible unbeatable sixth consecutive World Championship.

This was a fantastic period and I finish with all best wishes for the success of this book.

Giorgio Pianta

A modified 16v at play. Integrales were able to display their extraordinary abilities to even greater advantage on loose surfaces than on tarmac.

J651 WPY

1 Integrale Bloodlines

It was all very straightforward really, explained Ing. Sergio Limone, as he traced out the Lancia integrale family tree. Four stages from start to finish and that was it. He presented them this way:

Group B → HF4WD → integrale → 16V → evoluzione → ??

It was highly simplistic but displayed the evolution of the species perfectly – except that there was more, much more, to it than that...

Lancia and the Spirit of Innovation

Many historically significant cars are the result of Zeitgeist – they embody the spirit of their time. The all-wheel drive Deltas were definitively this but they should also be seen as one of the major steps in the evolutionary tale of Turin's most innovative and technically dynamic car company – Lancia.

The company's founder, Vincenzo Lancia, right from the start of the eponymous firm, established a determination to produce cars and trucks, not only of technical excellence, but also bristling with new concepts. These new concepts were not untried inventions but thoroughly tested engineering. This philosophy has held true throughout the near one hundred years that Lancia has been in existence.

But why should we go back so far into history when telling the story of a 1980s car? What possible contribution might it all make?

It is vitally important because a spirit of innovation has been the thread running throughout the life of Lancia the manufacturer. This spirit has clearly been carried forward through generations and was a dominant feature when the integrale concept was first tried and tested. It has a provenance, a clear historical lineage that makes it easier to understand the adoption of some, perhaps startling, solutions to problems as they arose. As it was in the 1920s, so it also was sixty and seventy years later. Okay, no one would deny that mistakes were made along the way but each successive innovation shone a light that illuminated the way forward.

Vincenzo Lancia, ideas man and inspiration behind talented engineers during his lifetime and after.

Vincenzo, like all good managers, was an ideas man. His ability to choose staff of the highest integrity and initiative stood him in good stead when it came to his other great quality: the art of delegation. He had the ideas; others devised the methodology and logistics to put them into practice. The innovations attributable to Lancia as a company before the Second World War were generally the result of the boss' inventiveness. Not only that, but he also had the ability to perceive problems and their possible answers before handing a project over to his talented engineers. He would then leave it for them to find sound engineering solutions.

Possibly apocryphal stories of Vincenzo's continual desire to ask why of situations, abound from the First World War period onwards. He had a summer house at Fobello in the foothills of the Alps north-west of Turin and would therefore have covered the 150km journey by car on many occasions. Italian roads had not developed very far, even by the end of the second decade of the twentieth century, and their surfaces left much to be desired. Severe potholes were numerous and consequently incidents were frequent. Cars of the period enjoyed front suspension by means of a rigid axle and cart springs for each wheel. On one occasion, Vincenzo was being driven by his chauffeur when a front wheel of the Theta they were travelling in hit a severe hole in the road. This was enough to wrench the steering wheel out of the driver's hands and break a spring. The frequency with which this sort of incident happened had started Vincenzo thinking that there must be a better way of suspending a car, in order to reduce the number of these time-consuming mishaps. What was basically needed was for the front wheels to be able to move vertically, but also independently, thus allowing the driver the chance of retaining more control in the event of difficulty.

Back at the factory, Battisto Falchetto was handed the problem and came up with several possibilities. Coincidentally, also on the back burner of his mind, Vincenzo had had to take a sea trip and, whilst watching the other ships, speculated to himself on how a hull could be adapted as the basis of the design of a car, where the main component would be a rigid passenger compartment and the ancillaries, such as engine and suspension, would be hung off this 'hull'.

Lambda

At a meeting in 1921, one of Falchetto's fourteen independent front-suspension proposals was selected for development and at the same time the ship's hull theory was put to the test. The resultant marriage of these ideas came together as Lancia's Lambda of 1922. After extensive prototype testing over Vincenzo's favourite roads to the north and west of Turin, some of which are still used by the factory today, the Lambda was announced to an astonished world as the first monocoque chassised and independently front-sprung production car. Not only that but it utilized the world's first V4 engine as well.

Built from 1923 until 1930, it evolved through eight stages of development and sold well, around 13,000 finding buyers.

Although Vincenzo had been a very successful racing driver in his youth, he had not encouraged motor-sporting activities within his own company. Even so, private owners were keen to take up the chance of driving Lambdas in competitive events and some remarkable performances were achieved. In 1928 Gismondi managed to reach second place on Italy's newly introduced flagship event, the Mille Miglia, before retiring close to the finish after a minor accident. Other top six placings were taken during this period and Casaro built a small number of shortened and lightened 'Corsa' Lambdas for racing.

The Lambda, then, was a vitally important car, both for Lancia and the global automotive indus-

The Lambda, pioneer of independent suspension and monocoque construction.

try, in that it kick-started the concept of the body not requiring the underpinnings of a heavy chassis. Perhaps, though, even Vincenzo was not entirely convinced, as his following models returned to the use of a separate chassis, perhaps because he was not sure that a Lambda style monocoque would work with a heavier car.

Augusta

This concern became academic with the introduction of the next innovatory Lancia design: the Augusta of 1933. This was a light four-seater saloon that took the principles of the Lambda a major step further. The Augusta was the first car in the world to utilize the body as a stress-bearing member. This was done in order to give the car maximum torsional rigidity for the lowest possible weight. In addition, for the first time a Lancia incorporated hydraulic brakes and was amongst the very first production cars to do so.

Innovation and inventiveness were once again Lancia watchwords. What the designers had created has since been adopted by every car manufacturer in the world and the concept is taken for granted. Whilst this innovation may not have seemed much of a big deal to the average consumer, it was incorporated four years later into the design of a car that was yet another innovative masterpiece to equal the headline-grabbing Lambda.

Aprilia

Enter the Aprilia. Sadly, Vincenzo was to die suddenly at only 56 years old before he could see it enter production, especially as there was a difference with this new car. Previously the use of the monocoque had been the main feature, but now Lancia's engineers wanted to move on and create further quantum leaps in the application of automotive technology. So, a replacement small Lancia was born in 1937 with aerodynamic bodywork that could seat five people and perform with considerable spirit. Independent rear suspension was utilized, as were inboard driveshaft-mounted rear brakes to reduce unsprung weight. The Aprilia thus took the stress-bearing body forward into another era. Despite being powered by an engine of only 1500cc, due to the aerodynamics, light weight and inherent good handling, the car was a lively performer and found homes with many motor-sport drivers, as well as the general public. After the war it resumed production and its advanced specification kept it selling well right up to 1950. A smaller version was also produced from 1939 called the Ardea that, from 1948, incorporated a five-speed gearbox to make the most of its 903cc engine.

Once the war was over, an initial indication of what was to come was provided by Carlo Abarth. He chose the Aprilia as the first Lancia for which his fledgling Turinese sporting company would offer a tuning kit. This consisted of a performance-improving twin-carburettor set-up, thus pre-dating a trend and relationship that was to flourish in the 1970s and later include the integrale.

Aurelia

The 1950s saw the arrival at Lancia of the legendary designer Vittorio Jano from Alfa Romeo, and immediately he became involved with the Aurelia. Another first for Lancia, this time the innovation of a V6 engine. The car was at first produced by the factory as a saloon, but soon Pininfarina designed the B20 version, a two-door coupé with sloping fastback, and this gave birth to the title GT to describe a sporting coupé. I will here only mention what was arguably Jano's masterpiece: the Lancia D50

Much appreciated as a road car by race and rally drivers in period the Aprilia set up new high standards of road-holding, performance and comfort.

Goodwood race paddock, an appropriate meeting place for Lancias which have impressed all who have driven them.

Grand Prix car of 1954, because although it bristled with innovation, it was purely a racing car and does not come within the parameters here of cars that could be used on the public road.

As the decade gave way to the 1960s, front-wheel drive was enthusiastically taken up and top quality engineering of great integrity continued as Lancia's trade mark, although the policy of engineering cars to a very high quality and then trying to sell them at a cost that made production an economic proposition, began to look decidedly precarious. So much so, in fact, that the cost of racing their technically advanced cars had precipitated a company sell-out to Carlo Pesenti in 1955. By 1969, Lancia was struggling again, this time being rescued by Fiat.

It became popular, even amongst Lancia owners, to deride Fiat's subsequent offerings as not worthy of Vincenzo's name and a clear indication that the standards maintained for so long had finally slipped. This was not the case, as other factors were allowed to taint public opinion. There is no question that the Lambda was, and is, one of the world's great cars, but the scope for quantum leaps in automotive development were inevitably becoming less likely. Every company needs to evolve and develop, and clear Lancia traits can be seen in the Beta series of cars, which were the first 'all Fiat' models to appear after the new owners had dabbled with updated Flavia 2000 sedans and coupés.

The fact is, the innovations just kept on coming. Third-generation Lancias introduced under the Fiat regime have been able to benefit from all the advantages of being part of a much larger group and with budgets that Vincenzo and Gianni could only have dreamed about. The coupé version of Lancia's small car, the Fulvia, enjoyed a very extensive competition history, which the Fiat group encouraged. Racing and rallying was undertaken, but it was the latter at which the car excelled. However, the development potential of the Fulvia was

The Aurelia was engineered to be driven hard on road and track by enthusiasts and competition drivers alike. It is not difficult to see where the integrale's genes came from.

rapidly running out of steam by 1970 and other ways had to be found of keeping Lancia, and thus the Fiat group, ahead of the opposition.

Stratos

The resources of Fiat made available possibilities that the old Lancia company could never have afforded to consider. The baton of innovation and inventiveness was picked up and kept running by Lancia's resourceful competitions manager, Cesare Fiorio. When it became clear that the Fulvia was running out of time, he went shopping for a car that would take the company's competition team into the future and make full use of the regulations at the same time. By coincidence, Bertone had presented a concept car at the 1970 Turin show that was an extremely aerodynamic mid-engined sports car. He called it the Stratos. Fiorio and his colleagues were quick to see the potential and the possibilities in the project, and so it was that Lancia innovation continued with the development of the car into a purpose-made rally winning machine. It was not that easy as there was no power unit in the Lancia range that would have been adequate for Fiorio's plans, so he had to look further afield, taking full advantage of the resources of the Fiat group.

The tentacles of Fiat influence by this time stretched as far as Maranello. By 1968 Ferrari was finding it increasingly difficult to find the necessary budget to continue its racing department at the level Enzo desired, so he looked to big brother Fiat for possible help. The outcome was that Turin took a financial stake in Ferrari and representation on the board. Collaboration had, in fact, already taken place as Ferrari had wanted to go Formula Two racing but the regulations required that whatever motor was used it had to be production based. This was way beyond the capabilities of Maranello, so a deal was agreed by which the unit in question, a 2418cc four overhead camshaft V6, would gain its 'production' credentials by being utilized in a Fiat car – the front-engined Dino spider and coupé. Ferrari themselves also used it in their own mid-engined Dino.

Fiorio found that the Dino V6 was exactly what his Stratos required. Thus, in 1972–73 this extraordinary device was let loose on the rally routes of the world and once again Lancia innovation brought home immeasurable success.

But, whilst the Stratos carried all before it, gaining win after win, Lancia was finding life more and more difficult when it came to shifting cars out of their showrooms. It has always

The Stratos was an inspirational idea from Cesare Fiorio based on a Bertone design. In 1986 he was responsible for instigating the HF4WD rally project.

been argued by those who took part that competition success led to an increase in company interest by the general public and that, in turn, was converted into increased passenger car sales figures. This was not happening with Lancia as the mid-1970s approached, and it became clear that something new and innovative was required in those showrooms to entice the public to spend their money again. In fact, it was becoming crucial.

The Birth of the Delta

The Lancia Delta was born out of a perceived necessity by the company's management – and Fiat's – for a car that would not only restate Lancia's image of engineering innovation and integrity, for it had been severely tarnished in some areas of the world's markets, but also kick-start their entry into what was then an emerging new market, that of the two-box, or two-volume, hatchback. The Delta was therefore seen as being the car that would turnaround Lancia's fortunes.

They had seen how the Golf had revived Volkswagen's flagging position after that company had relied for too long on sales of the Beetle earlier in the 1970s and had decided to go for a similar mid-sized two-box style of car. They had also made the decision to call in the darlings of Turinese styling, Giorgetto Giugiaro and Italdesign, to do the design work. After all, their work with the Golf was a pretty good CV.

Giugiaro had decided that the space and quality of the interior of the Golf, as it finally went into production, fell short of what he had really considered it should have been, so he made the decision to major on those two features in the development of the design of Lancia's new car. In particular, he had very clear views on what should be the distance from the pedals to the back of the rear seat.

The initial intention was that the Delta would be a two-box four-door with an opening for a boot below the rear-window, but pressure from Lancia's valuable French market and dealerships caused management in Turin to insist that in fact the car should be a hatchback. Giugiaro was not happy about this, as the strengthening required in the body shell to retain its rigidity would not only cause an increase in weight with consequent higher fuel consumption, but would also use up valuable passenger space in the rear of the car.

Whilst the two-box concept had been popularly initiated by Giugiaro, when asked at the Delta's launch whether the design of the Golf had seriously influenced that of the new Lancia, he replied that no, he did not think so and

Giorgetto Giugiaro was the first to come up with colour-coded bumpers and tried them on the Delta with success. This is an HF Turbo.

Lancia management were insistent that the Delta had more boot space than originally envisaged by Giugiaro. To disguise the extra length involved he included the louvres in the bodysides behind the rear doors. Behind is the Delta's blood brother, a Ritmo.

that if there were any similarities with any other of his designs then he felt that the 1973 Asso di Picche (Ace of Clubs) concept car, completed for Audi Karman, probably contained more suggestions of direction especially in 'its dihedrals and movement of side'.

The Delta was the first production car to appear with bumpers as an integral part of extended bodywork painted the same colour as the rest of the car. Almost every manufacturer in the world subsequently adopted this style, colour-coding as it became known. We are so used to seeing this styling ploy introduced on almost every new model in the world that it is remarkable to recall that Giugiaro took some time to ensure that the technology was actually available then to achieve his desired effect.

In addition to his boot proposal, other aspects of his Delta design did not come in for Lancia's wholehearted approval: they also wanted the baggage area to be increased. Giugiaro had originally intended that the car would only have a bootlid under the rear window, a small luggage area and a back seat that, rather in the style of his later Panda, could be adjusted to slide forwards and backwards depending on the number of passengers and quantity of luggage being carried. So, to him, the small boot was not seen as a problem. As early as 1975, this arrangement was seen by Lancia as too expensive to implement, and they also requested that an extra 80mm of overhang be incorporated into the rear to enlarge the boot area. This was definitely not received well by Giugiaro as already, in profile, the design had a clear mass of sheet metal behind the rear door and this extra 80mm would do the car's proportions no favours at all. The solution? Note the two louvres immediately behind the rear doors at the leading edge of this mass; they are there cleverly disguising the additional inserted length and stayed right through to the last of the line Evolution 2 integrales of 1993–94. Another Lancia insistence was the reduction in height of the tail end edge of the roofline by 20mm to suggest a more aerodynamic shape. This was also contrary to Giugiaro's principles of interior space and comfort, and did not meet with his approval, even if he had to acquiesce to the demand. Finally, Lancia decided that the actual tailgate should be of a more sturdy and robust construction than the

The Delta had to make use of the floor pan of the Fiat Ritmo, although Giugiaro was never allowed to see that car during the Delta's design process.

Giorgetto Giugiaro

Without the Delta there would have been no integrale, and without Giugiaro there would not have been the Delta.

Co-founder with Aldo Mantovani of Ital Styling in 1967, the company later became the world-famous Italian styling house, Italdesign. Mantovani's expertise was in being able to productionize Giugiaro's ideas and concepts, whilst Giugiaro has been responsible for many ground-breaking automotive styling ideas effectively giving birth to the people-carrier concept with his Lancia Megagamma, and starting the hatchback, two-volume trend, with the Volkswagen Golf. Perhaps his most enduring legacy is the 'vertical' car, which the public took to their hearts in the shape of the Fiat Uno.

Born in 1938 in Garessio near Cuneo south of Turin, he sometimes helped his father with restoring and painting frescoes, especially in churches. His mother was a seamstress working from home. So Giorgetto could not escape the vein of artistry that ran through his family. 'I often wonder if I would have been happier as a painter than a designer,' he once mused.

In the early 1950s he attended art college during the day in Turin and studied technical drawing in the evening. His professor happened to be the uncle of Dante Giacosa, genius designer of many fifties and sixties Fiats, so it was with a certain amount of inevitability that Giorgetto was found his first job in the special projects styling department at Fiat. This was not an ideal situation for a young man full of new energy and ideas. 1950s Fiat was not a company known for its flair; its conservatism led to Giugiaro maturing over the four years he was there but also experiencing dissatisfaction in not being able to see any of his ideas followed through.

He left Fiat in late 1959 for Bertone but soon after the Geneva Show in 1960 he was called up for National Service. Bertone's influence enabled him to be based close to Turin and continue his work, whilst serving his time with the army. His first serious styling success was the Alfa Giulia GT that he completed in his 'barracks'. He stayed at Bertone until 1965 when he was offered a managerial post at Ghia but left there when De Tomaso bought the company and the two did not see eye to eye.

He created ItalDesign in 1968 and soon after took on the Alfasud project. This was later followed by the first VW Golf and Fiat's Panda and Uno. In between there were many concept cars for car companies world-wide, as well as industrial design work for Nikon cameras and Fiat trains, the latter continuing into the late 1990s.

Despite the huge success of these flagship projects, it was the Lancia Delta that brought him his first 'Car of the Year' in 1980. Little did anyone suspect what would become of this boxy new car.

The end result of the Delta project won Giugiaro his first Car of the Year.

almost delicate style of Giugiaro's. They also required that it should extend down to the bumper, so the rear light clusters had to be redesigned vertically instead of horizontally, which Giugiaro had considered a more harmonious method of integrating them with the rest of the body's shape.

From the outset of the Delta project, the Fiat group's passenger car policy had dictated that in the future all their cars, whatever their final badge, would all be based upon a small number of common platforms. The Delta was thus to share the mid-sized base with the Fiat Ritmo and, although Giugiaro knew this and it obviously had a strong guiding parameter on his design of the Delta, he was never allowed to see the final shape of the Ritmo until it was announced to the public. With hindsight, the Ritmo's lines could generously be described as innovative but the model succumbed to a total facelift at the first opportunity. Giugiaro's Delta was clearly a well thought out Italdesign concept from the start and, other than minor cosmetic detail changes, never suffered a major facelift throughout its long production life.

Announced to the public at the Frankfurt Show in 1979, the Delta was well received and gained the accolade of Car of the Year in 1980.

Delta Turbo 4×4

The first indication to the public that there might be extraordinary development potential in the seemingly innocuous looking car came at the 1982 Turin Show. The press had already had a preview earlier in the year at the La Mandria test track and had been agreeably surprised by the car.

With considerable input from Italdesign, a Delta had been built incorporating four-wheel drive. Ing. Marascotti, now at N Technology but then with Fiat, remembers well that '...two cars were built by Italdesign. One was a concept [see Chapter 8] called the Orca and the other was what looked like an ordinary Delta but which had four-wheel drive. We worked hard at the Fiat Experimental Department to finalize the Delta and make it ready for its press presentation at La Mandria.'

The car certainly looked normal but had its title emblazoned along its flanks, making it clear that it was what was underneath that was so significant.

Lift the bonnet and there was a 1585cc twin-cam motor, as could have been found in Fiat's 132 or Lancia Beta. Mounted transversely as in a normal Delta, its power output was boosted by the addition of a Garrett turbo-charger, so that its output was 130bhp at 5,600rpm, with maximum torque at 3,700rpm; it utilized a five-speed gearbox with slightly altered final-drive gearing. Macpherson struts suspended the car at both ends with anti-roll bars. Overall weight of the added equipment meant an increase from the standard car's average 975kg to 1,100kg.

Italdesign collaborated with Lancia on the Delta Turbo 4×4 in 1982 but it was three years before the next all-wheel drive car – the S4 – was announced.

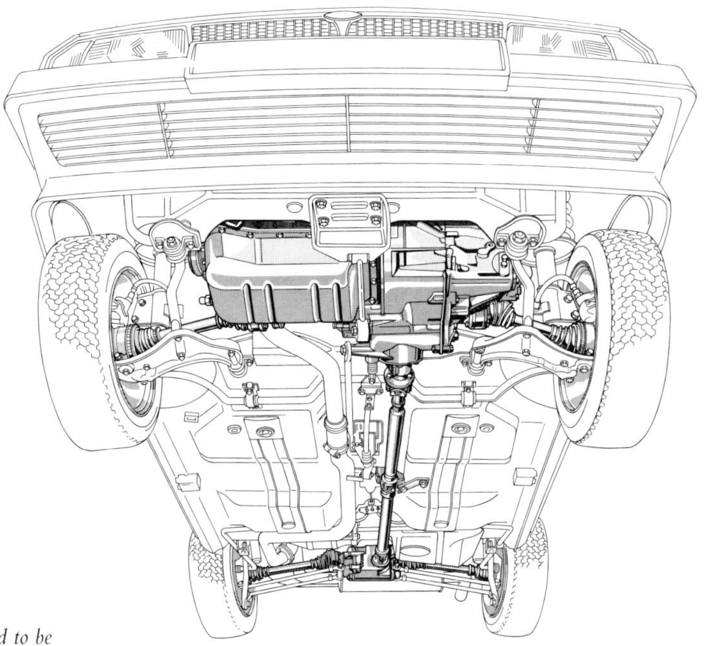

A transmission tunnel had to be fitted to the car for the special system's additional propshaft.

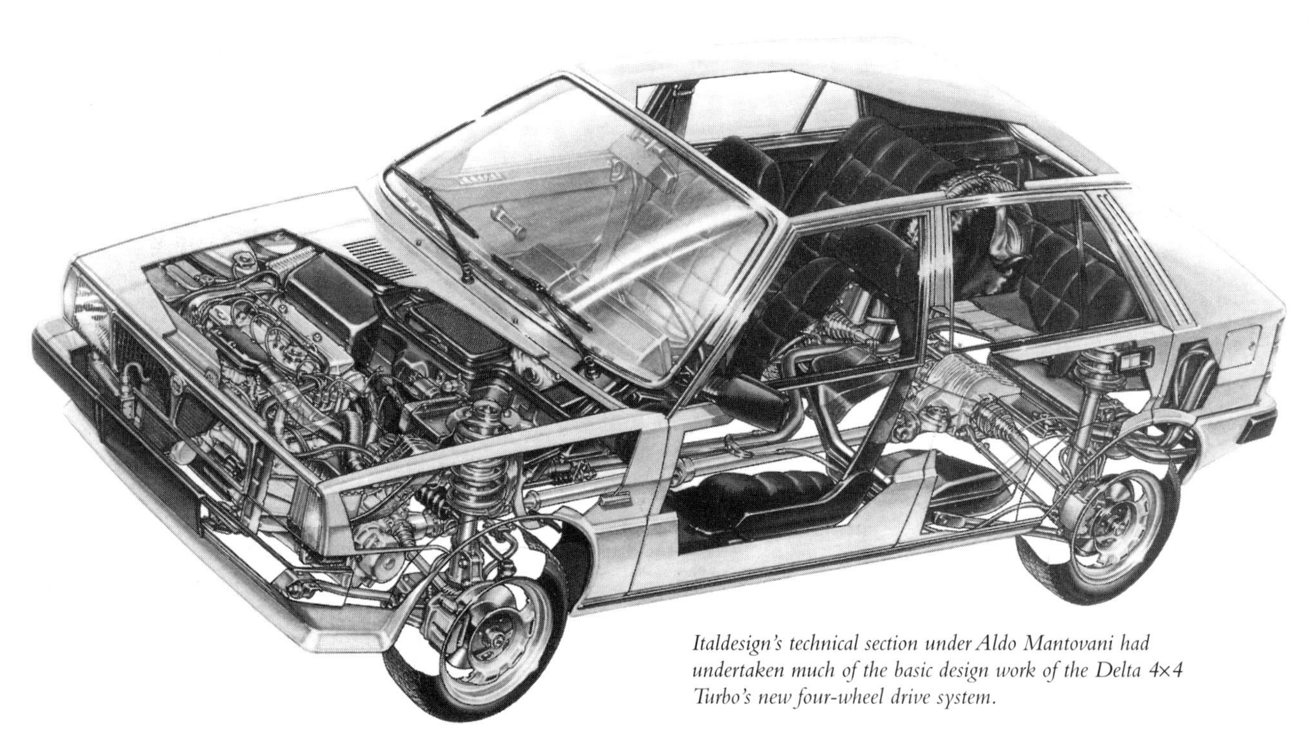

Italdesign's technical section under Aldo Mantovani had undertaken much of the basic design work of the Delta 4×4 Turbo's new four-wheel drive system.

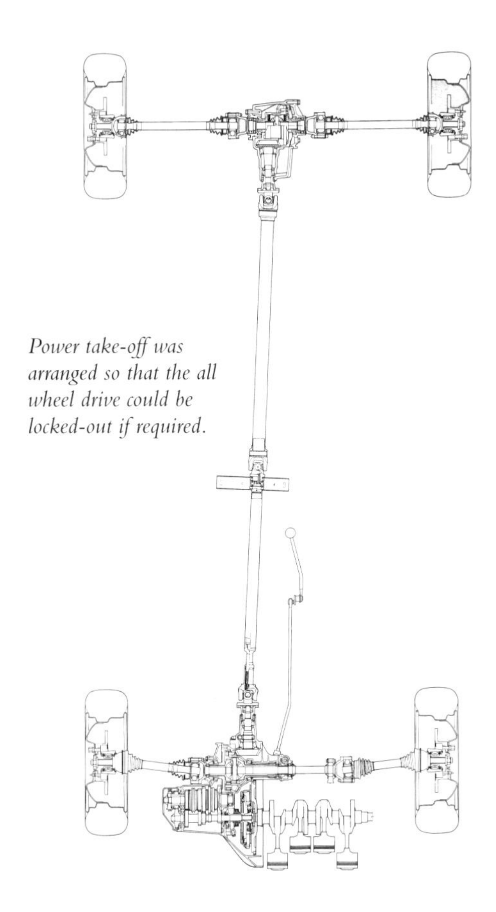

Power take-off was arranged so that the all wheel drive could be locked-out if required.

To accommodate the four-wheel drive, the shell was altered with the addition of a transmission tunnel and the exhaust system had to be re-routed, as well as a new fuel tank fitted.

Press reports of the day state that the car drove well with some under-steer, a preview of a 4WD bugbear that was to rear its head much later in the integrale's life. A third differential was built into the car's gearbox so that the system could be locked out if necessary. Italdesign had had much experience with 4×4 cars, their Mechanical Design Department having developed the Panda 4×4 two years previously.

To the outside world, the project seemed to have no lasting interest within the Fiat empire; but quite the opposite was, in fact, the case. It was just the start.

To complete the story of the integrale's philosophy and background, we must look at its other major bloodline – motor sport.

The Competition Genes

The innovative, technically advanced and highly successful Lancia Stratos had given way to Fiat's 131 Abarth as the group's World Rally weapon of choice; the latter had achieved champion status in 1980 in the hands of Walter Rohrl, but there was no room for complacency. With unsuitable tyres, Markku Alen's run on the opening event of the 1981 season had been a struggle to even approach being competitive. 'I can only wait for the new car,' he said and Fiat certainly needed one. Markku was a Fiat-group stalwart, his long connection with them driving competition cars from all the main constituent companies – Fiat, Lancia and Alfa Romeo – on special stages and race tracks means that, other than the Abarth team themselves, he was the human bloodline connection between the early days of the 131 right through to the development period of the integrale evolution. He worked with them all.

Markku Alen

The name of the Finn, Markku Alen, will feature strongly in the story of the total traction Deltas.

A stalwart of the Fiat group competitions department, he won the Finnish rally championship in 1969 and moved to Fiat in 1974. He was then loyal to the Turinese teams until 1990.

He drove Lancia Stratos and Fiat 131 Abarths before becoming an important part of Martini Racing with Lancia 037s, Lancia Delta S4s, Lancia Delta HF4WDs and finally integrales. He excelled in them all, gaining countless wins and the World Drivers' title in 1978, but, rather like Stirling Moss, is famous for never being quite in a position to win the World Rally Championship. This was probably as much due to his schedule of events as anything else.

The value of his input to the integrale story is far greater than his results would suggest.

Le otto Lancia mondiali.

Lancia Fulvia HF Campione del Mondo Rally 1972.

Lancia Stratos Campione del Mondo Rally 1974.

Lancia Stratos Campione del Mondo Rally 1975.

Lancia Stratos Campione del Mondo Rally 1976.

Lancia Rally 037 Campione del Mondo Rally 1983.

Lancia Delta HF 4WD Campione del Mondo Rally 1987.

Lancia Delta HF integrale Campione del Mondo Rally 1988.

Lancia Delta HF integrale Campione del Mondo Rally 1989.

The competition Delta had a formidable results heritage to contend with.

Quattro

For the 131 though, the writing was on the wall and Audi had written the script. The 1981 Monte Carlo event was the debut for their quattro, a car that was destined to have an everlasting effect on World Championship rallying.

The basis of the car was created by the adoption of four-wheel drive and a turbo-charged engine. This was the first serious effort at using this type of technology in world rallying. Previous years had seen alternative on/off road vehicles entered on an occasional basis in the rougher rallies, such as the Safari and Ivory Coast, but until Audi tried it, no one had put any serious development behind four-wheel drive for road or rally use.

The quattro was sensational right from the start, winning on only its second rally, the 1981 Swedish, and powering away from the opposition to win World Championships.

For Markku Alen in Monte Carlo, the future must have looked bleak, although Fiat competitions management and engineers did not necessarily have a feeling that they desperately needed to go out and develop a four-wheel drive car of their own. At that Monte Carlo rally they were quoted as saying that they were happy as they were, with more than one possible solution up their corporate sleeves. The Fiat competitions department (Abarth) on Corso Marche in Turin was effectively running the 131 Abarth as a holding situation in some rallies. Despite this, Markku took a win in Portugal and a second on the 1000 Lakes.

On the outside, from the public point of view, the team seemed to be wasting its time. There was plenty going on backstage, however, as a new rally weapon was being developed. It would have surprised many if they knew that it had already run over a month before that 1981 Monte Carlo rally.

The design was a synthesis of the Stratos and the 131 Abarth, rather like a rear-engined 131. The advantages of the mid-engined car were understood but they did not want to employ complex machinery, such as the Ferrari V6, as that would merely have created a 'Mk 2 Stratos'.

Besides, Lancia already had a successful mid-engined competition car up and running in the form of the Beta Montecarlo turbo.

Beta Montecarlo Turbo

After an analysis was made of the Audi quattro, team manager Cesare Fiorio decided 'not to copy Audi because the type of four-wheel drive it utilized was, essentially, that of an off-road vehicle and it was felt that at the rate of development and evolution looking likely to take place, the car would actually be obsolete within a relatively short amount of time'.

So, the die was cast, the new car was to have rear-wheel drive only, be mid-engined and, for reasons of low frontal area and therefore aerodynamic efficiency, it would be based on the existing Beta Montecarlo central section. The 131 carry over was to utilize the Lampredi designed twin-cam in 2-litre form but with the application of a supercharger.

Turbo-charger technology was available within the Fiat group via those racing Beta Montecarlos with their 1.4 and 1.8 turbo Lampredi twin cams and from Ferrari whose F1 cars were now using forced induction, but it was decided not to employ it. Lancia could also see a useful spin-off in terms of road-car application and so various models such, as the Beta and Trevi, included Volumex models in their range. This latter was the model name given to Fiat-group road cars that utilized superchargers. These also gave the rally car engine legality.

Lancia 037

The Abarth type number of the new car was 037 and supercharging its engine instead of turbo-charging it was considered vital to

Lancia gained much turbo-charging experience from its racing Beta Montecarlo Turbos. Here is Hans Heyer at the Nürburgring in July 1981.

maintain torque at all times. The key to the success of the compact new car was manoeuvrability, coupled to instant access to power, something which Audi always found difficult to achieve throughout the competition life of the quattro.

The car proved to be right for the times and it became the favourite rally machine for Markku Alen, winning the World Rally Championship in 1983. In order to comply with the regulations, which were the then new Group B rules, 200 road versions of any car used in World Championship rallying had to be built in order to allow it to be eligible.

This point is crucially relevant to the integrale. In the future, from the introduction of the 037 onwards, the Fiat/Lancia competitions department would have to develop, alongside its World Championship rally contenders, a stradale or road-going version to satisfy the FIA – the rule-makers. They would also have to ensure that the required number of these stradale versions had been built prior to the competition car taking part in its first event. Thus we can begin to see the whole reason for the eventual existence of all the integrale road cars, as the competitions department, still situated in the ex-Abarth factory on Corso Marche, had to produce new or evolution models of car every year to keep ahead of the opposition. The stage was set and the key players were assembled for a further act in which, through both tragedy and coincidence, the story leads ever closer to the conception of the integrale.

The pace of development in world rallying was, with the introduction of Group B, beginning to climb as steeply as that in Formula One.

The 037 provided necessary experience in supercharging as well as being a world champion along the way to the next step – the S4

Emphasizing the 'family' of competition Lancias, this group is headed up by a factory 037.

Effectively the rules allowed virtually anything so long as the requisite numbers of stradales were built. The 037 was heading for obsolescence almost as soon as it hit the rally scene. The engineers at Abarth realized this and, whilst developing it to its ultimate potential within the specifications that they had originally set down, they also started work on the car and technology that would replace it. Whilst the supercharger endowed the 037s engine with all the flexibility and immediacy that was asked of it, ultimately, continued development would lead to increasing engine temperatures and the absorption of power rather than production. The car had delighted drivers in the manner of its power delivery, so the engineers were reluctant to lose this advantage, but, the supercharger, as the revs rise, gradually becomes less and less effective; so, to start producing horsepower figures to equal those of the Audi (about 450bhp), manager Claudio Lombardi and his team began to consider the possibilities of the application of a turbo, of which they had some previous knowledge, whilst retaining a supercharger. The idea of this is that the supercharger provided the low down torque and seamless delivery, whilst the turbocharger took over for sheer high rev power. A test engine, to the maximum size allowed in the forthcoming rules (1750cc) was built and satisfied the engineers that the theory would work.

Lancia Delta S4

By the middle of the 037s championship year, 1983, plans were laid for the 038 and the first engine was running on the test-bench by Jan-

Combining four-wheel drive, turbo-charging and supercharging, the Delta S4 was an awesome contender in the ill-fated Group B rally series, as well as contributing a lot of useful data to the 4WD Delta project.

The stradale S4 was Lancia's second experience of having to build a road-car version of their current competition rally car, in order to satisfy FISA and ensure homologation acceptance.

uary 1984. Not based on any production engine in Fiat's then-current range, at 1750cc, this was the first purpose-built engine to be built by them for rallying.

Lancia's indomitable spirit of innovation had flourished once again. Not only did the 038, or Lancia Delta S4 as it was to be announced to the public, utilize this unique style of new engine but also, the car incorporated four-wheel drive for the first time. This consisted of a Ferguson viscous coupling, taking the power from the gearbox with self-locking differentials at both front and rear.

So now, in two areas, Lancia had embraced new technologies and concepts that would be relevant to the later integrale. They had adopted both turbo-chargers and four-wheel drive. They also had to build a stradale version of the car to comply with the regulations and this, like the 037, had to built as a minimum run of 200 cars.

Whilst Abarth had some experience of turbo-charging, they had had little in the field of four-wheel drive before the 038 and they had had a lot to learn. With this in mind, they had started work on the project with over two years to develop and finalize the specification

Abarth

Abarth was created in 1949 as the eponymous business owned by Austrian born Carl Abarth. He moved to Italy and soon after the war started to produce tune-up kits and accessories for some of the more popular Italian cars, such as Fiat and Lancia saloons.

He also started to construct a very few complete cars under his own name, and in all of this he was reasonably successful; but his business really started to accelerate when, in 1955, Fiat introduced their new small car, the 600.

Abarth based ever more powerful and flamboyant new versions of road and race cars on the little 600, eventually winning European championships, and many races and hill climbs throughout the world. He diversified into sports cars, still Fiat-based, and finally moved into sports prototype racing. As Abarth grew, Carlo moved the company into spacious premises in Corso Marche, Turin. By the end of the 1960s, although the cars were still successful, the business was clearly beginning to decline with the result that, in 1971 it was taken over by Fiat.

The car giant put an immediate ban on Abarth continuing in racing, but such was the good reputation of the name that it was applied to the future competitions department of Fiat and also used on their high-performance models.

Still based at Corso Marche, competition cars continued to be prepared there and included Lancia Stratos, Fiat 131 Abarth, Lancia 037 and Delta S4, and finally the HF4WD and integrales. Closure of the premises took place in 1992–93 and there was a move to Chivasso. There was also a change of name to Fiat Auto Corse and most recently, to N Technology, which is a triumvirate: 40 per cent owned by Nordauto, 30 per cent by Andrea de Adamich and 30 per cent by Fiat.

Ironically, from the early 1960s, Abarth had applied numbers starting at 001 to each of their new projects and these are still in use today, the list now reaching into the 070s. This explains the Lancia 037. The Lancia Delta S4 was 038, whilst the Delta's final evolution was 050.

The importance of the work, both pre- and post-Carlo Abarth ownership, that came out of the company cannot be over-stressed in relation to its impact within the Fiat Group and on world motor sport in general.

Claudio Lombardi, the Abarth general manager who made sure the all-wheel drive Delta worked and worked well.

of the car.

Four-wheel drive experience was not, however, totally lacking as, before the Delta 4×4 Turbo, test driver and manager Giorgio Pianta had masterminded the construction of a device called the Bimotore, based on the Lancia Trevi saloon. Displaying levels of technical innovation that would have raised even Vincenzo's eyebrows, Giorgio and his brother, Alberto, then in charge of Lancia's Chivasso plant, where their then-current road cars were built, arranged for a Trevi to be converted into a car that had all four wheels driven. As the Bimotore name suggests, this utilized two Lampredi twin-cam units of 1995cc, with both units supercharged, and all four wheels were powered with one engine at each end of the car.

Giorgio told me that he was very pleased with the car and '…Fiorio asked to borrow it after it was shown at San Remo. He took it with him to the mountains when he went skiing. When he returned it he could not believe how good it was saying this car is fantastic! But that was in the snow and anyway the fuel consumption was only three to four kilometres per litre!'

Back in the real world, by 1984–85, despite being out-classed and out-performed by the opposition, the 037s struggled on, sometimes producing good results; but in Turin, the emphasis was on superchargers, turbo-chargers and, above all four-wheel drive.

The 037s bowed out at San Remo in 1985 taking third, fourth, fifth and sixth places overall, but the next round, the RAC Rally, was to be the debut for the Delta S4. Actually the car had already appeared for testing purposes on the French Mille Pistes Rally and on the Algarve Rally in Portugal, but the 1985 RAC was to be its World Rally baptism.

The UK was experiencing a period of clear, still and bitterly cold weather when the RAC started, and it stayed that way for the duration of the event. Some stages were so icy they had to be cancelled; on others, cars slid off in increasing numbers. Lancia had come prepared and their service vans were always in the right places at the right time keeping their two S4s reliably on the move. By mid-rally the two cars had moved into the top two positions, continuing to slip and slide their way around England and Scotland, and finishing first–second in the order Toivonen–Alen.

A win at the first attempt for Lancia's new four- wheel drive car was beyond everyone's dreams, so to back it up with another at the following Monte Carlo Rally, the first event of 1986, seemed too good to be true.

Who were the opposition that Lancia was up against? Causing them by far the most serious problems was Peugeot with their 205 turbo 16, followed closely by Audi and their short wheelbase quattro S1. Occasional speed was shown by the Austin/Rover team with their 6R4 Metro and by Ford with their RS200, but neither of these was competitive enough to cause any worries. It is important to note that these manufacturers constituted the committed World Championship contenders. None of these cars had a future as road-going passenger vehicles in their parent companies plans; they existed purely for their own sakes. This was a key factor behind the initial success and development of the integrale family.

One area of innovation that never saw active service was the suggestion of using a CVT gearbox in the new car, but nothing came of it. The idea was that a constantly variable transmission would be able to deliver the immense power from the S4s engine to its wheels in an easier, more linear, fashion. Giorgio Pianta was very friendly with Frank Williams, who invited him to Silverstone where the Didcot Grand Prix team were experimenting with a CVT transmission on one of their Formula One cars. 'It was one second a lap quicker than the conventional car, the CVT gave incredible acceleration,' said Giorgio.

The S4 was not an easy car to handle, proving to be quite vicious approaching the limits of adhesion. Cesare Fiorio reckoned that none of his drivers ever seriously explored the car's outer envelope of performance. Add to these characteristics a prodigious amount of power, some 480–500bhp being mentioned as feasible, and even the idea of driving one flat out on a rally stage was a highly daunting prospect. Fiorio was also later to make the comment that 'at present the rules give the drivers more than they can cope with'. There was, perhaps, an air of inevitability that this gloriously indulgent and highly extravagant branch of motor sport should all come to an end but no one foresaw the escalation of tragic circumstances that would lead to its final termination.

At the Portugal Rally in March, the behaviour of the spectators, traditionally of a low standard, finally became inexcusable. So spectacular were the Group B cars that they attracted casual watchers in ever-increasing numbers. Problems in Portugal had been experienced in previous years but, in 1986, their total lack of concern for personal safety, or that of the cars and crews involved, became of epidemic proportions. Driving these Group B cars was difficult enough but rounding a blind corner or jumping over a brow, at the sort of speeds of which these latest cars were capable, and finding suicidal spectators standing in the road to get a better view or picture, was just too much.

After a car lost control, due to the proximity of the crowds, and crashed causing deaths, the leading drivers soon grouped together and refused to continue. Although most sympathized, some fingers were also beginning to point at the speeds being achieved by the cars. The rally continued for the remainder of competitors but the leading teams had withdrawn their cars and returned to their factories to ready themselves for the next round; the Tour de Corse.

Every rally enthusiast and motor sport commentator's eyes were focused on the event. Would there be a repetition of crowd trouble? Would Peugeot carry off a win on home ground? Would Lancia's incredibly quick driver, Henri Toivonen, extend his points position in the World Championship to take the lead?

Manager Giorgio Pianta recently gave an insight into how much, with the introduction of the Group B generation of cars, overall rally speeds had risen over the years: 'I had a good relationship with the authorities on Corsica and each year before the event we would arrange for the same 3km of road in the mountains to be closed for us for a while so that we could undertake final testing. In 1980 with the Fiat 131 Abarth, our fastest average speed over this piece of road was 72km/h. In 1983 we came with the Lancia 037 and this figure rose to 85km/h. For 1986 we had the Delta S4 and guess what the speed had gone up to – it was 120km/h – incredible!'

With every sign that Henri intended to stamp his mark on the event, he drove his Delta S4 with blinding speed over the narrow twisting roads of Corsica, easily establishing an early lead, but the worst possible happened. At high speed Henri rounded a corner and, from the lack of tyre marks to be seen on the road later, the S4 simply left the road at a point where there was an unprotected vertical drop to some trees. Early arrivals on the scene said that it looked as if there had been a light aircraft crash. There was no chance of survival for either Henri or Sergio Cresto his co-driver.

Jean-Marie Balestre, president of the governing body FISA, reacted with almost knee-jerk spontaneity. It was almost as if he was waiting for the chance to pass sentence. He had decided that the Group B rules would continue only to the end of that 1986 season. They would then cease to exist and be replaced. The cars involved would become obsolete in World Championship rallying and their place would be taken by acceptable makes from the Group A category, which meant that they would have to be to effectively modified showroom specifications.

The rest of the 1986 season became irrelevant, just a championship that had to be played out. Whilst Lancia may have been going through the motions on the special stages of the world, back at home in Turin the final step was taken that was to link all that had gone before to the integrale that was in Lancia's competition future. Why? Because Balestre's decision, now ratified by the FISA, was extremely serendipitous for the Turinese company.

Lancia's HF4WD seemed an innocuous-looking model from the outside when it first appeared.

Following the immediate post-Toivonen accident period, the FISA and many involved and not-so-involved parties, were tripping over themselves issuing statements on rallying's past and future. Some were useful, others considerably less so; but the one hard and fast point that everyone had to take on board was that World Championship rallying would be run to Group A touring car rules on and from 1 January 1987.

The big three manufacturer rally teams, Audi, Ford and Peugeot, anxiously scanned their new car brochures to find a car that would be suitable for them to run under the new rules. Peugeot admitted defeat and retired from top-line competition. Audi decided to give their 200 saloon a go but realized that it was too big and unwieldy, and was really only suitable for tough rallies, such as the Safari, which required stamina. Ford fell back on their Sierra, which in 4×4 form only utilized their mundane V6.

Lancia, on the other hand, were very happy, for they had just introduced the perfect car to fit the regulations – the Delta HF4WD. This was purely fortuitous, as the company had developed the model as a high-tech flagship to head their Delta range for use purely as a road car, but its specification was almost tailor-made for the new rallying regulations.

Bloodline Fusion – Lancia Finds its 4WD Feet

What was the Delta HF4WD? How did it come about? In 1980 the Delta was still only an above-average, up-market, comfortable five-door hatchback powered by either 1.3 or 1.5 single-camshaft engines. Nothing there to suggest that it had any serious development potential or that it might set hearts racing like no other car could.

The introduction of a GT1600 in 1982 started factory production of a performance Delta for the first time. This was an updated car utilizing the Lampredi designed twin-cam 1585cc carburettor engine.

At virtually the same time, after some years of successfully racing their World Sports Car Championship winning Beta Montecarlos, the turbo-charged engines they utilized had given the company a huge amount of feedback on this technology, which the engineers in Turin eagerly translated into possible road car use. These engines were basically the same as that in the GT1600, although with forced induction and race modified. A marriage of the Delta and a turbo-charged engine seemed a natural course of action and the first fruits of this line of development appeared in 1983 in the form of the HF Turbo. Still with front-wheel drive and the same block dimensions as those on the GT1600, the addition of a Garret turbo-charger boosted engine power to 130bhp in initial carburettor-fed form and at last endowed the Giugiaro hatchback with serious performance.

Stepping back one year to 1982, Giugiaro returns to the story with the presentation to the world at that year's Turin show of the previously mentioned innovative Delta 4×4 Turbo. This was the first turbo-charged Lancia intended for the road but, more significant than that, as the name implied, it was also the first Lancia passenger car to be fitted with four-wheel drive. Fiorio and the competition team may have dismissed the Audi quattro as utilizing a technologically stagnant drive system and opted for two-wheel drive on their rally cars, but Lancia as a company could see the benefits that a four-wheel drive development programme would bring. Not only would they be seen to be wholeheartedly embracing new horizons, but also they would be demonstrating their abilities and interest in what was, at that time, a very fashionable automotive concept. There was money to be made but they never knew then – nobody knew then – where this was going to take them, for the 4×4 turbo was very definitely a one-off concept and development machine.

The Delta 4×4 turbo must be seen as an important step in the bloodline of the inte-

Celebrity motoring reporter Tiff Needell tried the Delta Turbo 4×4and enjoyed himself, despite his dislike of front-wheel drive handling tendencies.

grale. Indeed, there was evidence to suggest that not only was a production total traction Delta considerably more than just a concept or wishful thinking, Lancia admitted that the 4×4 was part of a continuing development exercise. It is, perhaps, revealing, certainly in retrospect, that the opening line of the 4×4 turbo's press release reads 'La Lancia Delta turbo a trazione integrale…'. The latter words translate into literal English as 'complete traction', the perfect description of what was to come.

Celebrity test driver, Tiff Needell, was able to try the car when he went to Turin to test the Rally 037 for *Autosport* magazine in June 1982. Pointing out that it was the first transverse-engined road car to be fitted with four-wheel drive, his dislike of cars with inherently front-drive characteristics did not stop him from commenting that, although the car was 'very much a prototype, no development work having been done on the suspension, the car was well-finished and acceleration impressive'.

For a further four years this car was the only outward sign that Lancia had even half a mind on the likelihood of a four-wheel drive car for the public, but their fearsome S4 rally car was to give the possibility considerable impetus. Vast amounts of data on the subject were created by the S4 project. The drive system itself was completely re-engineered, compared to that of the 4×4 turbo, and incorporated its own original features. The success of the S4 and the fact that four-wheel drive was then the most fashionable high-performance car accessory and therefore a sure-fire selling point, finally prompted Lancia into introducing their first total traction production passenger car.

Lancia Delta HF4WD – Introduction and Features

By May 1986, the Delta had been around for seven years and so Lancia gave it a facelift. This is standard procedure by many motor manufacturers, as it prolongs a model's life for a period of time and allows a final boost to its sales figures before it is made obsolete and replaced by a completely new, redesigned car. Fuel injection was introduced on the GT1600 and HF Turbo, and some slight styling alterations were introduced, such as revamped front-ends, different headlamp arrangements and black side-window surrounds on the higher-performance versions. All of these changes were to update the cars in an attempt to keep the Delta abreast of emerging fashions and trends. For the model in general though, by far the most significant announcement concerned the arrival of the HF4WD.

It was difficult at first glance to distinguish this new model from the revamped version of the previous top of the heap, the conventionally front-wheel drive propelled HF Turbo ie. The only external differences were a new four-headlight system with the addition of two fog lamps mounted in the front spoiler, small side skirts with small HF4WD badges located just ahead of the rear wheel arches, further badging on the front grille and rear hatch, and two raised air-intakes towards the rear of the bonnet. The net result was an understated high-performance car, this concept being very familiar to anyone who had taken any interest in previous sporting Lancias.

This new total traction Delta was, however, only available from the factory in left-hand drive configuration. In fact, although there was some initial speculation in the UK that right-hand drive would eventually be an option, Lancia was not prepared to commit the investment and tooling to enable this to happen, so all the cars emerged as new with left-hand steering and that goes for all subsequent integrale models as well. If you see a right-hand drive example, it will have been specially converted. Two Lancia dealers in the UK were prepared to undertake this work contemporarily – Mike Spence and John Whalley – but numbers completed were small and steering gear from other Fiat range cars had to be utilized in order to fit.

Gone was the 4×4 turbo's drive system. All that S4 knowledge and expertise had been put to good use. Innovation and engineering integrity combined to put the HF4WD several steps ahead of the opposition. Ford had upstaged Audi's 4WD system with viscous couplings on their Sierras. Lancia had moved another leap ahead by utilizing a Torsen differential at the rear axle. The secret of the Torsen (a contraction of 'torque sensing') unit is that it never locks up like conventional diffs. It senses what each rear wheel is doing and feeds different proportions of torque to each wheel. Thus the drive system reads the road conditions at all times and the wheels never skid or spin. The HF4WD's front differential was of the free-floating type, whilst the centre differential incorporated a Ferguson viscous-coupling unit-controlled epicyclic gear set on the other. Previous four-wheel drive cars had tended to have the percentage of torque split sent to the front and rear wheels biased in favour of the rear, or certainly no more than 50/50 front/back. Indeed, the S4 ran most of the time with a 25/75 set-up. The HF4WD was set at 56 front and 44 rear, thus retaining some of the conventional Delta's handling characteristics.

To help cope with the added stresses of the new car's higher performance capabilities compared to the HF Turbo ie, the basic suspension system remained the same with the Macpherson strut independent arrangement incorporating dual-rate dampers and helicoidal springs. The struts and springs were set slightly off-centre, however, and flexible rubber links were introduced to the suspension/body interface to help further damp out road shocks and noise. The suspension was also fine-tuned to include altered damper rates, and front and rear toe-in. Also, the angle of incidence of the powered steering rack was changed, along with ball thrust bearings being introduced instead of roller-type to help reduce steering effort.

The badge that introduced the legend.

Despite the plain exterior appearance, the dynamics of the HF4WD immediately won over many motoring journalists.

Aurelio Lampredi

The engine that powers all HF4WDs and integrales has a long bloodline heritage of its own. Designer, Aurelio Lampredi, sprang to prominence as being responsible for the engine that powered Ascari's Ferrari to win the 1950 British Grand Prix against the previously all-conquering Alfa Romeo 158/9.

Before that time, Enzo Ferrari had been relying on supercharged V12 motors designed by Giaocino Colombo, but Lampredi convinced Enzo that what was needed was a relatively simple and less stressed normally aspirated unit.

In Ferrari lore Lampredi came up with the 'long-block'V12 and this superseded Colombo's 'short-block' unit. Formula One rules changed and Lampredi produced a 2-litre four-cylinder unit for 1952, which went on to be the most successful engine GP racing has experienced.

In 1955, Enzo took over the racing remains of Lancia's D50 project and Lampredi left Maranello.Very soon he was snapped up by Fiat and designed many successful road-car engines into the late 1950s and early 1960s.

By this time Fiat was in need of a new unit that could be produced in large numbers and in differing capacities for many different applications. So Lampredi came up with an engine that not only could be produced in the required different capacities but could also utilize either pushrod or twin overhead camshaft valve actuation.

The twin-cam version started life in two versions of 1438cc and 1608cc. Perhaps the most significant feature of these units was their utilization, for virtually the first time in mainstream production (the small German company Glas having also tried it), of a cogged rubber belt to drive the camshafts in place of the traditional chain.These two engines were used in Fiat saloons and sports cars from the mid-1960s. Many different capacities were eventually offered and one was of 1995cc. This engine tended to be used in premium and sporting Fiat and Lancia cars. In particular, just before the arrival of the Delta HF4WD, it had been fitted with a turbo-charger and used to power the flagship of Lancia's Thema luxury saloon range, the Turbo ie.

Without doubt, Lampredi's 'twin-cam', as it became simply and affectionately known, was one of the most successful road-car engines in the history of the motor car. Its last incarnations, after the demise of the integrale, were in Fiat's coupé and Lancia's Kappa coupé in the late 1990s.

The front seats were supplied by Recaro and the only upholstery colour option was grey alcantara, which was a suede-like material used only by Lancia.The seat inserts were trimmed in grey/blue diagonal-striped cloth and this design was repeated on the door trims. Six colours were available: white (bianco Saratoga), red (rosso monza), grey metallic (grigio scuro), blue metallic (blu dry), maroon metallic (Bordeaux), black metallic (nero).

To give added status and performance to the HF4WD package, the largest engine yet carried by a Delta was included. This was taken from its upmarket top-of-the-range saloon stablemate, the Thema ie Turbo, and was the 1995cc version of Aurelio Lampredi's multi-use twin-cam four, here in turbo-charged form. Intercooled, it put out 165bhp at 5,250rpm with 188lb ft of torque at 2,500rpm. There was also an over-boost facility that came in if the throttle was kept wide open whilst accelerating. This acted on the wastegate valve temporarily increasing the feed pressure and thus briefly increasing torque, so that 210lb ft would then be available at 2,750rpm. The engine had twin counter-rotating balancer shafts running in roller bearings to increase smoothness, and the whole unit was electronically controlled by a Marelli-IAW ignition system. All of this pushed the Delta HF4WD from 0-60 mph in about six and a half seconds. Whilst it undoubtedly became Lancia's fashionable flagship model, it was also in the frontline of then-current performance technology and for a year the situation stayed that way.

Motor magazine in the UK sent Mark Hales to Italy to drive one and he commented, 'the abiding impression is of a nicely balanced chassis, smooth powerful engine, good ride and clever 4WD system'.

Car magazine's Richard Bremner was moved to say in December 1986: '...make an extra [driving] effort and the Delta HF4WD will course through the countryside with blinding ability… there can be very few cars capable of covering ground as quickly as this with so little fuss… [it] raises the competitive hatch battle on to a new plane'.

It was actually not quite the first production four-wheel drive Lancia to enter the showrooms. That accolade goes to the Delta's booted sibling, the Prisma, a total traction version of which was announced at the same time and reached production just in advance of the hatchback, although this did not enjoy the sophistications of a viscous coupling and a Torsen rear differential.

During their world launch, Ing. Marascotti, later at Abarth and now at N Technology, had spoken with Lancia's marketing people and asked them what they considered the percentage sales proportions of the two models would be. How many Prisma 4WDs did they expect to sell compared to Delta HF4WDs? The answer was 'about seventy Prismas to every thirty Deltas'. How wrong could they be! Little did they know what was going to happen: the actual figures were more like ninety-five Deltas to every five Prismas!

So, after the Tour de Corse, the FISA had called for an immediate end-of-season ban on Group B cars and a change to Group A touring car rules. Whatever car was chosen from a manufacturer's range had also to incorporate a competent chassis, adequate power but, above all, development potential.

One can almost imagine that in the summer of 1986 Abarth managers were giggling slightly uncontrollably to themselves as they realized that they had exactly what was required. The first examples were already rolling off the production line and the car fitted the basic rally specification requirements on virtually all counts.

That car was the new Delta HF4WD. The two bloodlines of innovation and competition had finally merged together.

Little did anyone realize what this car would lead to when it was announced in 1986.

2 The HF4WD Evolves

'Some are born great, some achieve greatness, and some have greatness thrust upon them' although, in the case of the HF4WD, a fourth option, a slice of all three, would be more relevant.

In 1986, Lancia had introduced this exciting new model as a flagship road car. All who drove one proclaimed it as something very special and agreed that it was one of the fastest point-to-point cars they had handled. It was born great. At the time no one knew it but it was to achieve greatness on the special stages of the world. Before that though, it would have greatness thrust upon it.

This is a very rare HF4WD right-hand drive conversion, probably carried out by Mike Spence Lancia dealers in Berkshire UK.

Impact of the New Rules

Little did Lancia know where things were going. Rallying under Group B rules had been axed under FISA. Hand on heart, nobody was really surprised that FISA had reached such an immediate knee-jerk decision after the tragic events in Corsica, but practically, what did the new rules, which had immediately been laid down – after all, they were not just proposals – mean to the manufacturers?

First indications were that the adoption of Group A touring-car rules required cars entered in the 1987 World Rally Championship to be based on a production model of which a minimum of 5,000 should have been built. Modifications would be allowed but to strict parameters. FISA also stated that engines would be restricted to a maximum power output of 300bhp, although no one in the organizing body as yet had any plan as to how this was going to be checked.

As we have already seen, these new rules did almost nobody any great favours. They required that, to be successful in 1987, a company that envisaged competing had to have in production a car that fitted the requirements, not only in terms of size, weight and power output, but most of all, potential. There was also the small matter of there being only six months in which to start a new competition car project from scratch and develop it into a likely World Rally Championship round winner.

To put this into perspective, Lancia had started development of their Group B Delta S4 in June 1984 (serious planning had preceded this since April 1983) and the car was not deemed ready enough for the international stage until late 1985, when it debuted on the RAC Rally in the UK. Sixteen months had been spent honing the car and added to that time another thirteen months had been spent in the planning.

Homologation and Group A

Before a car can compete on an important event – one that has Federation Internationale des Automobiles agreement – it must have evidence of having been 'homologated' by its manufacturer. This consists of documentation registered with what was then the FISA, but which is now the FIA. This documentation, virtually a birth certificate, lays down all the essential dimensions and characteristics of a particular model, so that at any time an event's scrutineers can check that a competing car complies exactly with its manufacturer's declared specification.

As cars coming off a production line will inevitably vary slightly, there was a small leeway in some of the dimensions. All this was done to ensure a level playing field and that there was no cheating. The problem though was that an inventive or creative engineer could interpret these parameters in a way that would suit a car's competitiveness. Thus the overall specified width could be, and was, expanded by a legal amount and that would be enough to fit wider wheels or tyres. This was all part of the game when required numbers built were as low as 200, but FISA really moved the goalposts by announcing a 5,000 minimum.

With the earlier low numbers, many are the stories of officials being invited to count the cars made and being shown a number of them before lunch in one place then being shown some more in another location after a cordial meal. The morning's cars merely having been moved from one place to another! Eventually the authorities had to bring in a firm of international auditors to ensure that a manufacturer was telling the truth and this took a lot of time, as will be seen in the case of the HF4WD.

It was not only numbers either. With the introduction of the new 1987 rules, all engine, suspension and many other parts, had to have a photograph provided to ensure that they all complied with original factory specification, but this did not mean that Group A, from 1987 on, was totally restrictive...

Group A

All cars run in international motor sport come under their relevant FIA sporting code groups. In Group B the rules as to what was allowed were almost totally liberal, hence the dramatic machines that resulted.

The more restrictive Group A had always existed under those rules for any manufacturer who wished to run cars that could take advantage of the way they were written. A perfect example of this was the Alfa Romeo Alfetta GTV and GTV6, which could be made to go very quickly under the pre-1987 Group A. Few exploited it and when the 1987 rules were announced with the 5,000 minimum requirement, this became the crucial point and immediately outlawed, not only the intended Group B, but some cars that were running under the pre-1987 rules as well. Not only did the minimum-number situation cause some cars to withdraw, but new internal dimensions were required as well, which in effect ruled out anything that was like a two-door coupé, hence the death knell of the Alfetta.

Steel bodies, front engines, rear fuel tanks and greater minimum weight all became compulsory. The 'evolution' concept of the past, whereby performance modifications to cars could be passed off as evolutionary development, stopped immediately. Any modifications or updating meant rehomologation and effectively a new model. This is the whole point concerning Lancia's enviable position at the announcement of the new rules and thereafter. Not only did they have a car that fitted all these new rules but also, most crucially, it was already tooled up and in production, and updates could be introduced as subsequent new models. Hence the integrale. It would have been logistically and financially impossible for anyone to arrange for the introduction of a new car that would fit as well under the required regulations as the HF4WD in the limited time available before the first rally of 1987.

In fact, so long as the dimensional and weight regulations of Group A were adhered to, a manufacturer could fit what were virtually Group B standard modified parts under the shell, so long as they homologated them first. This is what Abarth did very successfully, with engineers 'interpreting' the rules to their advantage with items like six-speed gearboxes being fitted instead of the standard five-speeds.

During the second week of May 1986, FISA had announced that their new rules would become effective from 1 January 1987, but more to the point, the manufacturers had to have their new cars on the line ready to start the Monte Carlo Rally, which was the first round of 1987s World Rally Championship, on 17 January. They therefore had eight months in which to decide which car they would run, prepare it for competition, test it and be competitive right from the word go.

For most, choosing which model to use was the difficult decision. Group B rules had allowed an 'anything goes' atmosphere to pervade rallying, now manufacturers had to sort through their sales lists to find a car that might be a world winner.

The fact that Group B had been abolished, due to serious incidents on rallies, could never have been predicted by anyone, so it was only pure coincidence and luck, serendipity as was once suggested, that Lancia had recently introduced their Delta HF4WD.

Even so, Cesare Fiorio seized the opportunity immediately, realizing instantly that it had Group A potential. The car was obviously no relation to the fire-breathing Delta S4 – any similarities that they had were there purely for company marketing reasons. The HF4WD had, however, benefited from the technical developments of the S4, and incorporated ideas and lessons learnt from the use of its novel four-wheel drive system. The production engineers at Lancia had tamed the concept for road use.

So, whilst Peugeot contemplated with resignation its 205 hatchback and Audi wondered how their driver's would fare threading the big 200 quattro turbo saloon around Corsican lanes, Abarth was already pulling an HF4WD apart in Corso Marche, Turin under the direction of Ing. Sergio Limone, with the intention of trying out all manner of modifications on it. They were also looking to see how far they could go under the new rules.

The 165bhp of this first Delta four wheel-drive turbo motor was set to double by the time the 1992/3 rally cars took to the roads.

What they had to work on were the basic specifications of the road HF4WD including power courtesy of the 8-valve Lampredi twin-cam in 2-litre form with turbo-charger, as used in the company's Thema turbo saloon. This produced 165bhp and it drove through a five-speed gearbox that then directed power through a Ferguson viscous differential and, by shaft, to the Torsen differential at the rear, with a classic arrangement at the front. Weight in road form was 1190kg.

Creating the Competition HF4WD

Claudio Lombardi, Sergio Limone and the development team set to work at Abarth to turn the HF4WD into a potential winner. They were, of course, helped by the fact that the transmission had been developed from the S4 but all else was new. The basic requirements would be to increase power, reduce weight, and improve handling and road-holding.

By 6 August 1986, the engineers at Abarth had the first prototype competition HF4WD ready for testing at Fiat's La Mandria test track north-west of Turin. Weight had been reduced

Lancia Delta HF4WD

Layout	
Unit construction steel body/chassis structure. Four-doors plus hatchback, front engine/four-wheel drive.	
Engine	
Type	831.B5.000
Cylinders	Four transverse
Cooling	Water
Bore and stroke	84 × 90mm
Capacity	1995 cc
Valves	Four per cylinder worked by twin-overhead camshafts, which are driven by cogged belt from the crankshaft
Compression ratio	8.0:1 (Group A 7.5:1)
Fuel supply	Weber 1AW electronic fuel injection with Garrett T3 turbo-charger and intercooler
Max. power	165bhp @ 5,250rpm (Group A, 260bhp @ 6,250rpm)
Max. torque	29kg m/210lb ft @ 2,750rpm (Group A, 38kg m/275lb ft @ 3,000rpm)
Transmission	
Type	Permanent four-wheel drive with central epicyclic train type torque distributor with Ferguson viscous coupling and automatic Torsen rear limited slip differential (Group A cars had an additional limited slip differential at the front)
Overall gearbox ratios (:1)	Top 3.50
	4th 2.235
	3rd 1.518
	2nd 1.132
	1st 0.928
	Reverse 3.583
Final drive	2.944
Suspension and steering	
Front	Independent with McPherson type struts
Rear	Independent with twin-parallel lower transverse suspension arms, longitudinal reaction arms and coil-spring struts (Group A anti-roll bars front and rear)
Steering	Rack and pinion with power assistance
Tyres	185/60-HR14 (Group A 210/580-15)
Wheels	5.5J-14 (Group A Speedline 7J-15 for asphalt, 5.5J-14 for gravel)
Brakes	
Type	Discs on all four wheels with the fronts having a larger diameter (Group A 280mm ventilated discs with Brembo callipers 4 pot at front 2 pot at rear)
Dimensions	
Track	Front 1,410mm/55.7in (Group A 1,434mm/56.5in)
	Rear 1,405mm/55.3in (Group A 1,440mm/56.7in)
Wheelbase	2,480mm/97.6in
Overall length	3,890mm/153.1in (Group A 3,895mm/153.4in)
Overall width	1,620mm/63.8in
Overall height	1,380mm/54.3in (Group A 1,360mm/53.5in)
Unladen weight	1,190kg/2,624lb (Group A about 1,120kg/2,470lb)

The advantage for Lancia of Group A rallying with the Delta was that it was directly connected to cars the public could buy.

by the adoption of carbon-fibre components, in particular in the transmission, power had been increased to over 200bhp utilizing a Garrett turbo-charger, the same as on the production car as required by the rules. Road-holding and handling were not so easy to improve. The rules would not allow the use of tyres and wheels that protruded outside the wheelarches. The first test cars, TO 55066F being one of the earliest, had to make do with wheels from the factory Group A Fiat Uno turbos and this was to prove a headache for the team, with early testing being punctuated by the cars losing their wheels. This problem was a fundamental reason behind the introduction of the next important model development, the integrale, but that is moving ahead too fast. The gearbox on the first car of August 1986 was still of the standard-production type. The definitive box, by ZF, was not to arrive until early autumn and development testing of the completed competition package did not start until October on the island of Elba, where the team was able to test on both gravel and tarmac roads. By late September, legendary Abarth manager and engineer Giorgio Pianta had had his first test in an HF4WD.

To raise the specification of the road-going HF4WD to that of a Group A car involved a lot of work on the engine, then ensuring that the transmission, brakes and suspension could make most use of the extra power.

Engine power was increased from 165bhp at 5,250rpm to 258bhp at 6,250rpm, whilst retaining the standard conrods. A new, bigger, more efficient intercooler was fitted along with better water and oil radiators. A four-coil capacitative discharge mapped electronic ignition from Magnetti Marelli was added, and new pistons and newly designed valves in new material were fitted. The camshafts were of a new design reprofiled for increased lift and phasing, and modified composite material air filters and pipes aided efficiency, as did an exhaust system made of titanium with reduced back-pressure. Turbo-boost pressure was raised and the injection control unit was reprogrammed.

The gearbox internals were modified and made of stronger materials, whilst the central torque-splitter received different tooth geometry to allow for a variation in torque split

Giorgio's experience is second to none. Here he teases Mercedes competitions manager Norbert Haug after his Alfas had just beaten the German's cars at Silverstone.

front/rear, depending upon the conditions of an events, for example, the differences between the Safari and the Tour de Corse. The rear Torsen diff was arranged so that it could be set up to cope better with differing conditions. The propshaft was made of carbon composite materials and more robust drive-shafts and couplings were fitted at the front.

The rules did not allow considerable changes in the suspension, so the front struts were relocated allowing the use of larger tyres. Larger wheel bearings and improved brake disc ventilation to bigger brakes with bigger calipers, were joined by new anti-roll bars and stronger suspension arms. The brake-servo was removed and provision added for manual regulation of braking power between the front and rear wheels.

In addition to all of this, the interior was altered with racing seats, rollover protection and specific safety and rally equipment.

Fine-Tuning!

By mid-October the team was able to unveil a fully Martini-liveried car to the press and public, when TO 09449F was displayed outside the Royal Hotel in San Remo on the occasion of the rally of that name.

The marketing men loved the concept of rallying the Delta. Here a dressed up HF4WD raises the profile of a turbo diesel version.

Giorgio Pianta

Giorgio was born in Milan in 1935, his father was in business in textiles and there was no spare money for motor sports, but he persisted and started in regularity runs in 1957 in a Fiat 1100/103. These were competitive events involving little hard driving, just precision timing over a set distance. In 1958 he acquired a Fiat 500 sport and raced in hill climbs and circuit meetings. In 1961 he bought an Abarth 750 Zagato but ended up in hospital after a practice accident. By 1962 he had an Alfa Giulietta Ti saloon with which he took many class wins in events before being invited to drive an Abarth 1000 TC with the son of Dragoni, who was chief press officer for Ferrari.

After a terrific dice at Monza, where Cesare Fiorio's father was watching, Giorgio was offered a works drive for the 1963 season with Lancia in racing and rallying. He stayed with the team until 1965, having driven Appias, Flavias and Flaminias. In the latter he remembers a great race in the Motor 6 Hours race at Brands Hatch, battling with Graham Hill who was in a Jaguar Mark 2. After one fraught event in Italy Giorgio hit the headlines, his father sees them and finally gives his son his blessing to continue in motor sport.

More variety came his way in the 1966 Monte Carlo Rally when he drove a yellow Ferrari 275 GTB and was only 45 seconds slower than Makinen's Mini Cooper S over the Chartreuse stage. Meanwhile in Italian races he co-drove Tarramazzo and Nicodemi in their Ferrari 250 LM and GTO, and drove for Autodelta winning a touring car long-distance event at Monza in an Alfa GTA. Moving through Formula Three he had some good drives in Porsche 911s in the European touring car championship with a second in Budapest and a win in Belgrade.

He worked with Abarth as the sixties turned into the seventies, and also drove a Lola Cosworth sports car in the Targa Florio.

From 1973 he worked alongside Abarth designer Colucci with the Fiat 124 Abarth spiders and was with the Corso Marche organization from then on. In a vast collection of competition and championship wins his winning drives in the Giro d'Italia in the Abarth 031 prototype, and later a 24-valve Stratos, stand out. He became a senior Abarth test driver before dividing his time between that and management. He did most of the Delta S4 development, a lot of the HF4WD work and, after being called away to run Alfa's Indycar and saloon car race teams, he returned to Abarth for the Evolution integrale. His final job for the Fiat Group was to run Alfa Romeo's championship winning Deutsche Tourenwagen Meisterschaft touring-car teams when he was managing director of Fiat Auto Corse Spa from November 1995.

Speaking recently with ex-World Rally Champion Walter Rohrl, it was clear that the German had the utmost respect for Giorgio's testing talents. 'He could drive as quickly as us so I knew the cars would always be set up properly in advance,' he said. Sometimes for Giorgio the testing did not work out quite as planned. Amongst a huge wealth of anecdotes, Giorgio tells of the day he was testing a Delta S4 at La Mandria. The technicians called him in and told him that their telemetry showed he was not driving quickly enough through one particularly daunting corner.

'But I cannot go any faster through there as I will have a large accident,' said Giorgio.

'Nonsense, the figures show that you can, go out and try again,' said the engineers.

Off went Giorgio, trying harder than ever. Suddenly there was silence. After a while, a visibly shocked Giorgio appeared on foot carrying the mangled remains of the driver's door.

'Was that fast enough for your machines?' asked Giorgio. There was little else left of the car.

Giorgio is, therefore, enormously experienced, talented and knowledgeable. He was able to provide priceless feedback on development as he was, above all, a racer. Sergio Limone handed him the greatest accolade when he reckoned that there were few quicker than him at La Mandria in integrales.

The legendary team manager and racer Giorgio Pianta is uniquely involved in this story, as he tested and managed all versions of the Delta competition cars.

A press HF4WD, probably at Sestriere, with a show 'cassonetto fari' light pod. This was not used on the rally cars due to poor testing results.

Much wind-tunnel testing was completed to devise ways of avoiding lift, and considerable strengthening of the shells took place as testing showed up the weaknesses. At first, due to lack of space under the bonnet, the oil radiator was placed near the windscreen but early on this was found not to work. Sergio Limone said that cutting down weight and allowing as much air as possible into the engine bay were early priorities, and already the production cars were being affected by the requirements of the competition department. For instance, Abarth did not want to be forced to use fog lights on the Group A version, in order to lose a little weight and also release some space for air-intakes on the nose of the car. Such were the stringencies of the new rules, however, that many items that were shown as standard in the road-car's brochure would have to be included on the Group A version. Abarth therefore insisted that fog lamps were made only an optional extra for the road car, otherwise they would be an unnecessary obstruction on the competition car.

Autosport magazine commented that the team had 'geared production of the [road] car towards the necessary 5,000 units and were

Massimo Biasion

Massimo, or Miki as everyone knew him, was born in 1958 in Bassano del Grappa in north-east Italy. He began rallying in 1978 and joined Martini Racing in 1983, winning the Italian and European rally championships. By 1988 he had won the World Rally series and his importance was that he was the first southern European to break the mould of Scandinavian domination at the top of the rally business.

After five years with the Deltas, he left the Fiat group and joined Ford but did not find the same level of success there.

He has recently emerged from virtual retirement to conduct testing for N Technology's Junior 1600 World Rally Fiat Puntos.

expecting homologation to go through in December'. Homologation was the vital acceptance by FISA that the necessary number of similar cars had been built, so that they could then be allowed to take part in the World Rally Championship. Members of the press, who joined the Lancia Martini works team during final testing in the Italian Alps late in 1986, suggested that 1987 would be a strange year. Experience of the HF4WD for the first time clearly pointed out the differences between Group B and Group A. Miki Biasion, one of the team drivers chosen for 1987, was not downhearted however, confirming that it had been impossible to extract the ultimate from the ultra fast and powerful Delta S4. The reaction times required were far too short. In comparison the HF4WD, whilst obviously slower, allowed much more time for finesse, such as choosing the correct line for the next corner and achieving the best balance between braking and acceleration.

Engineer Lombardi was concerned about power, as the rules did not allow any basic changes. The engine was a 2-valve per cylinder unit and Abarth had to stick with that. He reckoned that with a production car developing 165bhp, then 230bhp or just over was feasible. The fact that some aspects of the S4 had been productionized for use on the HF4WD was good, especially as far as the transmission was concerned, but Lombardi fretted that their casings had to stay the same. Wheel sizes were also a problem, except that diameters could be increased, which would allow for larger brakes, but they could go for greater width. The production car utilized an all-synchromesh gearbox but straight-cut gears with no synchromesh were required on the competition car. Whilst the road car had a maximum speed of 210km/h (130.5mph) at 5,500rpm the rally car, with shorter gearing, was good for about 175km/h (109mph) at 7,200rpm, although this would depend on the requirements of the rally. Lombardi stated it would be very important to make the rally car strong and whilst this

The press were treated to some demonstration runs in a Group A HF4WD in the Alps in late 1986. Here Biasion gives a journalist an exciting ride.

may seem obvious, it had its practical issues too. The S4 had been developed as a car with a layout enabling all the items that could break or need replacing to be within easy and, more vitally, quick reach of the mechanics at a service halt. No such considerations had of course ever crossed the HF4WDs designers' minds so Lombardi hoped that gearbox and differential changes would not be required too often. In fact, whereas at first the mechanics were taking over an hour to change a gearbox, by half-way through the 1987 season they had managed to halve this time.

In an early interview with Lombardi, he hoped that the differentials would take about forty minutes to change, which was 'not bad, but if we have a failing in the gearbox, we stop and go home'.

That was, of course, a quip for the journalists as the Lancia team had proven itself to be far too professional an organization to actually do that, but it was a clear indication of the sort of difficulties facing everyone now that the cars had to be production-based.

Clearly identifying the Lancia team as being very serious about this new challenge was their choice of no less than six drivers for the forthcoming World Championship. Just before Christmas 1986 they announced that Markku Alen, Miki Biasion and Juha Kankunnen would undertake full championships of at least nine rounds but also that three other drivers would also be taken on from time to time. Michael Ericsson would switch between the Martini team and the Totip cigarettes Jolly Club run team, whilst Frenchman Bruno Saby and Argentinian Jorge Recalde would be taken on for national championships and specific World championship rounds.

No chances were being taken in Turin. Abarth made sure they had all possible angles covered as in addition to the Group A overall win assault, there would be two Group N class – showroom standard – HF4WDs entered for team manager Cesare Fiorio's son, Alessandro, and Vittorio Caneva. These cars would be entered and run by separately sponsored teams.

Group N

The rules according to what was allowed in Group A were different and were considerably more restrictive when it came to Group N.

This group was for 'normal', or large-scale production cars. Lancia was well placed to take advantage of these rules as well because the total-traction Deltas were being built in numbers never predicted for such a specialized car. The annual minimum was 5,000, as with Group A, although this was reduced to 2,500 from 1992.

The essential difference with Group N was that the cars had to run virtually unmodified and the only modifications allowed were for the inclusion of safety items like roll cages and competition brake materials. For this reason the category proved to be a popular starting point for new drivers in international events where they could receive recognition and possible promotion by factory teams to Group A cars.

Despite this potential strength in depth, it might all have gone to waste as Abarth was facing great problems with the homologation of the car. The road car employed a Garrett turbo-charger, but Lancia claimed that some were fitted with a KKK unit and therefore the rally car could also utilize this unit. Rival manufacturers were not happy about this and were quick to criticize Lancia. They saw the possible adoption of a KKK turbo-charger as being a devious method of extracting more power than would be available with the Garrett. Lombardi had already admitted at earlier press conferences that he was worried about the limitations of power development placed upon the engineers by the use of the Garrett.

First Racing Season

In particular, Tony Fall of General Motors Opel rally team was very upset that the

HF4WD had been passed by FISA as homologated, subject to the requirement that the requisite number of identical cars would have been produced by 15 February. This meant passing the car in advance of a date that was after the opening rounds of the World Championship. Lancia's rivals became even more concerned after the opening stages of the Monte Carlo Rally that started on 17 January. The HF4WDs had immediately leapt into the lead and, after fifteen stages and nearly three days of driving, were first and second, with the huge margin of some five minutes ahead of third-place man, Walter Rohrl in his Audi 200 quattro.

A quick weight check during the rally after the overnight halt at Aubenas revealed that the Biasion HF4WD was 1,196kg/2637lb, Carlsson's Mazda 4×4 was 1,160kg/2558lb but Blomquist's Sierra 4×4 was no less than 1,304kg/2875lb.

Lancia's dominant performance included one of Lombardi's dreaded gearbox changes and they did not go home, the mechanics did the job in thirty-eight minutes. In the past, Lancia had won rallies because of the efficiency of their legendary service crews and the speed at which they worked, but this time, as the cars ran so well, the gearbox change actually gave the mechanics something to do.

At the end of the event, the HF4WDs still held first and second, with Biasion being allowed to take a controversial win as Kankunnen, who was in the lead at the time, was told to wait before the finish. They had held the gap to Rohrl's Audi at five minutes – but would the HF4WDs remain homologated thus allowing the results to be confirmed?

The situation was delicate. FISA had, of course, to a large extent, brought it upon itself. First, by its original knee-jerk reaction to the events in Portugal and Corsica, and second, by being extremely tardy at constructing clear and sensible rules for the future of rallying. In order to extricate themselves and the sport from a potentially chaotic situation, they decided that all Group A contenders should be checked again, as there was now some doubt over the turbo-chargers used by the Mazda 323 4WD team.

At the same time, these Mazdas were proving themselves to be Lancia's most serious competition, as one of them won in February on the Swedish Rally. Not without some contention, however, as FISA decided that their Japanese-only market turbo-chargers should be investigated further before ratifying the results.

Markku Alen was also beginning to have reservations about the concept of Group A touring cars in world class rallying, stating that before 'where the S4 would have been in first or second gear, now we are approaching bends flat out in third'. He added that if the cars continued to be driven in this way on rougher rallies to come, such as the next one in Portugal, he doubted if they would last. Sergio Limone echoed these thoughts recently when he said that by Portugal in 1987, Abarth had developed the HF4WD into a good car but not really good enough to survive rough rallies for long.

FISA complicated matters still further by stating that they had decided already that they were not going to allow whatever result occurred in Portugal to stand, until all the relevant competing cars there were checked after the event. And this was the pinnacle of the sport, the World Rally Championship; many began to think it was a farce. During testing at their La Mandria test circuit, Abarth admitted that the Group A HF4WD was lapping in times that were becoming very competitive in comparison to those of the previous Group B S4 supercar. This indicated that speeds would soon be enabling point-to-point special stage times not far short of those in 1986 Croup B – with FISA-inspired supposedly standard-based touring cars. No wonder Alen was worried.

Portugal Rally 1987

The governing body had still not confirmed anything when the Portugal Rally got underway on 11 March. Mazda were confident after much gravel road-testing, whereas Lancia were not so certain.

One thing was for certain however. At last FISA finally recognized, on the eve of the rally, that the HF4WD was legal, that 5,000 identical cars had been built and therefore the team could breathe a huge sigh of relief and attack with a clear conscience.

Attack was just what Alen was all about and he took a lead after seven stages that he did not lose. Biasion was quick but suffered problems, and Kankunnen was hobbled by constantly overheating shock absorbers, a legacy of the fact that the cars were essentially production-based. Evidence that maybe FISAs reaction to Group B problems by imposing Group A regulations on rallying were not necessarily going to solve all the old problems was tragically highlighted by the death of one spectator and injuries to several others when a rally car left the road. This pointed a finger at the deficiencies of the organization and left a distinct feeling that maybe Group B was not quite so much to blame for all that had gone before, if only the public could have been sensibly controlled.

Although Limone and Pianta put in many hours of testing, in particular on car TO 88192F for the particularly difficult Safari Rally, Audi was able to display the mastery of the rough-road abilities of its big and heavy

By the time of the Olympus Rally in the USA in July 1987, Martini Lancia had virtually wrapped up that year's Group A World Rally Championship. There were plenty more of them to come.

Not only Group A fell to Lancia but Cesare Fiorio's son, Alex, claimed the showroom Group N world championship in 1987, as well.

200 quattros when they won that event in April. The HF4WDs also displayed some all-tarmac surface deficiencies when the team was beaten on the Tour de Corse by a Prodrive run BMW M3, although the rear-drive road racer was ideally suited to the twisty tarmac stages.

In between times, the works team went to the national level Costa Smeralda rally in Sardinia and Kankunnen/Piironen took a win ahead of the privately run, Totip cigarettes sponsored, HF4WD of Cerrato. This was good training for the notoriously rough upcoming Acropolis rally in Greece, for which the team were probably grateful.

Acropolis Rally 1987

The Greek round, starting in late May, flattered Miki Biasion at the beginning only to deceive. The Italian pulled out over two minutes lead on his Scandinavian team mates before his turbo-charger blew late in the event and with not enough time to arrange repairs. Markku Alen lucked into the lead followed by Kankunnen. In Group N, the rough roads and extraordinary pace of the event – the organizers provide little or no respite time for service or even petrol – took their toll on the Lancia team cars. Caneva had his front suspension break mid-stage, whilst team mate Fiorio was stuck for much of the event with only first and second gears, finally struggling through to twentieth place. Without the turbo, by the way, the Group A car of Biasion, normally rated at 260bhp, was left with 80bhp only and the need to be refilled with oil on every occasion possible for the rest of the rally.

Lancia won again on the Olympus Rally in the USA, which meant that the trip down to

Markku Alen dominated the 1987 1000 Lakes rally and won by the huge margin of over 5min.

Argentina for their round in August had the potential of delivering the team yet another manufacturer's world championship but this time their first with four-wheel drive.

End-of-Year Tally

This time Miki Biasion did the necessary work and delivered the goods, finishing first, with team mate Jorge Recalde second. The Martini Racing sponsored, Abarth developed and run Lancia team had succeeded with the HF4WD in its first season and only the driver's title was left to be decided. It had been far from a complete walkover, however, and it was clear that an evolution car would be needed to keep Lancia at the top. Their new model, with more space for greater amounts of suspension travel and with a bigger turbo, had already been under development. Lombardi said in Argentina that at that moment the Group A HF4WD was, per kilometre, almost within one per cent of previous Group B S4 stage times and that he hoped the new car would be directly comparable with the old supercar. So much for FISAs Group A utopia of slower rally cars. It was particularly naïve as history has always shown that, given engineers of the standard required at this level, whenever authority forces rules onto them to effect a general increase in stage or lap times, they perceive it almost as a challenge that they should develop a car that is as quick, or quicker, than the outgoing machines.

At the end of the year, the final tally for 1987 was that out of the eleven rounds that made up the FISA World Rally Championship, the Martini Lancia team had taken victories on eight of the events. Closest challenger Audi had won once, on the Safari, an event to which their 200 quattro was perfectly suited.

Seventy-three drivers had scored points during the year and thirteen of these had been driving Delta HF4WDs. In addition, amongst these drivers were Cesare Fiorio's son, Alessandro, who won the Group N World Series, whilst the European Rally Championship was also dominated 1 – 2 by the Deltas, with Dario Cerrato taking first place.

When the project had started, Claudio Lombardi had pushed interpretation of the regulations to its limit to see just far he could go. He had, backing him up, his highly experienced team of Giovanni Roffina, who was responsible for engines and Sergio Limone, who took charge of car design and development, and who is still masterminding the similar activities of Alfa's 156 European Touring cars. Very successfully too, as they now have two recent overall championship wins to their credit. Trying to find a special advantage is common practice amongst experienced motor sport teams and has been so for many years. The art of interpreting the rules for homologation in such a way as to find benefits, where none seem to exist, is one of the crucial abilities of the most professional teams.

In the case of Group A, the rules stated that whatever model of car was chosen to take part in the World Rally Championship, 5,000 identical examples had also to be built for sale to the public. But, reasoned Lombardi and his team, maybe we could persuade the FISA that there were detail variants available within those 5,000. At the time there was a Delta HF Turbo model, which utilized a KKK turbo unit, so they decided to offer up the HF4WD for homologation with the option of either a Garrett unit, which was standard, or a KKK. Other teams saw this purely as a means to obtain more horsepower, which was one of the few aspects of the car that the team found difficulty in improving to their desired level. The opposition were fairly astonished when they saw the Lancias for the first time at Monte Carlo in 1987, as their front ends incorporated considerably more cooling slots and vents than the standard car. Much discussion took place amongst these opposing teams, but a spokesman for Mazda opined that Lancia, as probably the most experienced and professional team in rallying at the time, apart from Audi, had simply shifted the boundaries and pushed the rules to their ultimate limits. Whilst other teams considered that the FISA decision to change from Group B to Group A in 1987 meant a return to touring cars. Lancia, however, had set out from the beginning to build the ultimate vehicle they could, making use of any loopholes in the rules that they could find.

Despite all this though, it became clear early on in the life of the HF4WD project that the car actually had little or no future in rallying. Lombardi clearly told the press on many occasions that he was not happy with its restricted power output, restrictive wheel arch sizes and suspension travel, and the message was that a successor was, even at the time of the HFs debut in January 1987, being developed with the intention of introducing it for the 1988 season. Lancia simply could not afford to stand still, as their interpretation of the rules and methods by which they had applied them had so stirred up the competition that 1988 was clearly going to be a battle against seriously determined opposition who had, literally, been stung into action by the Turinese team.

Put simply, Lancia had applied the same professionalism and determination to build a winning car that they had displayed in the past with the S4, 037 and Stratos. Other teams had viewed Group A touring cars as a soft option in comparison to Group B and had entered 1987 with a bemused view. Their attitudes changed immediately on seeing the HF4WD, so effectively had Lancia upped the stakes and stirred up a hornet's nest.

Official Factory Lancia HF4WD Works Cars (Abarth SE 043)

GROUP N 1987

TO 55052F	
TO 55060F	
TO 55061F	
TO 60624F	
TO 60995F	
TO 30144G	
TO 30145G	
TO 39357G	
TO 56781G	

GROUP A 1987

TO 55066F	Later converted to integrale
TO 60994F	
TO 60996F	
TO 60997F	
TO 66483F	
TO 66484F	
TO 66485F	
TO 66486F	Later converted to integrale
TO 66487F	Later converted to integrale
TO 66488F	
TO 82978F	Later converted to integrale
TO 82979F	
TO 88187F	Later converted to integrale
TO 88188F	Later converted to integrale
TO 88189F	
TO 88190F	
TO 88191F	Later converted to integrale
TO 01766G	Later converted to integrale
TO 01767G	Later converted to integrale
TO 01768G	Later converted to integrale
TO 01769G	
TO 01771G	
TO 01772G	Later converted to integrale
TO 74226G	
TO 74227G	Later converted to integrale
TO 74228G	Later converted to integrale
TO 74230G	
TO 04201H	Later converted to integrale

Herein lie the genes of the following succession of four-wheel drive Deltas. When Lancia had debuted the HF4WD road car, it did so with no intention that the car would participate in world-level competition. The model existed as a flagship for the Delta range and represented what was virtually a swansong for the model. There were no plans to continue with the Giugiaro Delta as it stood and its heavily revised successor – with no planned total traction version of any sort – was well advanced.

Lancia now had a dilemma on its hands. To continue the success of what it considered an obsolete model in international-level competition it had to update the HF4WD and doing so would have resulted in what would have been termed an evolution version. The Group A rules did not allow for this, so, if Lancia was serious about continuing it would have to develop a completely new car.

That they were totally committed to the concept and the project itself is illustrated by the fact that the HF4WDs successor was in the minds of the designers and engineers before the HF even appeared at its first event.

By mid-September 1987 the truth was out, as the new car made its public debut at the Frankfurt Show. It was to be known by that descriptive word integrale, first mentioned in connection with the Delta in the press release of the 4×4 Turbo back in 1982.

The whole philosophy of the four-wheel drive Deltas had now changed. From turning a road car into a competition car in the case of the HF4WD, Lancia was now in the process of ensuring success on the rally stages of the future by reversing that principle. It was incorporating all it needed to enable it to win in future motor sport events into its road cars of the present. In other words the Delta four-wheel drive project had changed from road-

Alen's 1000 Lakes winning HF4WD was fitted with a 45/55 front/rear drive set up and Martini did not appear on the car as alcohol advertising was banned in Finland.

PIRELLI
SIEM

car led to competition requirement led. At San Remo in 1987, Lombardi commented that Lancia was struggling to find enough power with the HF4WD 'because the production car came first'. The roles were now being reversed.

So, following the Frankfurt show debut, all Lancia had to do was build 5,000 integrales in time for the 1988 season – oh, and develop it into a new rally winner.

End of season results: Lancia wins 1987 World Rally Championship for both drivers and constructors in two categories: Groups A and N.

In addition Lancia also finished first and second in the European Rally Championship with HF4WDs driven by Dario Cerrato and Patrick Snijers.

The flat bonnet used on the HF4WD and the first HF integrale (second from the right here) is very noticeable in this line-up.

3 Integrale – Addressing the HF4WD's Problem Areas

Claudio Lombardi and his team were well aware of the shortcomings of the HF4WD as far as use at World Rally Championship level was concerned.

The key areas were excessive weight, insufficient wheel arch space for increased width tyres and greater suspension travel, and a lack of front-end air-intakes to allow enough cooling to take place in and around the engine. The latter was vital to the development of more power in any turbo-charged engine. As a road car, the HF4WD had a perfectly adequate area of air-intake space dotted around its front end, but this was totally inadequate when it came to use in competition.

None of this, of course, was in the designer's mind at the time of the car's conception, and the public certainly were not concerned. Lancia's sales of the Delta had consistently increased due to the success and exposure the works team had generated during 1987. These increased sales came at a time when Lancia's management were effectively expecting the model to slip down the sales charts. After all, eight years was considered a good innings for any car and a new model was already taking shape.

So, Lancia's management had a dilemma to deal with. At a time when the Delta should be entering its last phase, they had to accept that it was, in fact, entering a new phase and showing the potential of enjoying a new lease of life. The car for which Lancia was already developing a replacement had recovered yet another wind. Success never comes cheap.

Clearly Lancia's production men had no further interest in the model, so roles had to be reversed and the competition department was now to call the shots. But how long could this situation be allowed to go on? Whilst Martini Lancia and Abarth were winning there was justification for the large budgets involved. But what if they failed?

The determination to ensure that this latter situation was unlikely to happen had been clear when prototypes of the HF4WDs replacement were noted during the summer of 1987. Then the production model's debut in September at Frankfurt was followed only days later by pictures in Italian magazine *Autosprint* of a car in partial works Martini livery undergoing testing. As Sergio Limone made clear to

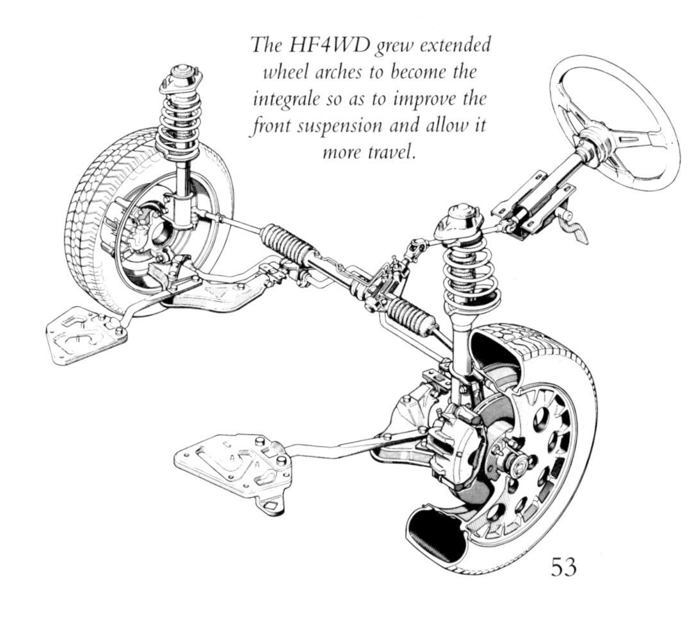

The HF4WD grew extended wheel arches to become the integrale so as to improve the front suspension and allow it more travel.

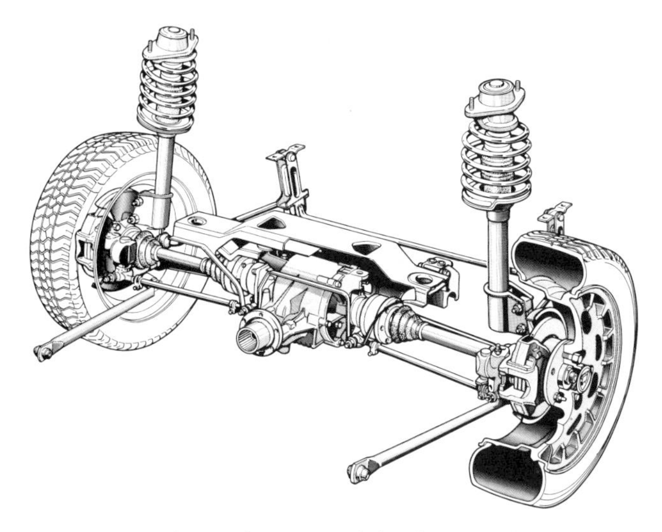

As at the front, so at the rear. Those flares gave the engineers at Abarth much more scope for rear suspension development.

me when I first started this book: 'The reason for all the integrales was that they were due entirely to the pressure of competition.'

The Road Integrale – Introduction and Features

What was so different about the new car, full name Delta HF integrale, compared to the HF4WD?

If the Delta could continue winning World Rally Championships, then the resultant publicity meant that there was every reason for Fiat to continue underwriting the cost of further total traction development of the model. It cannot be stressed too strongly that from this point on the road cars would simply never have existed if Abarth had not seen a future in the model as a World Rally Championship car. This is why right-hand drive was never available from the factory – the competition department had no need for it, so there was no point in Lancia going to the expense of tooling up for the option.

In order to continue winning rallies the engineers had to tackle the HF4WDs weak points. Taking and addressing those previously mentioned areas of deficiency, namely, the problem of limited suspension movement

From the archive of Ing. Sergio Limone comes this shot of the very first Martini integrale – still without proper wings – under test at Fiat's La Mandria track near Turin. An HF4WD stands behind.

Chivasso Factory

Until the end of 1961 all Lancia cars had been built in the company's factory in Turin, but it had become clear that a new plant would be needed and at the same time more space.

A site had been found on the edge of Chivasso, a town to the north-east of Turin and a purpose-built new factory was built there and opened its doors in 1962. This was the only plant where all models of total traction Delta were produced.

Moving forward into the late 1980s and early 1990s, it was clear that Lancia needed to improve efficiency and cope with a severe reduction in demand. New factories had been opened by the Fiat group in financially depressed areas of Italy and so diversification of Lancia production took place rendering the Chivasso plant virtually obsolete.

The introduction of the Evoluzione integrale allowed coach-builders Maggiora to capitalize on the situation, so they bought part of the now ex-Lancia Chivasso plant and started construction of the cars themselves in 1991–92, but this is moving too far ahead and the full story is described later in the relevant chapter.

and restrictive availability of tyre size, resulted in a new road car on which the most obvious immediate difference was the provision of flared, widened wheel arches on all four corners.

These were simply add-ons in the best tradition of competition car requirement. Speed of availability of the new machine was the priority, so the arches were grafted on to the shell. Every HF4WD and integrale made was built at the Lancia factory in Chivasso about twenty kilometres north-east of Turin.

New Integrale Features

The new integrale therefore differed visually from its predecessor in the areas of the four corners and the front air-intakes. The extra space that the engineers found allowed the road-car's tyre size to be increased to 195/55 VR 15 from the HF4WDs 185/60 VR 14. Rim width was up also to 6in. Those wider arches required the bumpers to be restyled and they now wrapped around to meet them at both front and rear. At the front new larger air intakes were included to assist in increased engine cooling and, in the UK market cars, rectangular auxiliary driving lights were fitted. As Ing. Sergio Limone pointed out though, these were not standard items, as Abarth did not want the extra weight on the rally cars.

Cosmetically, the twin door-mirrors were finished in body colour and the side skirts were faired into those new wheel arches and carried

The shaded areas on this integrale diagram show the most obvious differences from the outgoing HF4WD.

HF

The capital letters HF appeared on many Lancias, whether in the actual name of a particular model or figuring prominently somewhere on a car's bodywork.

The significance of the letters has its roots in the creation in 1960 of an exclusive club for loyal Lancia owners. Named the Hi Fi Club, a contraction of High Fidelity, membership was governed by strict rules that centred on the requirement for a potential entrant to have bought a certain minimum number of Lancias new. Rather like a very upmarket version of today's loyalty points schemes.

Soon after this the letters started to appear on sporting Lancias competing in the upper levels of national and international motor sport. The first of these, in 1961, were the Pininfarina Flaminia coupés campaigned in what was then a European touring car series of races. One of these was driven by Giorgio Pianta. These were followed by Flaminia Zagatos and Flavias in both races and rallies.

The letters became definitive when they were included for the first time in the name of a Lancia model, in this case the Fulvia HF of 1966. The successes of the factory entered examples of these cars in rallies meant the letters became known throughout the world and were, perhaps, enhanced even more when used in the title of the immortal Stratos HF between 1974 and 1978.

The factory Lancia rally/race team started from an unofficial group of amateur owners in 1963 and these became an official team as from 1965.

The letters were revived for the Delta HF Turbo, HF4WD and this first integrale, and were further enhanced by the addition of a small galloping red elephant with the introduction of the final Evolution cars.

Back in 1953, Gianni Lancia had chosen it as a good-luck symbol for the first official factory racing sports cars. It would appear that it was important for the elephant's trunk to be stretched forward according to Eastern mythology. Most important though was the way the insignia conferred and continued Lancia heritage and values.

the new badges, which were also fitted on the front grille and on the base of the rear hatch. These proclaimed the car to be an 'HF integrale'.

The engine's low potential maximum horsepower problem, inherent in the restrictive front-end arrangement of the HF4WD, was improved, not only by increased air-intakes on the new integrale, but by the inclusion of a bigger Garrett T3 turbo-charger with larger inter-cooler and overboost valve, which originally allowed pressure to be increased, for 30 seconds only, from 1.8 bar to 2.0 but now had the time-limit revised. New valves, valve seats, water pump and reworked engine internals enabled the engine's maximum power to be increased, in road form, from 165bhp to 185bhp at 5,300rpm. Maximum torque was 224lb ft at 3,500rpm. The extensive opening-up of the front end, with large areas devoted to ingress of air – even around the headlamps – was incorporated in the new road car's design, so that the homologated competition car would not be so lacking in this area, as was the HF4WD.

No changes were made to the essentials of the transmission system compared to the HF4WD. A shorter final drive ratio (3.111 compared to the previous 2.944) matched the new, larger diameter, 6J × 15 wheels, giving 39km/h (24mph) per 1,000rpm in fifth gear and the clutch was up to Thema 8.32 standards. To cope with the increased performance, front brakes were increased in diameter to 284mm. The rears received improved friction coefficient pads and a larger brake master cylinder and servo were fitted. New also were more substantial front springs, dampers and struts.

At first it was announced by the importers that the only colour available in the UK would be Monza red. No significant changes of any sort were made to the interior of the new car, which was effectively therefore the same in the HF integrale as it had been in the HF4WD, with Recaro front seats and alcantara edged cloth seats in grey with diagonal striping on the inserts.

More sophisticated than the engine of the HF4WD, the integrale's made use of improvements in electronics to help develop an extra 20bhp without sacrificing driveability.

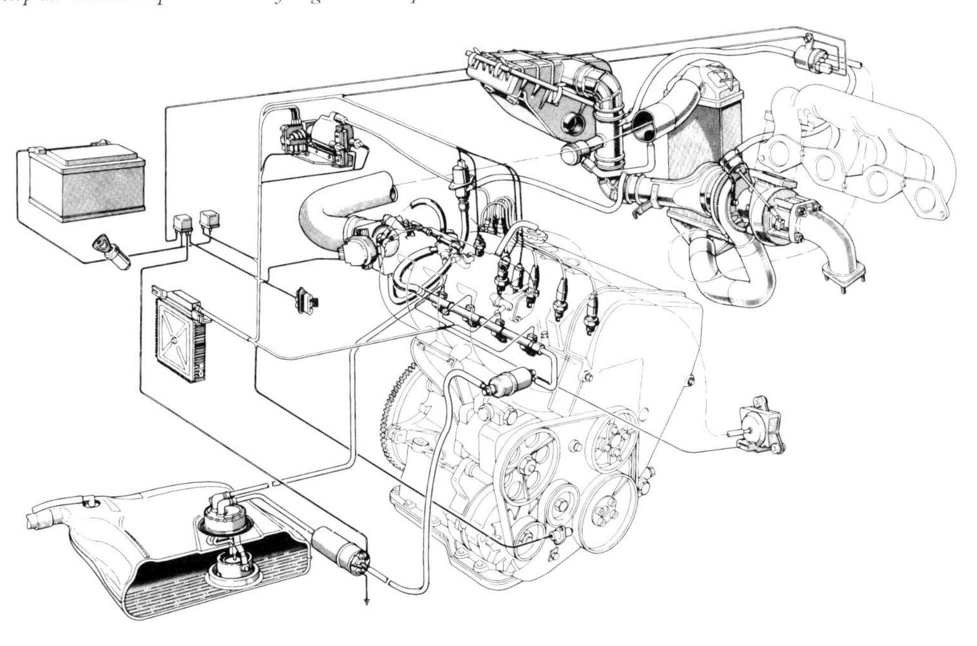

Twin camshafts were matched by twin contra-rotating balancer shafts to ensure smoothness in the HF4WD and integrale road car.

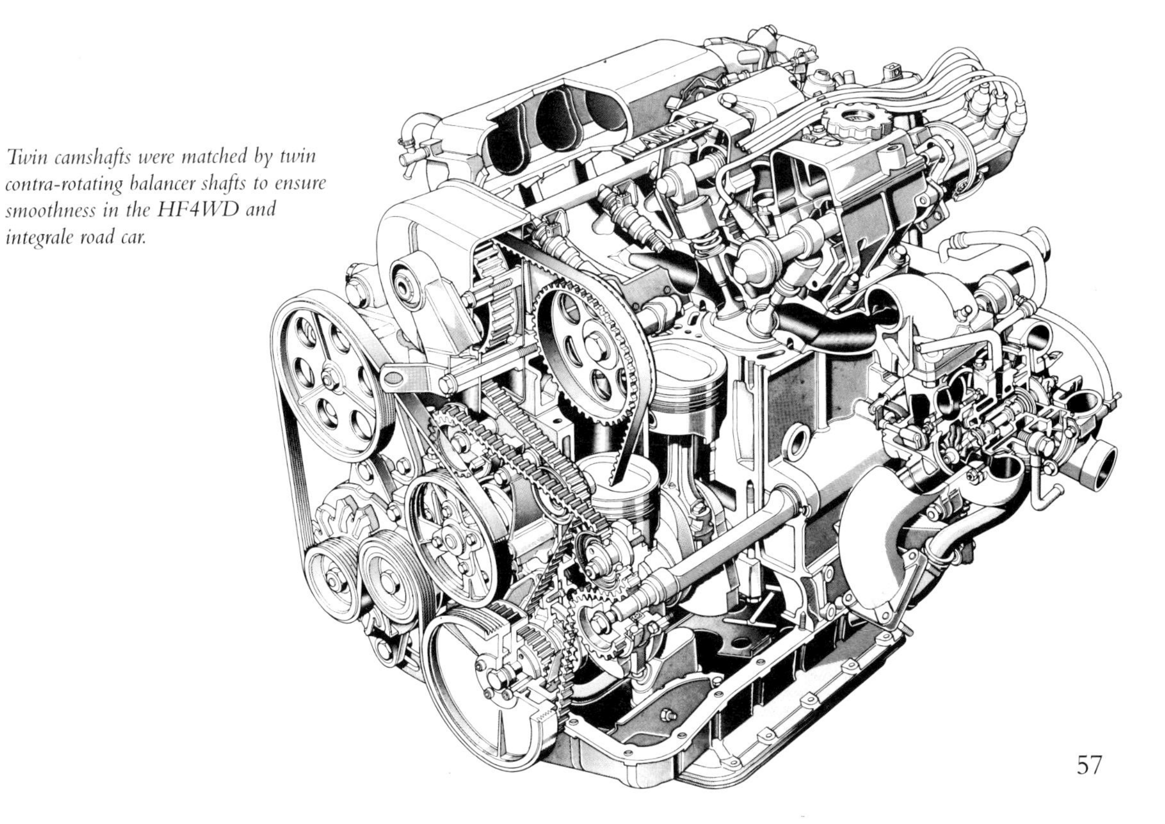

LANCIA DELTA HF integrale

Specification

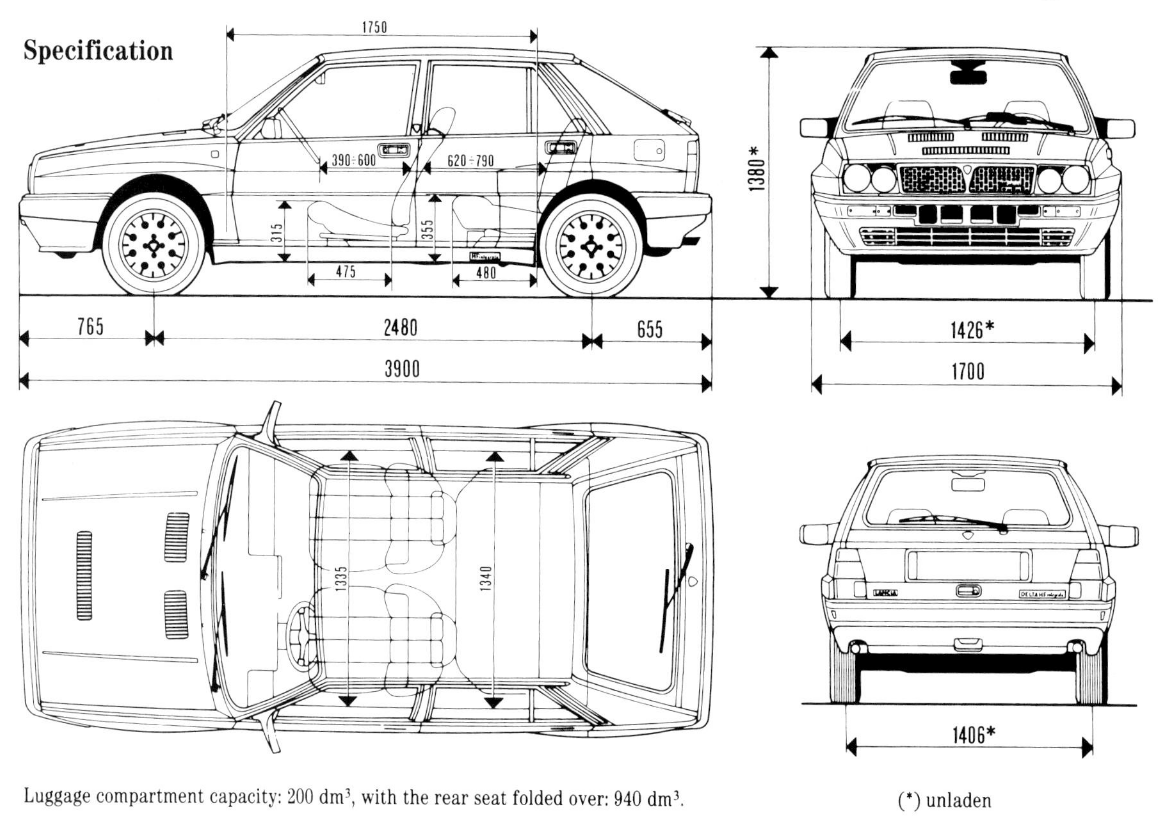

Luggage compartment capacity: 200 dm³, with the rear seat folded over: 940 dm³.

(*) unladen

ENGINE

Main features

No. of cylinders	4 in line
Cycle-stroke	Otto-4
Bore x stroke	87 × 90 mm
Cylinder capacity	1,995 cc.
Compression ratio	8 to 1
Max power output	185 bhp-DIN 5,300 rpm
Max torque (EEC)	31 mkg-DIN
at	2500 rpm - 2750 rpm
Fuel required	Premium, 4-Star

Structural layout

Arrangement	transversely-mounted at front
Cylinder spacings	91 mm
Main bearings	5
Cylinder head	light alloy
Cylinder block	cast iron with counter-rotating balancer shafts

Timing gear

Valve arrangement	at V(65°)
Camshafts	2 overhead

Timing control	by toothed belt
Phasing	phasing control play = 0.8 mm
Intake } beginning	8° before TDC
Intake } end	42° after BDC
Exhaust } beginning	42° before BDC
Exhaust } end	1° after TDC
Counter-rotating balancer shafts	2 in the cylinder block
Control	by toothed belt

Ignition

Type	electronic with mapped advance control and knock sensor, combined with the injection
Firing order	1-3-4-2
Spark plugs	Marelli F8LCR - Fiat/Lancia V45LSR Champion RN7YC - Bosch WR6DC

Fuel feed

Type	supercharging by turbocharger and air/air heat exchanger off the ignition and overboost automatically engaged at full revs
Fuel pump	electric
Injection	electronic IAW Weber combined with the ignition
Air cleaner	dry-type, with paper cardridge
Turboblower type	water-cooled Garrett T3
Max supercharging pressure	1.0 bar

Lubrication

Type	forced feed with gear pump and oil radiator
Oil filter	gear-type

Engine cooling

Type	water-forced by pump with radiator and additional expansion tank
Control	thermostat
Fan	electric, controlled from a thermostatic switch on the radiator

TRANSMISSION

Type	permanent 4 wheel drive with centrally-mounted epicyclic torque converter and Ferguson viscous joint; Torsen-type rear differential with 5 to 1 wheel torque ratio
Clutch	dry, single plate
Friction ring diameter ($Ø_e \times Ø_i$)	230 × 155 mm

Transmission ratios:

1st	3.500 : 1
2nd	2.235 : 1
3rd	1.518 : 1
4th	1.132 : 1
5th	0.928 : 1
Reverse	3.583 : 1
Final drive ratio	3.111 : 1 (55/18)
Bevel gear front/rear	2.263 : 1 (19/43)
Torque converter } front	56%
Torque converter } rear	44%

CHASSIS

Body	self-bearing structure
Braking system	front and rear discs with floating calipers, diagonal-split type hydraulic brake circuit with vacuum servo and brake effort proportioning valve acting on the rear wheels

Front discs	
- diameter	284 mm (self-ventilating)
- total front brake linings	50 × 4 = 200 cm^2
Rear discs	
- diameter	227 mm
- total rear brake linings	35 × 4 = 140 cm^2
Parking brake	acting on the shoes of the rear discs

Front suspension	independent MacPherson-type struts, lower wishbones, anti-roll bar, and double-acting hydraulic telescopic dampers
Flexibility at the wheel	0.55 mm/kg
Wheel wobble upper	78 mm
Wheel wobble lower	85 mm
Wheel position (unladen)	
- camber	- 40' ± 30'
- caster	2°50' ± 30'
- toe-in	- 2 ÷ 1.5

Rear suspension	independent MacPherson-type struts, transverse links, longitudinal reaction rods and anti-roll bar
Flexibility at the wheel	0.55 mm/kg
Wheel wobble upper	75 mm
Wheel wobble lower	125 mm
Wheel position (unladen)	
- camber	- 55' ± 30'
- caster	2°25' ± 30'
- toe-in	32 to 5 mm

Steering	servo-assisted rack and pinion
Turning circle	10.4 m
Steering wheel turns lock to lock	2.8

Road wheels	
Rims	light alloy 6 × 15"
Tyres	195/55 VR 15
Inflating pressure	
- front	2.0 bar - 2.2 bar (**)
- rear	2.0 bar - 2.2 bar (**)

Spare wheel	
Rim	light alloy 4J × 15" AH2-40
Tyre	115 × 70 R15
Inflating pressure front/rear	4.2 bar

(**) at high constant speed, fully laden

Electrical equipment	
Voltage	12 V
Alternator with built-in electronic voltage regulator	65 A
Starter motor	1.1 kW
Battery	45 Ah (service free)

WEIGHTS

Kerb weight (DIN)*	1,200 kg (2,645 lbs)
Distribution front	63%
Distribution rear	37%
Laden weight	1,665 kg
Distribution front	54.7%
Distribution rear	45.3%
Maximum payload	450 kg
Max towing weight	1,200 kg
No. of seats	5

(*) Inclusive of fuel, water, spare wheel, and accessories.

PERFORMANCE

Top speed (in 5th)	215 km/h (133 mph)
Max gradient climbable (laden)	58%
Speed at 1,000 rpm in 4th	30.9 km/h
Speed at 1,000 rpm in 5th	37.7 km/h
Power/weight ratio kg/bhp	6.57

	Acceleration		
	(2 adults + 20 kg)	(secs)	
	0 ÷ 100 km/h (0-62 mph)	6.6 s	
	0 ÷ 400 m	14.7 s	
	0 ÷ 1,000 m	27.1 s	
	Pickup from 40 km/h (in 5th)		
	(2 adults + 20 kg)	(secs)	
	over 1,000 m	36 s	
	over 400 m	20.2 s	
	40 ÷ 100 km/h	20.0 s	
	Conventional fuel consumption		
		(l/100 km)	(mpg)
	at 90 km/h	7.7	36.7
	at 120 km/h	10.2	27.7
	urban cycle	10.8	26.2
	ECE average	9.6	29.4
		dm^3	kg
SUPPLIES			
	Fuel tank capacity	57 (12.5 gals)	-
	including a reserve of:	6 to 9 (1.3-2 gals)	-
	Engine radiator, expansion tank, and heating system liquid	6.20	-
	Oil pan	4.9	4.4
	Total capacity of pan filter, radiator and ducting oil	5.9	5.2
	Gearbox and differential oil	3.8	3.4
	Rear differential	1.1	1
	Power-steering box grease	0.68	0.61
	Hydraulic brake circuits liquid	0.30	0.29
	Wind-screen and rear screen washer bottle	2.0	-

Meanwhile, development by the team at Abarth's Corso Marche factory in Turin continued so that by the end of September 1987, Fiorio was able to tell the press that about 270bhp had been extracted from the new competition car's engine but he doubted that they would be able to homologate the car until the spring of 1988.

Lancia Delta integrale Group A Differences

Engine	
Max. power	Group A, 280bhp @ 6,500rpm
Max. torque	Group A, 39 kg m/282lb ft @ 4,000rpm
Transmission	
Type	Group A, ZF 6-speed non-synchronized.
Wheels	Group A, 16in
Rim width	Group A, 9in
Dimensions	
Track	Front: Group A, 1,488mm Rear: Group A, 1,458mm

New regulations had again been announced by motor sport's governing body, FISA, and were due to be implemented from 1 January 1988. These were aimed, yet again, at reducing the performance potential of the cars, despite the fact that the year before, Group A cars had been heralded by that same organization as the dawn of a new, safer and slower rally car era.

Competition integrale

As an indication of newly reversed priorities, long before road versions were made available to journalists, Lombardi's team had announced the Martini works rally version of the integrale. Immediately prior to the start of the 1987 San Remo Rally, one of the two working prototypes was displayed, registered TO 55066F, and

It cannot be emphasized too highly that Lancia's road-car sales benefited greatly from the Delta's World Rally Championship success.

this was, in fact, an old friend already having been Sergio Limone's first development HF4WD and therefore was a conversion.

Part of the FISA rule change was their insistence that all turbo cars should compete with a standard sized intercooler, which meant that for 1988 it would be about 35 per cent smaller than that on the competition 1987 car. Conversely, the turbo cars' coefficient, as applied to engine capacity, was changed – turbo cars' engine sizes had had to be multiplied by 1.4 in 1987, which meant they were the equivalent of a 2.8-litre normally aspirated car and thus fitted into the under-3000cc class. For 1988 this equivalency figure was increased to 1.7 making 3391cc, which was one class 'bigger'. This handed the advantage to Lancia of being able to run larger wheel rim widths of up to nine inches. This was the reason for those big, butch-looking wheel arches. One-and-a-half inches more rubber on the road all round was going to make a considerable difference. To make full use of all those holes in the front end of the car, water and oil radiators were 20 per cent bigger on the integrale, enabling the engine to run on average six degrees cooler than before. The cooler a turbo can run, the more power it can develop. There was an increase in the turbo-charger size, allowed by the new rules, so the net result of additions allowed here and subtractions there is that Lancia expected to start the integrale's campaign with as much power as they had finally managed to extract from the HF4WDs set up, which was 260bhp. As the new integrale would not be fully homologated until the Portugal rally in March 1988, the team would have to continue using the HF4WD until then. This would also be subject to the new rules so, because they would not have the larger turbo, intercoolers and air intakes, the

net result of those rules on them would mean a reduction in power from 260bhp at San Remo and the RAC in 1987 to 240bhp at Monte Carlo and Sweden in 1988.

Bigger turbo-chargers though result in more power being generated at higher revs and thus a narrower power band. The team had foreseen this eventuality and developed a six-speed gearbox for the competition integrale. This was particularly useful on the Safari rally, where top speed was high but good low-gear acceleration was also needed. The ratios had to be agreed with FISA before the season started so, on a fast rally, the use of higher ratios and the five-speed box would have left the cars with too high a first-gear. Using the lower ratios available with only five speeds would have cured the low-speed acceleration problem at the expense of a higher top speed. Homologation of a six-speed ZF gearbox solved this problem. The rules allowed for teams to specify an alternative Group A gearbox.

The marketing men at the factory had to work hard at conferring the abilities of its rally winner onto the more mundane showroom versions, otherwise the integrale would have had no commercial justification and its rallying would have stopped.

With its extended wheelarches, the integrale impressed all just standing still.

The standard integrale was designed to run on 15in wheels, an increase of 1in over the 14in on its predecessor. The integrale competition car was thus able to use 16in if necessary. Larger brakes had also been incorporated into the integrale specification and correspondingly larger items were therefore planned to complement the integrale's 16in wheels.

Common on many cars now, and an indication of how competition improves the technology of road cars, the rally integrale heralded the arrival of separate coils for each cylinder

Whilst the engineers beavered away down on Corso Marche to ensure more rally wins, other Lancia designers had been contemplating the idea of completely different badging for the integrale.

The minute differences – size of lettering, rounding off of the 2.0 'box' – are a good example of Lancia's insistence on quality detail design.

because, as Lombardi stated, 'Cylinders theoretically work in the same way, but not in reality, so it will be possible to monitor and adjust each cylinder independently'. Lombardi publicly expressed his disappointment that a 4-valve per cylinder engine had not been chosen – little did anyone realize what the future held.

Weight of the road integrale was up, by some 25kg, to 1,215kg over the HF4WD, but Lombardi thought the new rally car could be kept down to around 1,120–1,130kg, especially on the Tour de Corse, a tarmac rally that required the cars to be as light as possible. The increase in weight was mainly due to the longer – by 40–55mm – suspension arms required by the new wide track availability because of the new flared bodywork.

A big change for the rally cars in 1988 would be a switch by the Abarth team from the use of Pirelli tyres to those from Michelin, although Lombardi also remarked that the private Jolly Club Team would stay with Pirelli '...so we will have to develop the car for two different types of tyre...'. A situation unheard of today.

A myriad of consequent engine modifications also involved the valve seats, pistons, gaskets, oil and water pumps, air filter and fan, which all had to be changed. Other upgraded equipment on the integrale included shock absorbers, hubs, half-shafts, driveshaft couplings and springs, as well as larger brake calipers, brake servo and front discs.

The competition integrale also saw some considerable development in the field of torque splitting.

Production integrales were in Italian showrooms by the end of October 1987, but it was to be March 1988 before UK journalists were able to get their hands on one, although there had been a press launch near Turin in late October 1987 when *Autosport* magazine reported that Lancia 'made no bones that this is [the integrale] purely an homologation special'. As well as describing how Lancia had opened up the front of the car to let more cool air in, they had also cut louvres in the bonnet top to let the hot air out. This is particularly crucial on a rally car. Most rallies involve relatively slow running most of the time with

Ing. Limone and the team at Corso Marche tried many ideas to increase the integrale's competitiveness. Here are rear-mounted radiators.

plenty of slowing down and violent acceleration. Under these circumstances an engine in standard form will quickly overheat, whilst one modified to the extent of the works Deltas would even sooner expire without comprehensive cooling.

It was noted there was no ABS. Lancia decided that as rally cars did not need it then neither should the road version. Some journalists were critical of this but the fact underlined once again that no longer were Lancia's rally cars to be derived from their road cars, from then on it was very definitely the opposite way round. The road cars were there simply because they had to be; besides, the addition of ABS would have increased weight.

Meanwhile an early example of the integrale appeared in competition for the first time at the Rallye di Monza driven by Gianni del Zoppo in early December 1987. The new model was not homologated at this time and so the car, virtually completely standard, was

Torque Split

With a conventional two-wheel drive car 100 per cent of the torque produced by the engine is passed to the road through those two driven wheels. The situation is altered and made more complex when all four wheels are driven.

The distribution, to the front or back, of torque from the engine is controlled in the case of the four-wheel drive Deltas by the central viscous Ferguson differential situated alongside the gearbox. This can be set to provide however much torque should be sent to the front or rear. In the case of the HF4WD, during development as a road car 58 per cent was tried at the front wheels and 42 per cent to the rear. After considerable testing, however, it was decided to make these figures 56 per cent front and 44 per cent rear.

Lombardi and his engineers, when working with the competition cars, found that these figures were not always the most suitable. They may have been an ideal for day-to-day road driving, but could not really cope with the tarmac of Corsica, as well as the snow of Monte Carlo and Sweden or mud of the Safari.

Much work was carried out by the Lancia team to establish the best figures for various situations. Lombardi said that work was carried out experimenting with different values and even trying the possibilities of automatically being able to vary the torque split from inside the car. They found that 40/60 (front/rear) was best for tarmac and 50/50 or even 55/45 was best for mud, gravel or snow.

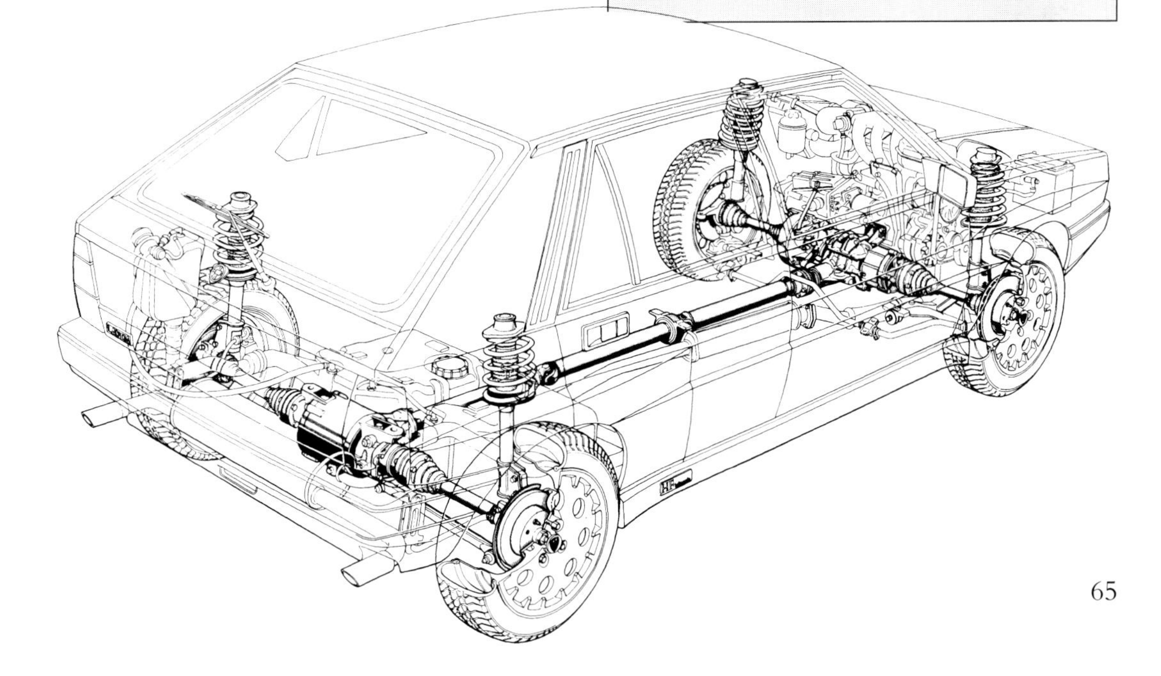

It took Abarth's engineers a lot of time to decide upon the best front/rear torque distribution figures. In the late 1980s this was non-adjustable from inside the car. That development came later to the industry and was never available on an integrale.

allowed to run in a special cars category. Even so, it was able to outrun a rally prepared Group N Ford Sierra Cosworth.

Last Rallies for the HF4WD

As predicted by Fiorio in the autumn of 1987, homologation of the integrale had not materialized by the time of the 1988 Monte Carlo in January, and it seemed as if Portugal in March would be the most likely date for completion of the necessary 5,000 cars and associated paperwork.

All of this meant that world rallying had not quite seen the last of the HF4WD just yet and it would have to bear the brunt of the rally workload at Lancia for the time being. So, despite effectively being obsolete cars, they returned to Monaco developing some 20bhp less than the previous year due to the new rules requiring the use of a series production-based intercooler. Thus the two works cars, on Michelin rubber for the first time, were developing 240bhp versus the previous years' 260. Yves Loubet, Bruno Saby and Miki Biasion were the drivers.

Despite their lack of homologation, integrales were conspicuous on the rally as they were being used by the ice-note crews that covered stages before the rally itself, relaying their findings of the condition road surfaces back to the team for driver information and to assist in making tyre choices. This was another small but significant example of the Lancia team's professionalism, as there was no doubt that the use of the cars and their performance was fed back into the development programme.

Two of the competing HF4WDs did not fare too well, however. Biasion's failed after three stages with a broken oil pump, whilst Loubet suffered a massive accident when pushing hard over the Puimichel stage. The car turned over after hitting the cliff face then shot over the edge of the hillside hitting trees before bouncing end over end down a ravine. Miraculously the crew were unhurt but very shaken. Loubet cursed himself for losing the rally but the spectators suggested that in fact, he was lucky. If he had had that accident in one of the previous Group B cars he would most likely not have got away with it.

Only one Martini works Lancia remained, that of Bruno Saby. He continued to push hard but there was a surprise after 3km of the Col de Turini, as reported by *Autosport* magazine. Fauchille, Saby's co-driver reported the appearance of a totally naked girl by the road and Fiorio spotted her too – but no other crews reported seeing her. It was assumed she was an over-enthusiastic Lancia supporter.

Still with one more event to go before works retirement, the HF4WDs had claimed yet another one, two; Saby beating Fiorio in TO 04201H. Their last rally in Martini livery was to be the Swedish. Where Saby's Monte Carlo car was again in evidence, this time in Markku Alen's hands, whilst Mikael Ericsson used Miki Biasion's from that event, as there was obviously not a lot of desire at the factory to build new examples of what was, for them, a dying breed. Especially as it would take up precious integrale development time.

Bruno Saby's integrale undergoes stiffness tests.

The main new aspect, as far as the works cars were concerned, were new snow tyres from Michelin with whom a lot of work was now being undertaken. The Martini team were taking full advantage of new rules regarding the number of studs in the tyres although, in the end, the weather was not as cold as was expected and, with rain, the snow tended to turn to slush.

Michelin Part One: Snow and Ice Tyres

Tyres for the Swedish Rally had always been a speciality, requiring narrow treads with deep gaps between the tread 'blocks'. These blocks were allowed twelve studs to be fitted per decimetre of tread, but the rules were eased to allow twenty. With 1988s new tyres having been tested with Lancia, there was an improvement in road-holding. This was gained by designing a tyre that would force the studs through the top surface of snow on the road and into the ice below to gain good grip.

Michelin put a thin strip of rubber compound between the stud and the casing of the tyre and as the casing itself vibrated all the time it caused the stud, as it hit the surface, to effectively be hammered into the surface as if with a pneumatic tool.

Stud technology had moved on in Sweden by this time to the point where they were glued into the tyre but, on this event, this was sub-contracted work not carried out by Michelin. On the other likely snow rally – the Monte Carlo – the requirement for the studs in the tyres was quite different. The Monte required bigger and wider based studs, which had to be sunk deeper into the tyre casing.

Guns are used to fire the studs into the tyres on the Monte Carlo and this allows them to creep out when the tyre is in action. When stationary the studs protrude 2mm but with movement they creep out to 3mm, so improving grip further.

Despite the fact that the number of studs per decimetre was raised in Sweden from twelve to twenty, Michelin found that the Lancias were faster on old tyres with only fifteen. One of the problems they encountered was 'snowplaning', whereby the gaps between the tread blocks on the tyres can be too narrow to allow snow to pass between them. However, the tyres used in Sweden were narrower than anywhere else and worked well, so Michelin found that this gave more pressure through the snow thus allowing the studs to work more effectively, proving that simply increasing the number of studs was not necessarily likely to produce an improvement in performance.

Having missed the Monte Carlo, as he was recceing for the Safari, Markku Alen was raring to go on the Swedish. Back on one of his highs, he was interviewed by Martin Holmes after the rally and showed huge enthusiasm for the Lancia Delta and Group A in general. 'The new formula is getting better and better all the time and it is safer as well. It is not boring like we thought it would be.'

Getting the cars to go and handle are the factors most would consider important in motor sport but Markku revealed that he had had 'a lot of problems on the first two rallies with the Group A Delta. I thought the car was stuffy. Later we discovered the trouble was solved by adding an extra internal window in the rear to protect us from petrol and exhaust fumes.'

Much of this enthusiasm probably resulted from his win on the Swedish. He reckoned he had the best HF4WD he had ever driven and by taking things easy, and never going faster than was absolutely necessary, he brought the car home for a swansong victory. Team mate Ericsson had gone out with overheating resulting from a defective water hose but an HF4WD took Group N honours in the hands of Soren Nilsson, although not without some drama. Leaving all others in Group N behind, Nilsson was romping away but began suffering from a lack of brakes, eventually having to appeal to the spectators for new disc brake pads. Someone found that Saab 9000 pads were an exact fit, so he was able to continue on his way to clear victory.

The reign of the HF4WD really was finally over; from the moment the Swedish Rally finished it was officially retired from active works competition participation, although many cars continued in private hands.

From the snow and ice of Northern Europe the teams were next due to clash in Portugal in March 1988. Not only the weather would be different. Lancia's integrale was to be homologated on 1 March – just in time for the Portugese Rally. Alen was delighted, in his interview with Martin Holmes he had said,'…the integrale is coming and I know how good that will be…'.

The HF4WD: Looking Back

The integrale had a lot to beat, as the HF4WD had set up an enviable World Rally Championship record.

From Acropolis 1987 it had won every round of the series during the remainder of that year and continued into 1988 whilst Lancia awaited the homologation of the integrale.

The full list of World Championship victories for the HF4WD is:

1987

Monte Carlo – Miki Biason
Portugal – Markku Alen
Acropolis – Markku Alen
Olympus(Usa) – Juha Kankunnen
New Zealand – Franz Wittman (private team)
Argentina – Miki Biasion
1000 Lakes – Markku Alen
San Remo – Miki Biasion
RAC – Juha Kankunnen

1988

Monte Carlo – Bruno Saby
Sweden – Markku Alen

Never assume an 8 valve car (on left) is inadequate compared to later evoluziones. Learn to get the best from one and there will be few who will even get close.

4 Integrale – Keeping Up Appearances

1 March 1988 marked the end of the beginning. The HF4WD had bowed out of works competition and its place was taken by the new integrale. The word is Italian for complete or whole, describing the transmission and drive, but also providing a good summation of the character of the new car.

Portuguese Rally 1988

In competition, the immediate start of its career was not totally auspicious. The organizers of the Portugese rally 1988 had arranged for the first stage to be televised and cars were sent off around a track laid out at the sometime Grand Prix circuit complex of Estoril near Lisbon.

During this super-special, as it was named, Markku Alen was seen to be slow-

Michelin Part Two: Puncture-Proof Tyres

After their new snow and ice tyres on the Swedish rally, Michelin used the latest versions of their new puncture-proof gravel tyres on the Portugese Rally.

Entitled ATS (appui temporaire souple) or temporary flexible system, the concept had appeared the year before on Audi and Renault at the Acropolis Rally but vibration meant they were too difficult to use effectively. Intensive development over the 1987–88 winter reduced the two main problems – weight of the tyres and vibration – to acceptable levels, and both Lancia and Mazda tried them.

The principle was that the doughnut, or mousse, inside the tyre is held compressed when the pressure is 1.8bar or greater – gravel tyres tend to run at between 2.1 and 2.4bar. If the pressure falls below 1.8bar the doughnut loses its compression and expands to fill the inside of the tyre before the carcass deforms.

The outside tyres were completely normal and the doughnuts were simply fitted inside them. It was possible for the drivers to continue at competitive speeds for up to 100km with a tyre supported only by the internal doughnut. Alen himself experienced a puncture and ran on the doughnut-filled tyre; he suggested that it was like driving with a worn shock absorber. The suspension seemed a little bit soft.

In fact, for Michelin technicians, it was difficult to tell when a car arrived at a service area whether it had a punctured tyre or not. The only way to tell was to press the tyre-valve. If no air escaped, it was flat!!

Every effort was made by the works development team to increase the amount of air circulating around the engine and turbo.

Martini Racing

Martini was the team sponsor and Martini Racing the public name of Abarth, the Lancia competitions department. Their livery first appeared on a rally Lancia in 1982, although they had been involved with the racing Beta Monte Carlo Turbos and later the Lancia LC1 and 2.

Consolidated over many years, it was a fully integrated team involving design, construction, development and an event team organization. Their main strength was having complete control of design and implementation of modifications all under one roof.

Overall boss was Claudio Lombardi, who had been with Abarth and Lancia since 1982; firstly, as head of rally engine development, and later as technical director. By 1988 he was general manager of Abarth and technical director of Alfa Corse.

Martini Lancia was divided into five sections:

- Engines: design, development and construction was responsibility of Giovanni Roffina who had been with Lancia since 1977.
- Vehicles: car design and development; the responsibility of Sergio Limone who had been with Lancia since 1978
- Transmissions: gearbox and differential design and construction was responsibility of Felice Garron, with Lancia since 1967.
- Electronics: engine management and electronic components were the responsibility of Enrico Alviano, at Lancia since 1980. On events, Giovanni Martina took his place.
- Rally Sports Organization: team logistics, management of materials and cars. This sector also looked after the sale of Group A cars to customers and after-sales service, such as the supply of spare parts, which included those for Group N cars.

They had priority customers such as Deutsche Fiat, Fiat France, Fiat Portugal, as well as the Italian teams such as Jolly Club and Grifone. This was the responsibility of Corrado (Connie) Isemburg who joined Lancia in 1986 and ex-co-driver Nini Russo, who had been with the Fiat group in rallying for many years.

Martini's contribution to the Delta 4WD story and its heritage must never be underestimated. Starting with the 037 they stood by Lancia for ten unforgettable years.

Miki Biasion heads for victory on the 1988 Portugal rally. This was the first world championship event for the integrale.

ing and finally stopped. His car had had total transmission failure based on problems with the central differential. Later, Claudio Lombardi stated that he had no idea what caused it and it would not be possible to assess the problem until a return to Corso Marche in Turin. The thought that it might have been caused by the extra stress of the integrale's larger wheels on the transmission caused some ripples of anxiety through the team. They were only able to use the five-speed gearbox from the HF4WD for this event; the stronger six-speed unit still was not ready.

So, whilst Markku spent the rally driving as hard as possible playing catch-up, Miki Biasion established himself at the front as early as the second special stage and never relinquished the position, whilst Markku finally ended sixth. He reckoned that the new car seemed to have less torque than the previous one, but there was a huge amount of potential in the integrale. He also considered that a small lack of torque would not be such a problem once the six-speed gearbox was in regular use.

A first-time-out win for the integrale was great news for Lancia, but Alen's and Ericksson's transmission problems gave some cause for concern. As far as bare results were concerned, Lancia's cup was full, however, as Jorge Recalde brought his Group N integrale home for the class win.

Occasional works drivers Fiorio and Loubet backed up the victory with second and third places in faithful HF4WDs.

Road Cars

In the UK, the first road cars were filtering through. *Autosport* and *Car* magazines were the first to commit their impressions to paper, suggesting that the rally championship-winning characteristics of the HF4WD had been translated well into what was effectively now a homologation model. Phrases such as 'very civilized' and 'competitively priced and packaged' were quoted.

Autosport suggested that the car should be driven in the wet first, before trying it on a dry road – otherwise there was a possibility of feeling a 'little disappointed'. Wet roads first, dry later and then the integrale will emerge as a truly outstanding all-round machine.

When Autosport *magazine first tested an integrale they recommended trying it first in the wet before going for it in the dry. A 16v proves the point.*

As on the special stages, so on the public road, *Car* magazine put the integrale up against the Toyota Celica GT-Four. This latter car was the Japanese company's hope in the struggle to topple Lancia on the special stages of the world. Price was a significant factor as the integrale could be driven away from a showroom for £15,455, whilst another £5,000 would have to be found for the Toyota.

Whilst the Japanese car had better brakes, courtesy of electronic ABS, which the Lancia eschewed, the latter was 'always the sharper, more eager car…never in danger of losing its performance crown to the tamer Toyota'. A telling comment is that the Toyota faithfully did as it was commanded, but dispassionately and without feeling.

The integrale 'shaped up as the performance bargain of the decade'. Whilst these accolades were being handed out in cold, wet, England, driving over Dartmoor, sometimes in snow, by comparison the works Martini team

In 1988, the integrale gave Lancia their first outright win on the gruelling Safari rally. Something they had been trying to achieve for many years.

were hard at it in ferocious heat. Once again the Turinese team was attempting to crack the Safari Rally. For years this had become some sort of Holy Grail to them. They had sent the Stratos more than once for Sandro Munari and later the 037 but they had never achieved a win. Success may have come relatively easily everywhere else, but in East Africa, try as they might, they just had not been able to make it all click into place.

Safari Rally 1988

The team had been testing since January and February with Markku Alen but because of the close proximity of the Corsica and Acropolis World Championship rounds, only two new cars were sent. These were for Miki Biasion and local driver Vic Preston Jnr who had been faithful to Fiat group products for some years.

The Martini team felt confident enough of their new six-speed gearboxes to use them for the first time, besides, they felt they had to after the worrying failures on the Portugese Rally with the previous five-speed unit.

Despite the greater suspension travel allowed by the integrale, it was not this that turned out to be the main advantage of the model over the previous year's car and that was surprising as the Safari is the roughest rally in the world championship. It became clear that the integrale's biggest advantages were the extra cooling available from the new air intakes and outlets, and a 30bhp increase in power, engines for the Safari being in a lower state of tune than those for sprint events.

Transmission problems did arise though, even with the new gearboxes, and caused the retirement of Vic Preston Jnr. Miki Biasion had some problems with the early pace causing overheating and a sticky 'box having to complete 400km in second gear. Perhaps worse was Vic Preston's experience of covering a long hilly section stuck in fifth gear.

Despite this, plus a blown turbo-charger, a broken driveshaft and an accident with a zebra, Biasion finally pulled off the result Martini Lancia had wanted for well over a decade. He won, but by only 15min, which is a very close call by Safari standards. The Fiat group had tried to gain this result thirteen times previously; now the virtually new integrale had finally got the job done.

The team had now won every World Championship Rally that they had entered since the Acropolis in spring 1987. They had also racked up maximum points at this early stage in the 1988 championship.

Tour de Corse 1988

After Martini Lancia's pleasure at taking first overall on the Safari, the team was in for a surprise on Corsica for the Tour de Corse. Whilst Yves Loubet – a driver chosen for his local knowledge of the stages - was clearly the fastest driver and car combination on the event, reliability problems arose as the gear linkage on his newly built integrale failed and he was never able to get back on terms with Auriol's winning Ford Sierra Cosworth. The other integrale, driven by Saby, suffered a puncture after running out of road and finished third.

Could any of this have been seen as an integrale weakness? A stronger performance on asphalt would have allowed a cushion to have been built up, which might have saved them from slipping back into the clutches of the chasing Sierra Cosworth, an acknowledged tarmac racer.

Technically the Martini cars were altered in several ways to make them more suitable for the fast but twisty tarmac stages. The closest possible ratios were chosen for the six-speed gearboxes and torque split was set at a rear biased 40/60. Very hard springs were fitted with soft shock absorbers and bigger diameter front brakes were included. The team claimed 275bhp from the engines but it was the transmissions that received the most interesting treatment. The Torsen rear differentials were locked so as to maintain maximum traction, even when the car was on three wheels, thus their handling was rather like driving a car with a rigid rear axle.

This rally was also the debut event for the car that was to become the integrale's greatest threat: the Toyota Celica GT-Four. Kenneth Eriksson achieving sixth place with the new car.

So it was defeat at last, at the hands of Ford, for Lancia's record-breaking team after an unprecedented run of wins. Was this the beginning of the end, or just a hiccup?

Kankunnen, in one of the new Toyotas, commented later that the main problem with his car was lack of power and an inability to run wide enough tyres on tarmac stages – the exact problems Lancia had experienced the year before. Ironically the overall speed of the winner on the stages set up a new record and it was the first time that the Group A cars had proven faster than their Group B predecessors. That it should happen on the rally that caused the regulations to be changed was missed by no one.

Acropolis Rally 1988

The pressure on the Martini cars continued into the following event but from an unexpected source. Whilst the team was aware that the all-tarmac format of Corsica would not necessarily be to the integrale's advantage – Lombardi admitting that any car with a weight distribution of 62 per cent front 38 per cent rear would be unlikely to display any other handling trait than a slight understeer bias – the team did not expect the Acropolis to present the same difficulties. Some of the team's crews still thought the understeer needed attention but their problems did not come from within. Instead, to everyone's surprise, the new Toyota Celica GT4 proved to be a very capable machine and in the hands of Kankunnen took the fight to Lancia, leading on many stages until engine failure put a stop to its performance. Such was its speed that the Martini cars were forced to use high boost pressures with consequent high engine temperatures. Biasion's gauge registered 120°C at one point forcing him to cruise for a while. The Lancia's were not proving inadequate for the job, however, as Alen, Biasion and Ericsson were taking their share of fastest stage times but already, at this relatively early point in the integrale's career, it was perhaps becoming clear that a further development of the car would be required.

As an indication of how hard the Martini cars had had to be pushed, reporters noted that after Biasion's eventual winning car had been cleaned and presented at the final holding control north of Athens, its roof was crumpled, displaying the intense strain placed on the shells of the cars by this extremely tough rally.

Despite all these inconveniences the records show that integrales finished first, second, third and fourth on the 1988 Acropolis, but *Autosport* magazine suggested, 'they should make the most of it, the tide is turning'. Even so, only one more

Markku Alen drove an 8-valve car to an early victory in 1988's Costa Smeralda rally in Sardinia. This was an extra-curricular event that the factory cars took part in for marketing and testing reasons.

win was required for Lancia to take the 1988 championship and when they did, the atmosphere was subdued as they succeeded on the very next event, the Olympus Rally.

Olympus Rally 1988

The Olympus is now all but forgotten as a round of the World Rally Championship. It had been invented as a means to take rallying to the people of the USA who knew little or nothing of the discipline and to a very great extent, cared even less. Started in 1986, the Olympus flame spluttered and died in 1989 by which time the major league teams had abandoned it.

In 1988, it was on Lancia's list but virtually no one else's. Barring John Buffum's locally entered ex-works Audi Quattro, the Martini team had only a Mazda, albeit in the experienced hands of Rod Millen and a team of Suzukis to worry about.

Martini only ran one car, for Miki Biasion, and it was his Portugal winning machine. Alex Fiorio's car was the same ex-HF4WD converted to an integrale that he had used on the Acropolis. The only real change to the works car was the adoption of Martini and Rossi on the livery.

Biasion duly dominated, came home first and Lancia won the 1988 World Championship in record time. No team had ever achieved this situation so early in the season but, as a local Tacoma newspaper man said – the event being based in that town – 'there are people in Paris, Rome and Helsinki who deeply mind what will happen here between now and Sunday night, but not, I think, in Tacoma'.

Giovanni del Zoppo was also on hand to take Group N for Lancia ahead of Recalde, both cars as used on the Acropolis.

So, sadly, a stupendous result for Lancia rather had the effect of a damp squib. What did get a number of rival teams nervous though were the rumours and stories coming out of the team concerning their 1989 contender.

Clearly the team was not resting on their laurels and the new threat from Toyota had got them working on how they were going to be able to keep the integrale on the roll that the HF4WD had started.

Expectations were that the 'Type 3' Delta would appear in time for the 1989 season, a daunting thought for the opposition. The only detail to emerge was that the car would feature a 16-valve engine that it was hoped would produce 200bhp in production form. By the time the Argentine round of the 1988 World Rally Championship occurred in the summer, it was reported that Biasion had tested the new car and that it had an electronically controlled centre differential but no other information was forthcoming.

Argentina Rally 1988

Two cars were sent to South America. Once again the Martini team were faced with little or no opposition. Private entrants in local cars made up the bulk of the entry and other than a couple of ex-works Audis as in the USA, Lancia had little to worry about. Except that Jorge Recalde, local ace, was in one of the Martini cars. On occasions, he was to enjoy a clear road, only for his teammates behind to find big rocks in their way. These mysterious circumstances caused Wittman's non-factory Lancia to lose a wheel and Biasion to lose time, but such was their superiority that they finished first, second and third with Recalde in front, much to the spectators delight. Lancia had entered Biasion because they hoped – expected – to clear up the Drivers Championship with the Italian winning, but that would now have to wait.

Road Car Tests

Whilst these shenanigans were going on in the Southern Hemisphere, back in the UK *Autocar* magazine was creating its own, by comparing a Ferrari Testarossa to the road going inte-

First owners of the new integrales were rightly proud of their cars. A gathering of 8-valve cars and HF4WDs like this would be difficult to replicate today – sadly.

grale. Other than proving that the former was actually a better car than expected, the magazine confirmed that, certainly as far as road-going cars were concerned, the latter was ' as good as ever...one of life's bargains'. In another test, *Motor Sport* magazine concluded by suggesting 'it is almost tempting to thank FISA for having created rally rules which force manufacturers to design and sell cars like the integrale'.

The car may not have had to fight too hard for commendations from journalists but Toyota was certainly beginning to cause it to have to fight hard in rallies.

1000 Lakes Rally 1988

At the end of the 1988, 1000 Lakes event winner, Markku Alen, said that seeing the broken Toyota was 'like Christmas, but I would like to fight all the way next time!'.

Maybe he would, but whilst it lasted, Toyota's Celica GT Four, once again in Kankunnen's hands, proved to be at times more than a match again for Martini's best. Under intense pressure, Alen fought Kankunnen stage for stage. At last it seemed Group A had reached maturity and with it a clear indication that Martini Lancia were not likely to have everything their own way in future.

This was all set against the backdrop of what proved to be the fastest World Championship rally yet held, beating the previous record set up in the heady days of 1986 by the infamous Group B cars. It had taken just 18 months.

Claus Billstam found Ericsson's works car had 'too much understeer'. Not something you want when the cars are geared for top speeds of 200–210km/h (124–130mph) and likely to reach those figures. Lombardi said that torque split had been set at 45/55 front/rear for the fast sweeping roads and Michelin had come up with a new gravel racing tyre for the Martini team. Power was 270/280bhp. In Group N there were three Lancias entered by the Italian Top Run team for Argentinian winner Recalde, Gianni del Zoppo and Massimo Ercolani.

To and fro, Alen and Kankunnen traded fastest time on the stages with neither driver ever managing to gain a lead of more than 10s. It was a frantic race between the two aces and at the end of the first day the Toyota led the Lancia by just 3s.

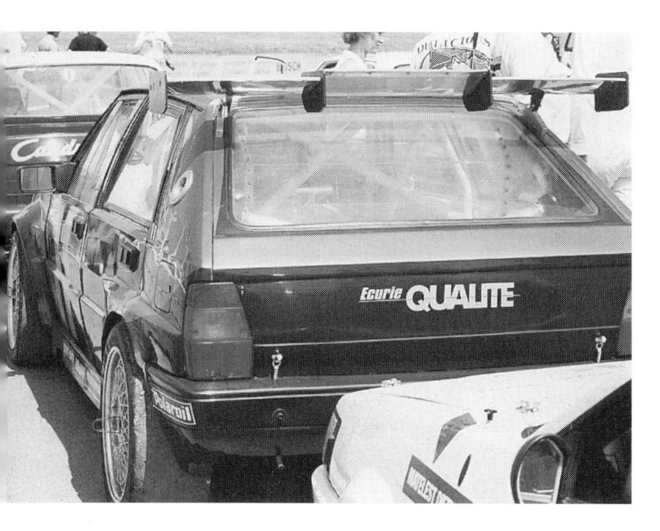

The first of three rare shots of a rare beast: an 8-valve integrale lines up in the collecting area of the Croix en Ternois circuit in France for a round of the French Super Production championship.

Battle was renewed the next day with the pair trading seconds on the stages. Kankunnen suffered a split oil-pipe, which was repaired, and Alen cut his lead to 2s even with a puncture courtesy of Michelin's run-flat tyres. So quickly were they going, that the battling pair had left Ericsson in third place over two and a half minutes behind.

With only five stages to go, the engine of the Toyota cried enough and all that remained was for Alen to reach the finish – hence his remark that he would have liked to have had to fight to the end.

So, was the integrale facing serious competition on a regular basis? The Toyota had proved a difficulty on the tarmac of Corsica, the rough stuff of Acropolis and now the smooth, fast gravel of Finland. Lancia were far from complacent back at Corso Marche.

Cyprus Rally 1988

Meanwhile the European Rally Championship had also been falling Lancia's way with Fabrizio Tabaton's Grifone-run integrale needing only a second place in the Cyprus Rally to take the series, then Toyota swooped again and Waldegaard took the Celica to its first overall win, whilst Tabaton drove carefully to his required second place.

The Toyota was not due to reappear until the Lombard RAC Rally in November – time for Lancia to make some announcements.

San Remo Rally 1988

Traditionally, the team had reserved the evening before the San Remo Rally in October for press releases and conferences and 1988 was no exception. In addition to the usual speeches concerning the driver line-up for the following year, two technical introductions showed that Abarth was forging ahead, not just with car performance development in expected areas, but that they were also using innovative ideas in order to find that performance quantum leap that they would need to keep the opposition behind them.

In the pits during practice 23 July 1989 Croix en Ternois. This integrale was driven by the Frenchman, ex-Formula 3 driver Bernard Lagier.

Entered under the Ecurie Qualite team title, this is, as far as I know, the only integrale ever to take part on a regular basis in an international track racing championship.

First it was revealed that a two-pedal electronic clutch system had been under development since March 1988. The work was being undertaken with Valeo and involved the deletion of the clutch pedal. The changing and selection of gears being accomplished by electronically managed automatic control. The gear lever was retained.

They appeared in all sorts of events. Here is a Belgian 8-valve car being subjected to rallycross on a dreary winter's day at Brands Hatch.

Not content with just an automatic clutch, Lombardi also announced that four-wheel steering was on their list of future developments and that an old Group B Delta S4 was to be so equipped for research, as the racing suspension made the job easier. Fiorio also confirmed that a normally aspirated Delta was under evaluation and that work was continuing on the 16-valve integrale.

After these revelations, the rally itself came as something of a disappointment, especially to the assembled press. By the finish, Lancia were extremely pleased to take the top four places with Miki Biasion winning and thus confirming himself as World Rally Drivers Champion of 1988, despite dreadful weather conditions that caused many problems throughout the field including, tragically, one fatal accident.

Valeo Electronic Clutch – How Did It Work and What Were the Advantages?

The criteria behind the development of an electronic clutch, as far as rallying was concerned, were the optimization of the rate of acceleration from a standing start, by making use of the ability to change gear at exactly the right time. This leads to less stress on transmission parts and therefore makes life easier and less tiring for the driver, who is then free to develop a different driving technique – maybe using left-foot braking at the same time as operating the throttle. The system automatically engaged and disengaged the clutch by the use of an electro-mechanical actuator. An electronic control unit operates the gearbox depending on what information the sensors send it. There is a pushbutton on the steering wheel to manually engage or disengage the clutch when required, such as when idling.

To engage a gear, the gearlever (3) is moved and this initially disengages the clutch, whilst it is re-engaged when the gearbox-engaged gear sensor (6) tells the system that the gear has been selected. The speed with which this takes place is directly affected by the sensor (5), which keeps a check on the angle of opening of the fuel intake butterfly valve. So, if it is fully open, and therefore the accelerator pedal must be fully depressed, the system works faster than if it is partially open. Gearbox and engine revs are picked up by sensors (7 and 8) and it is all controlled by a central electronic processing unit (1).

Under normal circumstances, below 1,200rpm engine speed, the gear required to start from standstill is selected by moving the gear lever. When the revs rise above 1,200rpm the clutch engages and the car moves.

Under extreme conditions, say when the car is leaving a stage start and more revs are required, the button on the steering wheel (4) can be held depressed until the revs required are reached; releasing it will cause the car to start moving. Sensors (2) were also available to provide a form of traction control depending on whether the surface was tarmac or loose.

The point of any automatic clutch/gearbox actuation in a competition car is to save time and Alen thought that on ice or snow he would, by utilizing this system, only have to use the brake and accelerator.

Prophetically, Lombardi predicted that the system would eventually find its way onto production cars; Ferrari in particular being mentioned.

We can say then that this integrale system was a founding father for all Formula One paddle gear changes and, retrospectively, can be seen as a direct predecessor of today's 'F1' and Selespeed systems on twenty-first century Ferrari and Alfa Romeo road cars. Lancia was once again to be seen taking the lead in technological innovation.

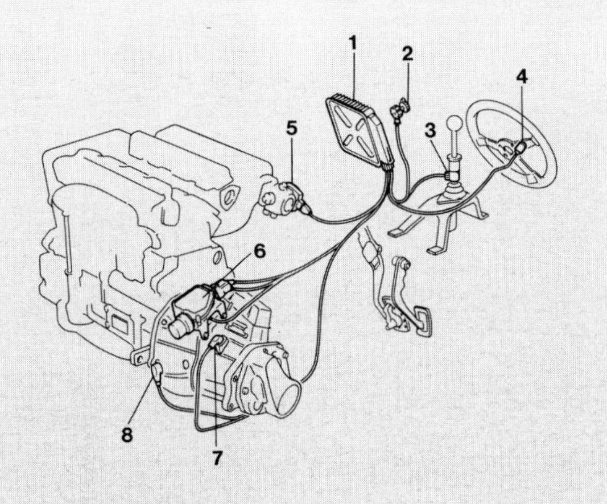

The electronic clutch, developed in conjunction with Valeo, allowed two-pedal driving and eventually led to the F1 and Selespeed quick-change mechanisms available today on Ferraris and Alfa Romeos.

All the integrales, both Martini and Jolly Club entered, were always within striking distance of the lead, but Toyota and Ford, both good on tarmac, were constant threats until retirement and accidents allowed Lancia to virtually cruise home.

For tarmac, the Martini cars had their torque split at 40/60 but for gravel 50/50 was used for the first time, the drivers indicating that they were happy with the big improvement in handling that resulted.

The integrales, with maximum boost being required to counter the opposition, reputedly reached 290bhp on the tarmac roads, the highest power output yet quoted.

The team also brought another car for display purposes only. This was the Valeo clutch integrale, which was fitted with a seat with Lele Pinto's (the chief integrale test driver at the time) name on it. This car had been built as long before as the Corsica rally and had spent its time being used entirely as a development vehicle for the two-pedal system.

Although Martini Lancia had won both the drivers and manufacturers World Rally Championship titles, statistically in utterly convincing fashion, they decided to take part in the end of season RAC Rally in the UK. Turin had always had a love/hate relationship with this event, either ignoring it or trying to dominate it. Previously, if the team was in this position they had not bothered to come, but now there was a chance that Markku Alen might break his jinx and at last win the RAC.

RAC Rally 1988

Martini entered two cars, the one for Alen being Biasion's San Remo car and that for Ericsson was Alen's San Remo car. There was a third, ex-works, car that had been purchased by shell preparation experts, Safety Devices, and this was in the capable hands of Pentti Airikkala.

High drama and ever-changing fortunes greeted the crews as bad weather dogged the event from ice to snow. Through it all Alen seemed to be on a high, never falling far away from the lead and finally taking it near to the finish in Yorkshire, after main rivals Mikkola and Kankunnen, in Mazda and Toyota, both

Integrale interiors have been described as quirky, but, in 8- and 16-valve days, the seats were always considered to complement for the performance image of the car.

left the road never to return. Alen won at last, but Ericsson was another who went off, finishing his rally in Wales. Pentti Airikkala brought his five-speed ex-works Lancia home fourth after a quick roll in Yorkshire.

Other than sporting a 50/50 torque split for the first time, the Martini cars showed no innovations. Although back home the widely expected new 16-valve car was under serious development, there was no sign of its imminent arrival on the World Championship scene or in the showrooms so, as with the HF4WD, the integrale would be shouldering the brunt of Martini Lancia's responsibilities into a second season.

Team boss Cesare Fiorio later announced that Martini Lancia would be contesting every round of the World Rally Manufacturers Championship in 1989, and he also commented upon proposals to slow the cars down, adding that people had realized the cars were now virtually as quick anywhere, as the Group B models they replaced. The Valeo two-pedal automatic clutch system was to see event action for the first time when his son Alex was due to have a car so equipped for the Monte Carlo, first event of 1989.

End of Year Review

As 1988 drew to a close, how could Lancia look back on the year and with what confidence could they look ahead?

Their 8-valve road integrale had received rave reviews from all who drove it with perhaps some reservations, such as the absence of ABS. The Martini works rally team had statistically achieved an almost perfect set of results winning outright ten of the eleven rounds of the World Championship and being beaten into second place only once. Their drivers had taken the top three placings in the Drivers Championship, so Lancia could look back with satisfaction upon a year of what appeared, on the face of it, to be a virtually complete success.

Yet these results, despite having an extremely competent car with which to chase them, were achieved against a background of considerably increased competition. 1987 allowed Lancia the luxury of having the right car at the right time. The criticisms of the HF4WD had largely been addressed and the integrale initially displayed similar superiority to that of its predecessor. Over a year into the Group A regulations, however, the competition was beginning to catch up, not surprisingly. Toyota clearly had a potentially successful weapon in the shape of the Celica GT-Four, and Ford's immensely powerful Cosworth Sierra road-racers were formidable on tarmac. Conversely, Lancia had a car that it now knew inside out and a team that was organized above all others. With many drivers with differing talents on their strength they were able to enter horses for courses. There was a sea-change taking place in the nationality of world-class rally drivers also, possibly occasioned by the arrival of the Group A four-wheel drive cars. No longer were the Finns naturally at the top of team manager's wants lists. The success of Miki Biasion in 1988 showed the way for a new generation of non-Scandinavian drivers. As well as the Italian, there were Didier Auriol, Alex Fiorio, Bruno Saby and Yves Loubet. All younger talents rather than the 'old guard' from northern climes. Coupled to this, the team, probably more than any other, knew how to get their cars to the finish.

Complacency was not an option as the team had had some nasty surprises during 1988 and therefore were likely to have even more during 1989. Everyone knew that the subsequent 16-valve integrale was under development, and as Monte Carlo rolled around again for 1989 it was imperative that the new car was made available as quickly as possible. Biggest problem with the 8-valve car was understeer, and huge testing efforts were being made to improve the situation, although Lombardi considered that the problem could be partially solved by altering the front/rear torque split.

For the forthcoming 1989 year then, the team could not expect any help from the 16-valve car until August at the earliest, with homologation being expected on the first of that month. Meanwhile, the public were waiting with great expectations for the forthcoming road version, which was likely to break cover in the spring. The Delta's sales figures had increased still further with the success of the car's rally career, Lancia hoped the new version would further boost that situation.

Lancia won both 1988 World Rally Championships for Drivers and Constructors, taking the top three places in the former led by Miki Biasion.

Lancia also took the European Rally Championship with Fabrizio Tabaton.

Whilst not yet available to the Martini team, the 16v car was introduced to the press in typical 'rally' style pose.

Monte Carlo Rally 1989

Into the New Year, it was business as usual at Corso Marche. The team did not take part in the Swedish Rally, held earlier than normal that year and concentrated on Monte Carlo.

New driver for Lancia, Didier Auriol, was on the team strength when everyone assembled for the annual race around the Alpes Maritime.

Pressure from the Japanese was increased by the appearance of Mitsubishi with their new Galant and the highly talented Ari Vatanen behind the wheel. This car proved to be very quick, giving Lancia even more to think about than before. They had entered three cars, the other two being Bruno Saby in his 1988 Corsica car and Miki Biasion in a car new to com-

This is how Martini Lancia presented its 1989 driver line-up to the Italian press. Markku had been a Fiat group stalwart for ten years but his enthusiasm was wearing thin with the delays to the development of the 16v integrale. It can also be seen that the Scandinavian driver influence was on the wane.

petition. Alex Fiorio duly debuted the Valeo electronic clutch car and Cerrato brought along his 1988 San Remo mount.

Tragedy was stalking, however. Very sadly Fiorio suffered two offs. The first caused injury to spectators, whilst the second killed spectating driver Lars-Eric Torph, after Fiorio lost control and the car rolled down a bank hitting Torph and his co-driver who were standing at the bottom in a place where no one would reasonably expect to be at risk. Alex was immediately returned, devastated, to Italy.

The Toyota threat did not materialize as being as serious as Lancia expected, so the team was finally able to take a 1, 2, 3 with Biasion first, Auriol second and Saby third. The non-Scandinavians had made their mark convincingly on this snowy tarmac event. Monte Carlo had traditionally been the rally that mattered most to Lancia in terms of marketing power and ultimately new car sales but, although they had won again, it was a subdued victory.

Before everyone reassembled in Portugal at the end of February, Martini sent one car to the European Rally Championship round of Costa Brava in Spain for Yves Loubet who went on to take his first outright win.

More news was forthcoming concerning the debut of the 16-valve integrale. Conny Isemburg, who was manager of the Martini team on events, stated that it would definitely appear for the Rally d'Italia in October but that it was hoped it would be available for the 1000 Lakes.

In its never-ending quest for more effective tyres for the Martini team, Michelin had been concerned that both Auriol and Saby had suffered tyre deflations at the same point in the Monte Carlo so, post-rally, they returned to the exact spot to attempt a recreation of the problem and were surprised to find that the cause had been the effectiveness of the tyres on the Lancias. Their road-holding had been so good that, at the cornering force of 1.6G that had been developed, the tyres, in both cases, had pulled off the rims.

Portugal Rally 1989

Portugal was expected to be a show-down between Toyota and Lancia, and development of the 8-valve integrale had continued with weight-saving and time-saving in mind. New German-made springs were fitted with fewer coils. A more compact rear Torsen differential had been developed, coupled with driveshafts that fitted on splines instead of with bolts thus making them easier to change quickly.

Once again, Fiorio was in charge of the two-pedal car, whilst Biasion, Alen and Auriol handled brand new cars. Almost everyone was disappointed when the Toyota challenge faded early on and only accidents looked like getting in the way of a Lancia walkover, Alen having two.

Man of the moment, Biasion, was easily the winner – by 10min – from Alen and, at the finish, seven of the top ten cars were Lancias. The press asked how long it would be before the Japanese finally overcame the cars from Turin

Technical Sponsors

Martini may have paid the largest team bills, but who were represented by all the other stickers on the factory competition cars?

MAGNETI MARELLI: electric and electronic equipment (BORLETTI, CARELLO, WEBER).
OLIO FIAT: lubricants, coolants.
MICHELIN: tyres.
BILSTEIN: dampers.
BREMBO: brakes.
CHAMPION: spark plugs.
GARRETT: turbo-charger.
STEYR-PUCH: transmission (closely involved in the development of Delta 4WD system).
FERODO: brake pads.
ESSO: fuel.
TRW SABELT: seat belts.
SPEEDLINE: wheels.
SKF: bearings.
VALEO: clutch.

The 8-valve cars still had to bear the brunt of Martini Lancia's World Rally Championship efforts into 1989 but Biasion won again in Portugal.

that, seemingly, were stronger than ever. This was tempered by a surprise announcement, which detailed that Cesare Fiorio was, with immediate effect, leaving Martini Lancia to head up the Ferrari F1 team. His place at Lancia was to be taken by Claudio Lombardi, and many commentators were surprised by the promotion, some even suggesting that the team was likely to be wound down in the future.

Whilst all this was concerning the motor sport world, the Geneva Motor Show was the venue for a public announcement of the integrale 16-valve, to be known as the Lancia Delta HF integrale 16v. The 8-valve car had ceased production, but there was no news as to exactly when its successor would take over.

Safari Rally 1989

Back on the rally trail, Lancia then took the fight to the enemy. Having won the Safari rally for the first time in 1988, they returned even better prepared in 1989. Long the stronghold of the Japanese manufacturers, Biasion again took the win for Turin, thus notching up their fiftieth victory; but it had not been without problems. After a particularly long – 665km – section, both Martini cars stopped on the road out of fuel. Lombardi explained that they kept spare fuel quantities in the car to a minimum because of the possible effect the weight could have on the rear suspension. He was not particularly worried as it happened on a road section when time was not so important.

The cars, for Biasion and Recalde were new, but the Safari is an exceptional event and so a pump was fitted to the gearbox to allow an oil-cooler and fans were placed inside the cockpit air vents to keep car-crews cool. Fiorio, on his first Safari, was entered in a Totip-sponsored car that was fitted out as a high-speed service vehicle – Lancia were taking no chances. Despite the weight penalty, Fiorio brought the car home tenth overall in the results. One of the Lancia chase helicopters, however, caused something of an own-goal when it was flying near to Recalde. The pilot saw a car coming the other way, swooped to warn Recalde and disturbed some nearby sheep who promptly ran in front of the Lancia. Recalde hit them, puncturing the radiator and thus suffered retirement.

Three wins in three rallies put Lancia into a dominant World Championship position. At the same time, Cerrato won the Costa Smeralda event on Sardinia, where Lancia's domination in the European Championship event was even more impressive. Nine out of the final top ten finishers were Lancia integrale-mounted.

Tour de Corse 1989

All this winning was not interfering with the everyday issues of development, however. Next event in the World Championship was the Tour de Corse – Lancia's bête noir. A ferocious amount of work was directed at reducing the car's weight and improving the handling. The latter efforts involved a new Torsen with loading reduced to 80 per cent, whilst the team settled on a torque split of 40/60 front/rear. Where weight could be saved, the engineers found ways of saving it. For instance, even the wheel-brace was made of carbon-fibre and transmission linkages were made of composite materials.

Two cars were entered for Auriol and Loubet and a third ex-Monte Carlo training car was painted blue and white for Lancia France and piloted by Bruno Saby.

New boy, Didier Auriol, brought the team their first Delta win on Corsica in 1989.

LANCIA MARTINI
MICHELIN
MICHELIN
MARTINI
CARELLO
CARELLO

Lancia's determination was driven by two defeats in the previous two years; both at the hands of rear-wheel drive cars. This type of car was well suited to the all-tarmac rally being effectively road-racing cars. In 1987 it had been a BMW M3 and in 1988 a Ford Sierra Cosworth. Now Lancia was facing them again but this time they could at least feel they had done their homework.

Even so, brake problems early on stymied their efforts and allowed the Sierra Cosworth of Chatriot ahead. Turning up the boost to maximum on the Lancias allowed them to stay in touch but, as Loubet reported, 'We're not driving the cars, they are driving us!'.

On the Tuesday morning there was rain and the Lancias surged forward but still with brake problems until, after the retirement of Saby's French car, the Martini team commandeered the former's brake-parts. Their problems were solved, pointing the finger at sub-standard parts in the Martini team.

So Auriol broke Lancia's Delta duck on Corsica and at the same time took the company's fiftieth World Championship rally win. The Lancia Delta HF integrale was rapidly becoming the most successful rally car of all time, moving Juha Kankunnen, driving for Toyota, to remark in an interview, 'Rallying has become just a bit too much like a Lancia Cup rather than a World Championship' – at the same time Lancia announced that the introduction of the road-going 16v integrale was to take place within the month.

Road-Going 16v Integrale

By the middle of May the waiting was over. Lancia invited the press to Turin, where they were able to see and drive the new road-car and see the new 16v competition version in action.

The 8-valve car had been unexpectedly successful with over 10,000 units passing out of Lancia's showrooms, but the new 16v version needed to be homologated for rallying as soon as possible, therefore 5,000 had to be built to satisfy the rule. Production of 8-valve had ceased some time before, so that the factory could gear up for the new car and produce the necessary number to satisfy the FISA, and be able to cope with what was shaping up to be exceptional public demand. Production had started some time before the launch, so that Lancia were confidently able to announce that homologation would take place as predicted on 1 August 1989.

The difference between the two cars was the provision of two extra valves per cylinder on this new version, but there were also a considerable number of detail improvements. To house this new unit, the bonnet was fitted with a raised central area to clear the extra under-bonnet equipment; this was the only external difference on the road car. The new equipment raised the engine's maximum power from 185bhp in the case of the 8-valve, to 200bhp from the 16-valve unit. To handle the power, the suspension was altered with shorter and stiffer springs, bigger shock absorbers and front anti-rollbar, whilst the lower front wishbones were more substantial and 205/50 tyres were fitted. After the considerable testing that the factory competition cars had been subjected to in the area of torque-split, the previous 56 front, 44 rear arrangement was now altered to 47 front, 53 rear. At last, ABS was included in the package and it was initially reported that understeer had virtually been eliminated. There were a few grumbles about details such as ventilation and interior room but these were almost irrelevant.

These were substantial revisions for the road-car, but when translated onto the competition version there were many who did not believe the figures given to them by Lancia. The FISA, at the beginning of Group A, had set an arbitrary limit of 300bhp as being the maximum output allowed from any World Championship rally car. Lancia had always

A 16v car in 2003, another increasingly rare sight in original state with standard wheels and badging intact.

claimed figures below this maximum and, for the 16v car, quoted 295bhp, which, for 1990, would be reduced to 265/270bhp because of a new rule due to start on 1 January that year, requiring all turbo engines to incorporate a 40m/m air restrictor in order to reduce power outputs.

Competition car improvements were: automatically adjustable turbo boost, direct static ignition and larger oil and water radiators. A stronger propshaft sent power to the rear wheels and larger, 332mm diameter brakes, as just used in Corsica, would become standard. The Group N version acquired 7in wide and 15in diameter wheels.

To overcome the new restrictor rules, Lombardi stated that their engineers would have to come up with even more effective engine efficiency. He also suggested, once again, that four-wheel steering would be investigated and also an electronically controlled central differential. This latter point was especially important as on events run in high temperatures, the Ferguson coupling was proving to be less efficient.

Lastly, the new car was presented to the press in a red-based Martini livery instead of white. This had been designed by Giorgetto Giugiaro of Italdesign and was apparently in response to the fact that red shows better in photographs than white.

It would seem the Delta integrale's influence was unstoppable as, even in Russia, Scandinavian driver Tomi Palmqvist had won the Old Toomas Rally with his Lancia and so became the first four-wheel drive car to take victory in that country.

Jolly Club

Italy was a late-starter in Europe as far as increasing affluence and personal mobility were concerned. The introduction by Fiat of affordable small cars meant that private car ownership finally took off during the 1950s.

At first, Jolly Club was a touring organization set up to cater for these newly mobile masses. It provided help and assistance in much the same way as the AA and RAC used to before the advent of business diversification.

The Club also took a prominent role in motor sports, providing help in various forms for deserving race and rally entrants. It was an early form of sponsorship. By the 1980s, the Club had prospered and diversified itself and became involved in its own teams, drivers and cars. From being involved by entering one or two cars on World Championship rallies, it had become a promotional company, and was later able to take over the running of the Martini Racing integrales for the whole of the 1992–93 seasons. Nowadays the name is linked to motoring through Jolly Hotels.

Acropolis Rally 1989

Back on the championship trail it was time to visit the incredibly rough tracks of Greece for the Acropolis. The relentless war by the Japanese against Lancia's stronghold in the series was taken up by Mitsubishi, who proved more adept than Toyota on this occasion with Ari Vatanen mixing it in the top three places – Toyota was finding that reliability was not one of its trump cards in 1989.

But it waited to fight back and had the advantage at last of Pirelli run-flat tyres. For Lancia, it was probably their Michelin equivalents that saved the event for them, Auriol still setting fastest stage times even with punctures. Michelin explained that the run-flat mousse in their tyres now activated at a higher pressure than previously.

Lancia had entered two cars, the other was for Biasion and a Jolly Club example was run for Alex Fiorio, all with 50/50 torque split. Hungarian Attila Ferjancz ran his Abarth built ex-Wittman car and local driver 'Jigger', who had broken his leg earlier, appropriately ran an ex-works car with a Valeo clutch. Jorge Recalde was also present with Vic Preston's 1988 Safari car.

The very rough stages took their toll of the Toyotas with collapsed suspensions, overheated engines and snapped propshafts. Lancia was not immune with Auriol hitting a rock, finishing a stage with a front wheel under the car and Biasion's carbon-fibre sump-guard was split in two to the amazement of Lancia's mechanics.

With the loss of the Toyotas, the Lancias could cruise home holding their positions. Thus Biasion won from Auriol and Fiorio. Driver's characteristics could clearly be seen on this event with Auriol constantly attacking, whilst Biasion tended to bide his time. The shift of emphasis of rally-driving becoming a 'rest-of-the-world' pursuit was never more clear. The top six finishers consisted of two Italians, a Frenchman, a Scotsman, a German and an Argentinian.

Once again, the Lancias had lasted when their fiercest opponents had wilted, but newcomers Mitsubishi made it clear that they had arrived by challenging for the lead with their Group A car and winning the class with their Group N car. Lancia was under pressure – they needed those extra valves.

Lombardi later announced that the first event for the new car would be the Rally d'Italia 'for marketing reasons'. He also announced that they expected to continue with this new car until the end of 1991, although the Jolly Club, entrant of Alex Fiorio's World Championship car, said that they would not continue beyond the end of 1989.

Argentina Rally 1989

The 8-valve car still had three more events to go and four cars were sent to Argentina by the factory. Martini entered Auriol's Corsica car for Jorge Recalde and Baision's Portugal car for Mikael Ericsson. Jolly Club entered Alex Fiorio in Biasion's Safari winning car and the World Champion's Acropolis winner was brought as a training car. All had 50/50 torque splits and gearbox oil coolers.

With little in the way of competition, the Lancias ran at the top of the field virtually as they pleased finishing 1–2–3, setting up a new record in the process.

New general manager of Abarth, Claudio Lombardi, had plenty to make him happy after the event. With this win, Lancia had taken the 1989 World Rally Manufacturer's title in record time, having won all six events they had entered. Life could not get better – but it could easily get worse.

1000 Lakes Rally 1989

The 1000 Lakes Rally in August was not wanting for lack of entries. No less than thirty-four four-wheel drive Lancias were due to take part with Alen, Biasion and Auriol representing Corso Marche. Although it was scheduled to be the last event for the 8-valve car, Lancia had built three brand new cars for the rally.

For nothing, as it turned out. From winning the World Championship in record time, Lancia quickly became also-rans for the first time since the beginning of 1987. Ironically it was Mikael Ericsson, fresh from his Lancia victory in Argentina but not required by them in Finland, who won in a Mitsubishi. Markku Alen was the only Martini team driver capable of staying at the front but, in the process, the boost of his engine was turned up so much that head-gasket failure intervened and finished his run.

When Martini Lancia finally announced the World Rally Championship 16v car, it was painted in a new red livery that had been designed with the help of Giugiaro. It did not last long before the car reverted to white.

Official Factory Lancia Works-Built Integrales Used in 1988 (ABARTH SE 044)

– not including HF4WDs converted and carried over.

TO 34162H
TO 34163H
TO 34164H
TO 34165H
TO 34166H
TO 34758H
TO 54902H
TO 54904H
TO 66643H
TO 66644H
TO 66645H
TO 89092H
TO 89093H
TO 89094H
TO 89095H
TO 70780L
TO 70781L

Auriol suffered an off and Biasion put on a lacklustre display, finally finishing sixth after transmission problems added to the team's woes.

Worse was to come, the next round was in Australia and Alen was due to represent Martini with Fiorio as back up in his Jolly Club car. Their cars had already seen service on the Safari, then been sent directly to Argentina after which they went, directly again, to Australia.

Whilst it was a relatively low-key affair for Lancia, there is no denying that they were clearly beaten by Toyota. The 8-valve Lancias struggled against their opposition with better handling and more power. Rumours started that stalwart Alen was becoming disillusioned and wanted out, possibly to go to Subaru.

Lancia's long run of success had abruptly ceased, but all was not lost. Whilst Alen was making leaving sounds, he was also raving about the qualities of the upcoming 16-valve car – so were the press.

5 Eight More Valves – Enough?

Although the new 16v integrale had yet to make its world competition debut, the press had had time to assimilate the new machine under road conditions.

Whilst the cars needed to be sold in the required numbers for FISA homologation purposes, Lancia was also reaping the rewards of its extremely successful competition efforts. Considering the Delta was approaching its death throes at the end of 1986, the success of the four-wheel drive versions across the globe had pushed sales of the model up towards figures of which Lancia had not ever dreamed, and, prior to the introduction of the 16v, around 15,000 total traction Deltas alone had found new owners. For 1988 sales had been almost twice that of the previous year, up from 4,400 to 7,600 and they now accounted for more than 20 per cent of total Delta sales. Lancia's share of the European top performance, permanent four-wheel drive sector had by now steadily risen to 31 per cent.

In addition to the continued success of the Delta in World Championship rallying, the resulting positive publicity was creating its own momentum and, if it could be maintained, then the Fiat board were only too

'The finest all-weather driving experience on sale today' so said Motor Sport *magazine about the 16v.*

happy for the budgets to be found for the continuation of Abarth and its integrales in top-line rally motor sport.

Despite the reversal of emphasis from the HF4WD, where the road car provided a competition car, to the 16v, where the road car was the result of the competition car, Lancia continued developments that were more relevant to the road machine.

These were appreciated by the press. *Motor Sport* magazine in the UK, after trying a 16v road car for the first time in Turin in May 1989, commented that it was 'the finest all-weather driving experience on sale'. Italian showrooms had the new car available from early summer but it was to be later in the year before the UK was able to enjoy the experience of those eight extra valves. Colours available to British buyers were to be: white, Monza red, dark grey metallic, Bordeaux metallic and black metallic.

The UK had also seen Lancia car sales revert back under the wing of Fiat UK at Slough after Lancar in Crawley, briefly the importing concessionaire of the 8-valve integrale and its contemporaries, ceased to exist from 1989.

Integrale HF 16v – Introduction and Features

Anyone looking at the new car would have been hard put to it to identify any substantial changes compared to the outgoing 8-valve machine. In fact, the only significant external visual difference to the casual observer between the two models was a purposeful-looking bulge on the bonnet of the new car rising to a height some 3cm above the surrounding area. Why did it need this? The whole point of the newcomer was the addition of an extra eight valves in a new cylinder head to allow Abarth to introduce more powerful World Rally Championship cars. The resulting four valves per cylinder were arranged in vee formation and their inclusion increased the height of the engine, thus requiring the purposeful-looking bulge to be added to the bonnet. More observant and sharp-eyed enthusiasts may also have noticed that the 16v actually sat lower on springs that were stiffer and 20mm (0.8in) shorter. Very few changes of any sort were made to the seats and interior. The rev counter was slightly altered to make it more visible and an illuminated check panel was incorporated into the dashboard. This whole area was, by now, being referred to by Jeremy Walton in *Motor Sport* magazine as 'a sorry mixture of unsuitable colourings and sprawling switchgear'; but why should Lancia spend more money on developing something that would not have the remotest advantage in the heat of a World Rally Championship round attack. Buyers were attracted to the car by its dynamic ability and ever increasing fame and heritage.

Aiding the improved driving experience was not only the extra power provided by the heavily revised power unit but the way in which it delivered that power. The new unit shared the same block as the contemporary Thema 16-valve engine with the two camshafts opening and closing the valves directly via bucket tappets, also new, stronger con rods were fitted along with sodium-filled exhaust valves, whilst the crankshaft gained a torsional damper. Maximum torque was available at 500rpm lower than the equivalent figure on the 8-valve but maximum power was up to 200bhp at 5,600rpm. The Marelli-Weber IAW electronic injection now worked in conjunction with the ignition, fuel injection, turbo wastegate and the new ABS system. New, bigger, injectors were fitted and the intake and exhaust manifolds were redesigned and matched so that they were all exactly the same length, although these improvements were really only for the advantage of Abarth in extracting more power from the engine for rallies and the new Garrett T3 turbo-charger once again incorporated an overboost facility, but this time it operated with the advantage of electronic wastegate control. With the help of a proportional-acting sole-

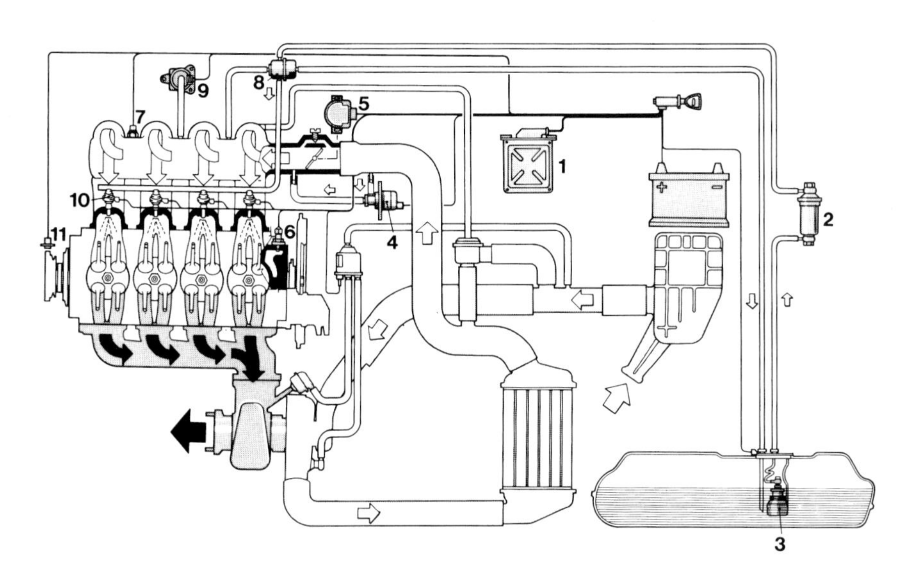

Key

1. injection/ignition central control unit
2. fuel filter
3. electric fuel filter
4. air valve
5. potentiometer sensor or throttle-valve position
6. engine coolant temperature sensor
7. iniet air temperature sensor
8. boost control
9. absolute atmospheric pressure sensor
10. electro-injectors
11. crankshaft location and rotation speed sensor

The integrale grew up alongside the ever-accelerating rate of electronics development and each subsequent model benefited from these advances with more integrated Marelli equipment providing improved efficiency.

noid, boost pressure was continually adjusted taking into account outside factors such as rpm and ambient temperature. The net effect was smoother progress and more efficient use of the turbo. Due to the fact that the addition of a 16-valve cylinder head onto an engine results in a unit that inherently develops its greater power at the top end of the revolution range the engineers spent much time improving the new unit's low rev range power and torque delivery. The T3 was a new development and part of this work in that it was physically smaller than its predecessor, which meant that it enjoyed reduced inertia leading to considerably less turbo lag. The wastegate itself was now electronically controlled allowing it to work more efficiently at all times. To help keep temperatures down, the intercooler now had a larger surface area, although it was not bigger overall to the previous item. The new engine could run on both leaded and unleaded fuel and was able to return significantly better overall fuel consumption figures on the road.

The clutch was now hydraulically assisted and fed power to a new gearbox developed and strengthened by ZF from that used in the Thema 8.32 saloon. In particular, second gear ratio was higher closing the gap towards third.

Whilst the suspension was revised to take account of the new output with those lower, stiffer springs, uprated progressive action dampers were added to help along with a larger front anti-roll bar, reinforced lower front wishbones with new bump-stops and revised king pins incorporating ABS sensors. It also reflected the fact that weight distribution was such that 63 per cent of the 1,250kg-car was concentrated at the front-end. Despite the fitment of even larger tyres and wheels as standard: 205/50VR 15 tyres now on 7in rims, the engineers still found predominant front-end weight a problem. So, perhaps the most radical change to be included in the 16v specification over the previous HF4WD and 8-valve was that the torque-split had been almost reversed from 56/44 to 47/53 in order to dial out some of the inevitable understeer that was likely to develop. Lancia press department referred to the effect as 'a sportier drive'.

Bruno Cena of Lancia's experimental department said that when the extra weight of the 16-valve engine was first experienced in the road car, the amount of understeer increased considerably. He and his staff set to work to eliminate this with tyre and suspension alterations and tuning. They soon found out that none of this was going to achieve the desired effect, so that prompted the radical change of torque-split settings.

However, it was the addition of an ABS braking system that perhaps caused most comment from the media. When the 8-valve car had been introduced, Lancia had countered queries about its lack of ABS with comments ranging from 'there is not enough room under the bonnet' to 'a rally car does not need ABS anyway'.

Work had obviously been going on to rectify this gap in the integrale's CV. Perhaps, given what we know now about automotive electronics, the fitment of the system to the car may have presented few technical problems but, in 1989, Lancia brought in German electronics expertise from Bosch for help, as the job was anything but straightforward.

They could stop perfectly well, but with the introduction of the 16v came the addition of ABS for the first time. Much in demand at track-day events today the 16v has been described by some integrale specialists as the best model of them all.

above *Taking over a section of autostrada near Turin was not a problem for the Fiat publicity department and it allowed them to get great shots of Deltas and HF4WDs like this.*

right *Ramon Vilaro's 16v thunders up Le Mont Dore hillclimb in 1995.*

bottom right *Dashboards varied little from model to model. The 16v gained a check panel and there were further small changes for the Evoluzione. Here all possible warning and tell-tale lights are displayed.*

below *Never before seen publicity shot of 16v with helicopter. Pity it never made it to print.*

left *Puntegrale Grama 2 stands outside Maggiora's Chivasso factory in 1998.*

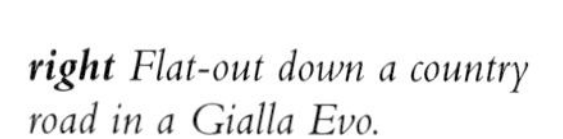

right *Flat-out down a country road in a Gialla Evo.*

below *Bruno Saby's works-built Fina 16v car on the French Championship Rouergue Rally.*

above *Evoluzione 2 engines had red cam covers.*

right *To honour the Fulvia Fanalone the Club Italia special edition integrales were given yellow and blue cam covers.*

below *From the left: Dealer Collection, World Rally Champion Verde York, Club Italia.*

top *The unique bronze car.*

above *The Viola car joins the factory's retained Final Edition at Chivasso.*

left *Still left in the factory after production finished, integrale Evoluzione bodyshells – now worth their weight in gold!*

above *One-off interior of Bianca Evo.*

right *Chivasso's Roberto Franco gives the Viola car a quick test-run especially for this book.*

below *The all-white Turin show Bianca Evo sees the light of day for the first time for many years.*

above *Juha Kankunnen splashes through a wet Welsh forest at speed during one miserable night of the 1992 RAC rally.*

above right *The setting sun catches a Martini 5 at speed.*

top *The unique Viola car, which carries Maggiora badges.*

right *A Martini 6 sums up 'simply the best'.*

above and below *More rare material from Japan featuring the Final Edition.*

Versione speciale della Delta HF Integrale costruita in pochi esemplari che possono prenotare solo i soci Hi.Fi.. Un'auto sportiva da collezione

DEDICATA HI.FI.

Una serie speciale della Delta HF Integrale in esclusiva per i Soci Hi.Fi..
La vettura 6 volte campione del mondo rally, immagine trainante della innovazione tecnologica Lancia, viene proposta ai Soci in una versione esclusiva per i colori, la selleria e particolari accessori che fanno della grande sportiva un'auto da collezione. Partiamo subito dai colori esterni che rendono questa Delta HF un esemplare unico. Il blu Lancia, scelto come colore base della carrozzeria, presenta una fascia centrale verniciata che percorre tutta la vettura dal cofano al baule. E' un richiamo alla tradizione sportiva della nostra Casa, che non mancherà di affascinare gli appassionati del genere.
La fascia giallo azzurra caratterizzava infatti le Fulvia HF, le gloriose campionesse di rally, che hanno fatto sognare i giovani degli anni '60 e '70. Elegantissima la personalizzazione esterna Hi.Fi., con due placche inserite nel

above *Rare publicity material for the HiFi special edition Evoluzione.*

below *Proposals for the internal badging of HiFi special edition Evoluziones.*

Never before seen shots of the unique Agnelli cabriolet under construction at Stabilimento Pilotta and after completion at traditional Abarth and Fiat Group photographic location, Campovolo, Turin.

Normal ABS technology relied on the fact that all four wheels on a car act independently of each other. The integrale's raison d'être is four-wheel drive, incorporating a viscous coupling and a Torsen rear differential, all of which was included to ensure that the very opposite happens and that whatever happens to each wheel is cancelled out, or enhanced, by a reaction from the others; all is controlled by the various couplings and differentials. ABS had been developed with sensors on each wheel, so obviously it would not work properly under these circumstances. A solution had been adopted by Ford and BMW, which resulted in the centre differential's effect being reduced so that it did not act so effectively in controlling each wheel. Lancia, however, was not prepared to take the easy way out, as they did not see the point of adopting ABS if it meant removing the whole dynamic basis of the integrale. Bosch developed a system that utilized four separate information channels, one to each wheel. Under normal circumstances only one went to the two rear wheels. These sensors could therefore detect slip but, in addition, two further sensors detected longitudinal acceleration/deceleration and lateral or cornering forces. Thus the ABS can pulse the brakes all round, if necessary, or it can work on only one wheel. Not only that, but Bosch worked with Magnetti Marelli to enable information to be exchanged between the ABS system and the engine's CPU, so that the engine idle speed could be increased when under sudden engine-braking situations, such as lifting off and braking suddenly whilst accelerating hard – in other words on roads with constant and violent speed and load changes, so that the risk of locking the rear wheels is lessened.

It all worked perfectly. Attempting to brake in the middle of a corner caused the *Autocar* to comment that the car came, 'quickly to a halt under complete control'. So the new 16v integrale won praise as being far more competition-based than its predecessor. It required greater commitment on the part of the driver but, in return, it gave far more back.

There was one drawback. The Lancia engineers could not rework the 16v engine to conform to the extremely exacting emission control standards of countries such as the US and, in Europe, Switzerland in particular. Thus Lancia introduced a new model that included all

After much press discussion and criticism over lack of ABS provision, the 16v was provided with a specially developed state of the art system, which complemented the car's sophisticated transmission.

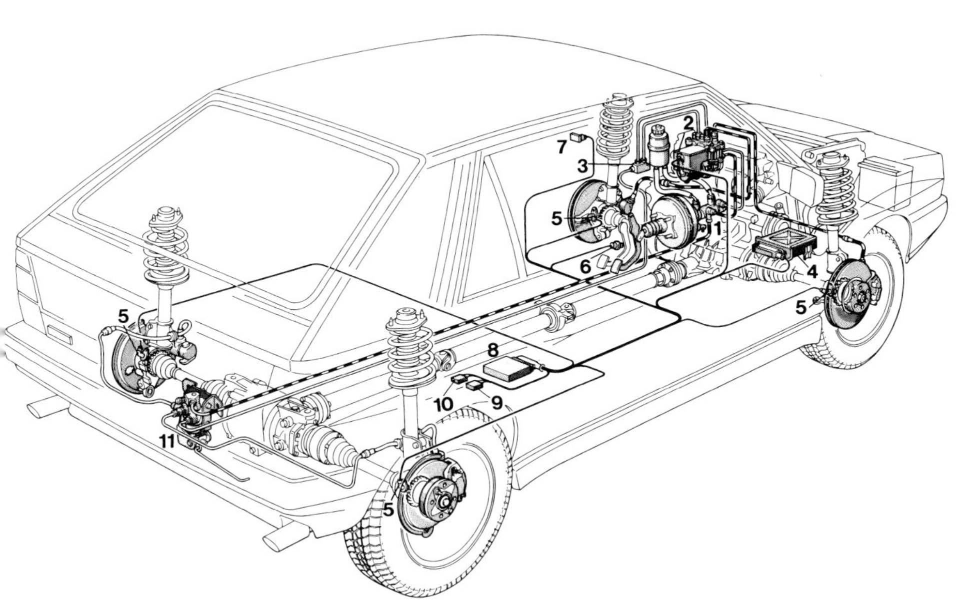

Key

1. brake fluid pump
2. electro-hydraulic actuator
3. three-way connector
4. electronic central control unit
5. toothed disc wheel sensors
6. brake pedal sensor
7. dashboard-mounted tell-tale light
8. injection/ignition cental control unit
9. transversel accelerometer
10. longitudinal accelerometer
11. brake-effort proportioning valve

LANCIA DELTA HF integrale 16v

Specification

(*) unladen

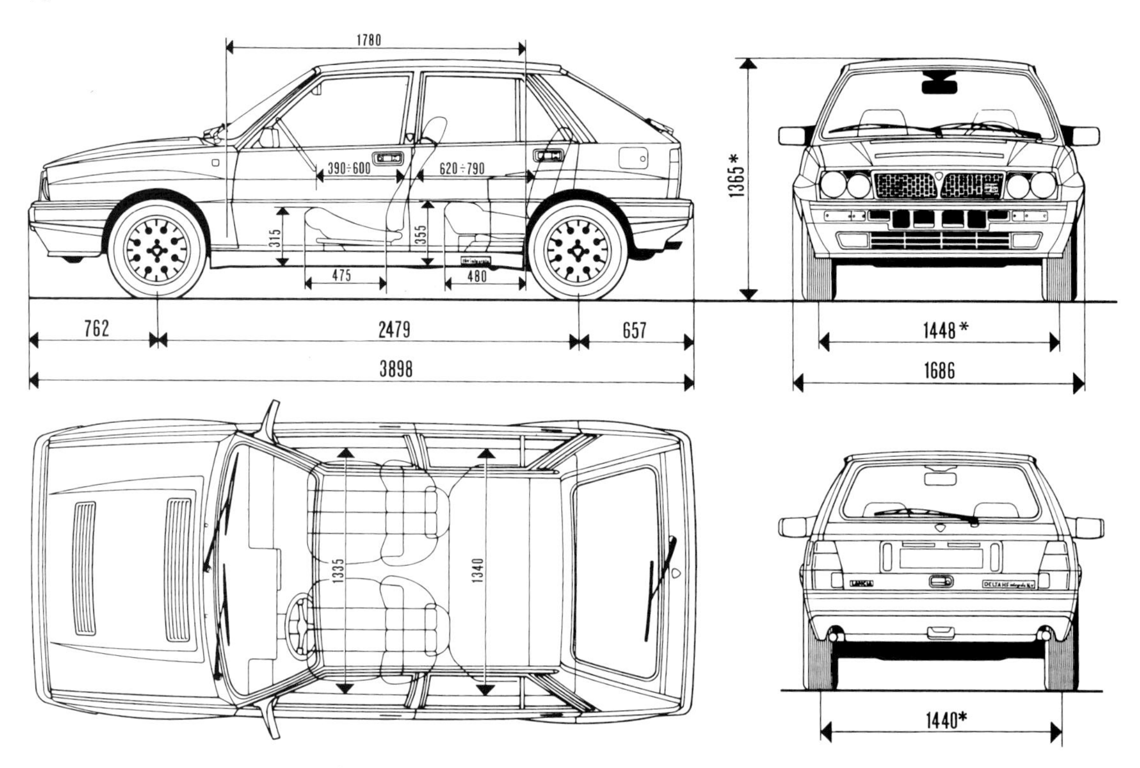

Luggage compartment capacity: 200 dm³; with the rear seat folded over: 940 dm³.

ENGINE

Main features	
No. of cylinders	4 flat
Cycle-stroke	petrol-fed
Bore x stroke	84 × 90 mm
Cylinder capacity	1995 cc
Compression ratio	8 to 1
Max power output DIN	200 bhp (144 kW-EEC)
	5500 rpm
Peak at torque DIN	31 mkg (298 Nm-EEC)
at	3000 rpm
Octane	leaded or unleaded petrol; lowest octane rating 95 (RON)

Structural layout	
Arrangement	transversely-mounted at front
Cylinder block	cast iron with counter-rotating balancer shafts
Cylinder spacings	91 mm
Main bearings	5
Cylinder head	light alloy

Timing gear

Valve arrangement	at V(65°)
Camshafts	2 overhead
Timing control	by toothed belt
Phasing	phasing control play = 0.8 mm
Intake — beginning	8° before TDC
Intake — end	35° after BDC
Exhaust — beginning	30° before BDC
Exhaust — end	0° after TDC
Counter-rotating balancer shafts	2 in the cylinder block
Control	by toothed belt

Ignition

Type	electronic with mapped advance control and knock sensor, combined with the injection
Firing order	1-3-4-2
Spark plugs	Champion RN7YC - Bosch WR6DC - Marelli F8LCR - FIAT-LANCIA V45LSR

Fuel feed

Type	turbocharging and air/air heat exchanger (off the intake) and overboost automatically engaging at full engine revs
Fuel pump	electric
Injection	electronic IAW Weber combined with the ignition
Air cleaner	dry-type, with paper cartridge
Turboblower type	water-cooled Garrett T3
Max turbocharging pressure	1 bar

Lubrication

Type	forced feed with gear pump and oil radiator
Filter	cartridge-type

Engine cooling

Type	water-forced with radiator pump and extra expansion tank
Control	by thermostat
Fan	electric, controlled from a thermostatic switch on the radiator

TRANSMISSION

Type	permanent 4-wheel drive with centrally-mounted epicyclic torque converter and Ferguson viscous coupling; Torsen-type rear differential with 5 to 1 wheel torque ratio
Clutch	dry, single plate, hydraulically controlled
Friction ring diameter ($Ø_e \times Ø_i$)	230 × 155 mm

Transmission ratios:

Gearbox	
1st	3.500 : 1
2nd	2.176 : 1
3rd	1.519 : 1
4th	1.132 : 1
5th	0.929 : 1
Reverse	3.545 : 1
Final drive ratio	3.111 : 1 (56/18)
Bevel gear front/rear	2.263 : 1 (19/43)
Torque splitter — front	47%
Torque splitter — rear	53%

CHASSIS

Body	self-bearing structure
Braking system	front and rear discs with floating calipers. Diagonal-split type hydraulic brake circuit with vacuum servo and

	brake-effort proportioning valve acting on the rear wheels. Antilock Braking System (ABS) optionally available.
Front discs	
- diameter	284 mm (ventilated)
- total front pad area	50 × 4 = 200 cm²
Rear discs	
- diameter	227 mm
- total rear pad area	35 × 4 = 140 cm²
Parking brake	acting on the discs of the rear brakes
Front suspension	independent wheel struts with lower wishbones, anti-roll bar and double-acting hydraulic telescopic gas-operated dampers
Flexibility at the wheel	0.50 mm/kg
Wheel wobble { upper	60 mm
Wheel wobble { lower	103 mm
Wheel position (unladen)	
- camber	- 1° ± 30'
- caster	3°10' ± 30'
- toe-in	- 2 to +1 mm
Rear suspension	independent wheel struts with transverse links, longitudinal reaction arms, anti-roll bar and hydraulic, telescopic double-acting gas-operated dampers
Flexibility at the wheel	0.51 mm/kg
Wheel wobble { upper	60 mm
Wheel wobble { lower	125 mm
Wheel position (unladen)	
- camber	- 1°30' ± 30'
- caster	2°30' ± 30'
- toe-in	3 to 5 mm
Steering	servo-assisted rack-and-pinion power steering
Turning circle	10.4 m
Steering wheel turns lock to lock	2.8
Road wheels	
Rims	light alloy 7 J × 15"
Tyres	205/50 R 15 V
Inflating pressure	
- front	2.0 bar - (2.2 bar**)
- rear	2.0 bar - (2.2 bar**)
Spare wheel	
Rim	light alloy 4J × 15" AH2-40
Tyre	115 × 70 R15
Inflating pressure	4.2 bar

(**) at high constant speed, fully laden

Electrical equipment	
Voltage	12 V
Alternator with built-in voltage regulator	65 A
Starter motor	1.1 kW
Battery	45 Ah (service free)

WEIGHTS

Kerb weight (DIN)*	1250 kg
Distribution { front	62.4%
Distribution { rear	37.6%
Laden weight	1700 kg
Distribution { front	53.5%
Distribution { rear	46.5%
Maximum payload	450 kg
Max towing weight	1300 kg
No. of seats	5

(*) Inclusive of fuel, water, spare wheel and accessories.

PERFORMANCE

Top speed in 5th	220 km/h (80 km/h) (*)
Max gradient climbable (laden)	58%
Speed at 1000 rpm in 4th	30.6 km/h
Speed at 1000 rpm in 5th	37.3 km/h
Power-to-weight ratio kg/bhp-DIN	6.25
Power-to-weight ratio kg/kW-EEC	8.7

(*) Max permissible speed when mounting the low-section spare wheel

Acceleration	
(2 adults + 20 kg) (secs)	
0 to 100 km/h	5.7 s
0 to 1000 m	26.1 s

Pic-kup from 40 km/h in 5th	
(2 adults + 20 kg) (secs)	
over 1000 m	30.5 s

Conventional fuel consumption (l/100 km):	
at 90 km/h	7.9
at 120 km/h	10.5
urban cycle	11.2
ECE mean	9

SUPPLIES

	dm^3	kg
Fuel tank capacity	57	-
including a reserve of:	6 to 9	-
Engine radiator, expansion tank and heating system liquid	6.2	-
Oil pan	4.9	4.4
Total capacity of pan, filter, radiator and ducting oil	5.8	5.2
Gearbox and differential oil	3.8	3.4
Rear differential	1.1	1
Servo-assisted power-steering	0.75	-
Hydraulic brake circuits liquid	0.40	-
Wind- and rear-screen washer bottle	2	-

CHARACTERISTIC ENGINE CURVES

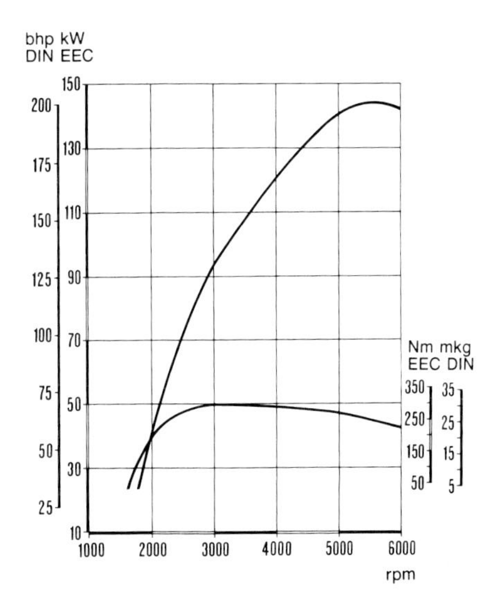

The outward sign that a catalyser is fitted and power is down to 177bhp for the Swiss market.

the advantageous new equipment of the 16v car but was powered by a low-emissions legal specification 8-valve engine of 177bhp. Not so quick, but blessed with the latest specification shell and chassis, they also included a three-way catalytic converter in its exhaust system. It was reported that at the time of homologation of the 16v car, which was 1 August, five of every sixty integrales built were in low-emissions configuration. No factory exports were ever made to the US.

At last the Abarth competition department in Corso Marche, Turin learned that the necessary 5,000 16v cars had been built to allow it to succeed the 8-valve car on the world's rally special stages.

It had already been announced that this would happen on the San Remo-based Rally d'Italia in October 1989, but meanwhile the now beleaguered rally team, having been beaten in Group A by Toyota and in Group N by Mitsubishi, found it was due to lose the services of stalwart Markku Alen at the end of the year. He had agreed to join Subaru for 1990, partially perhaps because the Japanese manufacturer was able to offer the Finn a full season.

Markku had been with the Fiat group for 16 years – an unprecedented length of time for any driver/team combination. It was common knowledge that Lancia was seeking Juha Kankunnen from Toyota as a replacement.

At the traditional Lancia press conference before the San Remo event, Kankunnen's appointment was confirmed. This left Carlos Sainz at Toyota and the combination was seen as a considerable threat to Lancia.

Integrale 16v Group A Car Engine and Weight Differences

Max. power	Group A, 295bhp @ 7,000rpm
Max. torque	Group A, 41kg m/297lb ft @ 4,500rpm
Unladen weight	Group A, 1,100kg/ 2,426lb

San Remo Rally 1989

It was time for the new 16v integrale to stand up and be counted. Lancia hedged their bets entering two of the new cars painted in an eye-catching red-based Martini livery, designed by Italdesign's Giorgetto Giugiaro. These were for Auriol and Biasion. Jolly Club cars, in 8-valve configuration, were present for their usual drivers, Fiorio and Cerrato.

Would the 16v integrale prove capable of maintaining the tradition set up by the previous two Delta rally cars and win its first event outright?

At first the Toyotas could not match the pace of the Lancias, which were running in the order Auriol, Biasion, Fiorio. Auriol went off the road and retired in Tuscany and Biasion suffered a flat tyre, so Fiorio took the lead in his 8-valve car only to hit gearbox trouble allowing Sainz to power ahead in the Toyota, but there were 150km of tarmac stages to go in the final night, which would benefit the Lancias.

Biasion pushed hard and in the morning was in the lead, whilst Fiorio took advantage of problems with Sainz to establish himself in second place. Only 25s covered the top three finishers – a very close finish for a World Championship rally. Biasion had finally succeeded in not only adding the 16v integrale to the list of Lancia's first-time winners, but he also wrapped up the World Rally title for the second year in succession.

Once again, on the face of it, all seemed to be going to plan, but Sainz and Toyota's performance in Italy made it clear that Lancia could not afford to stand still, new 16v car notwithstanding.

Very soon came an announcement that Lancia had cancelled their entries for the RAC Rally in order to concentrate on testing and development, so clearly they were concerned and the Lancia team, as always, showed total commitment to its future. Much criticism was levelled at the team from the UK for this decision but the first event of 1990, the Monte Carlo rally, was only three months after San Remo and Abarth knew that the new year would bring a redoubled effort from Japan.

Probably the best place to explore the prodigious performance – and the possibility of nasty surprises – is at a track-day.

Lancia won both the 1989 World Rally Championships for Drivers and Manufacturers with Miki Biasion and Fiorio backed him up in second place.

Lancia also won the European Rally Championship with Yves Loubet. In 1989, by mid-year alone, from Tasmania to Russia and the Arctic, all-wheel drive Deltas had taken forty overall Group A victories and nine Group N category wins in important national and international rallies.

Monte Carlo Rally 1990

Although Lancia now had the advantage of their 16v integrale, the rules were forcing them to run with a 40mm (1.73in) air restrictor. Then they lost the undoubted talent of Markku Alen, but that was balanced by the arrival of Kankunnen. As the new decade opened, the Lancia Martini team once again lined up to start in Monte Carlo with Biasion and Auriol in the other two team cars alongside the Finn.

Juha's return did not last long as on only the fifth stage he spun his car into retirement after hitting a solid post. It was Auriol though

who was setting the Lancia pace, trading fastest times with Sainz' Toyota, both of them moving away from Biasion. The battle at the front was fierce. The Martini car, now back in traditional white-based livery, ended the penultimate leg dead-heating with Sainz. The last stages were expected to be very exciting indeed. To aid their bid for victory, Toyota had brought along tyre warmers to raise the temperature of the rubber before key stages. Lancia were running a new tyre developed by Michelin and specially designed to reach working temperature in 400m from the start of a stage. They looked enviously at Toyota's warmers wondering if they were missing out somewhere but reconciled themselves to the knowledge that their get-warm-quick tyres were probably just as effective. In fact, they managed to get some warmers sent from Arese by the Alfa Romeo saloon racing team – another example of the huge resource back-up available, to the team when they needed it.

Lancia was not too happy about the new 40mm air-restrictor rules, as they had previously been using 48mm (1.9in) inlets. This compared with Toyota and Mitsubishi who had only to reduce theirs from 42 and 43mm (1.65 and 1.69in), respectively. This was more an indication of the fact that the Japanese engines were of more recent design and technology than the Lancia's and were thus more efficient in the first place.

Although Didier Auriol won, it was not a convincing victory. Everyone had seen this situation before but always the Lancia team had been able to grab the advantage. The strength of the team should not be underestimated. Respected Italian journalist Franco Lini suggested that, even at this early stage of its career, the latest integrale was on the ropes as there was no new car scheduled to replace it and Toyota clearly now had all the attributes for becoming a potential regular rally winner.

16v cars started to be used in many different motor sport applications and some thought that the car's abilities would be well suited to hill-climbing. In the French Hillclimb Championship round at Le Mont Dore 6 August 1995, they were still popular and hard to beat. Here is Gael Lesoudier tackling the Auvergnat hill.

Only time and hard work on the part of Abarth would tell and hard work they were used to. With all this as a background, it should be noted that a 16v integrale also took the Group N award in the hands of Frenchman Bertrand Balas.

To remind the public just how good the dynamics of the road-going16v integrale really were, *Autosport* magazine tested one immediately after the Monte Carlo rally and suggested that it was a difficult car in which to relax 'because the urge to explore the power, dynamics and the excitement is nearly irresistible'. They concluded with 'it is near perfect if dynamics are what you seek'.

Auriol's win was, however, contested by Toyota, who claimed irregularities with the turbo-charger had taken place during the last night of the rally, allowing the Frenchman to go faster. The subsequent FISA Court of Appeal in Paris turned down Toyota's appeal, confirming Lancia's win. The latter could also take some comfort from the fact that coincidentally, 16v integrales finished the Catalunya Rally, the first important round of the prestigious European Championship, in 1–2–4 formation, being split only by an 8-valve car. Cerrato won in a Fina/Jolly Club car, followed by Loubet in a Martini version.

Portugal Rally 1990

More was to come. By the end of March's Portugal rally, anyone looking at the results would assume that happy times were here again for Lancia. It would be difficult, on a World Championship round, given the new competitiveness of the Japanese teams, to better a straight 1–2–3–4–5 result. Oh, and throw in a 1–2–3 in Group N as well. Not one single front-line Lancia dropped out of a rally that saw the decimation of Mazda, Toyota and Mitsubishi. It was the greatest result for a single marque in the history of rallying and nothing else could so underline the strength in depth of the team and its reliability. After the uncertainty of Monte Carlo, Lancia could not have wished for more. The result was a triumph for teamwork and reliability, which was good, but not entirely the way that Lancia wanted to win rallies.

Technically, much work had been done on the engine management system allowing the team to claim that the 1990-restricted 16v motors were developing only slightly less than the 1989 unrestricted 8-valve units.

Safari Rally 1990

Nobody believed that the result in Portugal was a pointer to the rest of the season, although Lancia felt that after several months of practising in Africa they were likely to reap the rewards on the Safari rally.

Unfortunately the weather changed from dry to wet just before the start, turning the roads into deep mud. Despite opting to use 8-valve engines for reliability, the Lancia team suffered engine problems that put both Fiorio and Biasion out, leaving Kankunnen second at the finish, beaten by Waldegaard's Toyota.

The Safari is always a difficult rally to place. The conditions are so different to any other, even so Lancia were disappointed not to take a hat-trick win, especially when Markku Alen took the start, for the first time for 16 years, in a non-Fiat group car and led everybody until retirement in his new Subaru. Lancia had another fully competitive Japanese runner to worry about.

Tour de Corse 1990

Markku Alen was not present for the Tour de Corse in May, so it was the usual baying pack of Toyotas and road-racing BMW M3 facing up to the Martini and Fina Lancia entries. The result was a mixture of very hard and precise tarmac driving by Auriol, which kept his Martini car in contention throughout. Saby spent most of the rally just trying to keep in touch with the leading three in his Fina car, whilst Loubet retired with an interesting problem: he suffered two driveshaft breakages on one stage and spun violently to a halt. Once these were replaced, he

Tyre Warmers

Although portable tyre warmers were common in Formula One, the technology, nor for that matter, the requirement, had yet to become even a choice in rallying until 1990s Monte Carlo when Pirelli set the pace with new equipment and, at the same time, set Lancia and Michelin thinking.

A tyre warmer is basically a wrap-around, electrically powered blanket that is used to cover a tyre before use so that it can be at its most effective working temperature immediately a car starts away from the line at the beginning of a stage.

Michelin admitted that they were not sure how useful they were, whilst Pirelli were employing them, not only at the beginning of tarmac stages, but also when the surface was going to be gravel. They heated the rubber to 60–70°C in advance and Michelin accepted that maybe 'the system cannot be bad', adopting it themselves for harder compound tyres only – never when run-flat mousses were being utilized.

Bruno Saby was occasionally part of the MARTINI Lancia driver team but here he is in action, in a factory built car, on the 1990 French rally championship round of Alpin Behra, where he finished second.

suffered another driveshaft problem causing retirement. After later investigation it proved that the car had twisted its chassis in the earlier incident causing the driveshaft to run out of true and eventually pull out altogether.

The legendary Lancia Martini teamwork helped Auriol to victory during the latter stages of the event when he was forced to stop for a new front differential. The job normally took 40min but he was on the move again in less than 25.

It was becoming clear that the 16v integrale was an excellent car but, unlike 1987, it was not just a good car that won rallies. Lancia definitely had an edge over its rivals in that it seemed to have all angles covered at any time, and they now led both the Manufacturers' and Drivers' Championships but there was no room for complacency. There were no technical developments for Corsica, just two new cars for the Martini team.

Acropolis Rally 1990

The Greek rally was not particularly a specialist event. Lancia had been beaten before on Corsica and on the Safari but that was by cars specially suited to those events. This time it was in a straight fight with the team that had been threatening for some time.

Lancia had arrived with three new cars for Kankunnen, Biasion and Auriol. There were, again, no new technical innovations, but unreliability hit Auriol in the shape of a broken crankcase and Biasion with transmission problems, and both suffered intermittent power-steering problems, which had never occurred before.

Kankunnen fought hard for all three days but whenever he pulled in front of the Toyota, Sainz seemed to have an answer and retook his lead soon after.

After the Acropolis Rally in June Miki Biasion was quoted as saying, 'The Toyota combination [with Sainz] was unbeatable this time'. What many had imagined was unthinkable, since the beginning of 1987, had happened. Not only had the Lancia team been beaten comprehensively, but also by doing so, the winners, Toyota/Sainz, had grabbed the lead of the World Rally Drivers Championship. This was the first time that Lancia had lost its grip on this series since Group A started in 1987.

Sainz Moves Ahead

Sainz was surprised at the next round in New Zealand that Lancia did not turn up, but the team had always viewed the World Rally Constructors Championship as their basic reason for being involved in the sport, so a round that was only likely to improve driver's situations was not seen by them as worth pursuing. In a world where the media spends most of its time obsessed with personalities, this is a philosophy that is perhaps difficult to grasp but it is important to do so for a greater understanding of the workings of the team.

For two events, Sainz was able to increase his drivers' lead, whilst Lancia, although they entered the Argentinian rally, made no effort to send the drivers who would most benefit from a good result. In fact, Biasion won with a reliable run, whilst Sainz suffered three rolls in an accident and finished second. Auriol was third, helping Turin to go further ahead in its chosen category.

The drivers' crown slipped further away when Sainz won again in Finland on the 1000 Lakes Rally. Lancia had entered two Martini cars for Kankunnen and Auriol, plus Fiorio in his usual Jolly Club machine. These were all new cars employing steel propshafts instead of carbon-fibre and in lightweight gravel specification with torque-split set at 50/50. The limitations of the Delta shell, even in wide-arched integrale form, were beginning to show again as the shock-absorbers were now fitted with automatic water-spray cooling, due to the requirement for ever wider wheels within the limited wheelarch space. The larger the wheel, the less air space remained. Banal unreliability hit Kankunnen when in the lead, as his throttle cable snapped. The five-minute delay ended any challenge he might have for Sainz and Toyota. Auriol and Fiorio were racing each other, but for eighth place until the former crashed out and the latter's gearbox failed.

All the indications were beginning to suggest that the integrale was on the wane. In fact the situation was already very similar to that of exactly one year previously when the 8-valve car was beginning to display its inadequacies. There was no sign of a new car being developed or even talked about, although a rumour appeared in the UK *Autosport* magazine that a

Few 16v cars were used in the UK motorsport but here is Rodney Bennett in his on Salisbury Plain during a British club rally.

'Dedra coupé' was being considered. With 20/20 hindsight it would seem that someone had seen what was to become the Delta's eventual road-car replacement and jumped to conclusions. There had even been rumours that long-term sponsor Martini was likely to abandon the team in 1991 and turn to track racing with Alfa Romeo. The situation reeked of uncertainty.

Lancia Fight Back

Quite suddenly, the rot stopped. At the Australia rally in September, Kankunnen won convincingly from Sainz, although Auriol eliminated himself with an accident, which resulted in a blown engine. A torque split of 50/50 was again utilized and the Martini cars' specifications were as normal for gravel rounds with 1000 Lakes suspension settings. They had one innovative advantage, however.

The previous year had seen the first win by Toyota and this was partially attributable to a special effort by Pirelli to produce tyres suitable for the unique road surfaces found in Australia, which consist of fine bauxite. After some testing Michelin felt they had succeeded in finding the solution by hand-cutting some of the tread on their usual tyres. It was only later that a veteran mechanic from the Martini team, Rino Buschiazzi, suggested a different approach. His idea was tried and the cars went quicker than ever. He had proposed removing separate blocks of tread and the spaces thus revealed on the tyres filled up with stones, which acted as if they were studs thus improving road-holding.

Kankunnen took a convincing victory that allowed Lancia to breathe again, especially as it put the manufacturers title virtually beyond anyone else's reach.

Less than a month later at San Remo, Lombardi was able to announce that Martini had actually agreed to continue as Lancia rally team sponsor for a further two years, as there had been speculation that this might cease. He also said that he was satisfied with the development position of the 16v integrale and that yet a further evolution of the model was being readied for 1992. He added that he felt the 16v car was not yet at the peak of its development.

Once the rally started, Miki Biasion, returning to the team having had a back injury attended to, disappeared into an ever-increas-

A 16v car poses on the historic north banking at Monza.

It is South London and Barry Waterhouse gives his 16v an airing at a Crystal Palace sprint in the late 1990s.

ing lead. Lancia had entered three new cars for Biasion, Kankunnen, and Auriol, whilst the Jolly Club runners were Cerrato in Kankunnen's 1000 Lakes car and Fiorio used the car he had had on the same rally. Michelin had spent time developing the new tyre treads they had used in Australia and the two-pedal car put in another appearance for relatively low-key development purposes in the hands of Piero Liatti.

The new Michelins turned out to be of no help to Biasion as he crashed out after losing concentration on seeing damaged bodywork debris. That was a result of a roll by Sainz who continued but dropped way down the leader board. The last night of the event was the opportunity for the Spaniard to attack, as he needed to finish in the top three to take the Drivers' Championship for Toyota away from Lancia for the first time since 1986.

At the finish everyone was happy. Auriol had taken up the mantle of Biasion and drove a storming rally to finish first, beating an off-form Kankunnen into second, but Sainz had taken his all-important third place to win the 1990 drivers' championship. So Lancia had taken their third manufacturers' title in a row. In a season when the integrale's run of success had several times shown signs of finally faltering, Turin was very happy to take the victory and, despite doing so, they had arranged entries on the British RAC Rally in November – an event they seldom attended. Ex-teammates Kankunnen and Alen battled through the cold, wet forests at first before Alen retired his Subaru and Sainz joined in. Kankunnen and Auriol had their San Remo cars, whilst Biasion used Kankunnen's 1000 Lakes' machine. Sainz took another win after Kankunnen suffered a horrifying accident on sheet ice being extremely lucky to escape without injury.

Lancia won the 1990 World Rally Championship for Manufacturers and in addition, won the European Rally Championship with Robert Droogmans. Whilst it was clear that the works team was facing formidable opposition, it is important to emphasize that the integrale was far from dead in national rallying as these cars had, in 1990, won outright the rally championships of: Austria, Finland, France (gravel), Germany, Greece, Hungary, Portugal, Spain (tarmac), Sweden and Turkey.

1991

It had been a long year from which the 16v integrale had emerged with honour, but a nagging question still remained – what next? There were rumours of a new car having been seen in Turin and a grabbed shot of one appeared in the UK *Autosport* magazine before the end of 1990. Its appearance was dominated by even larger extended wheelarches than those on the current 16v car indicating that more suspension travel and space for even wider wheels had been the priority.

There was no question that the 16v integrale was virtually bursting at the seams, but it was not showing its age in itself, merely displaying all the disadvantages of being based on a car that had been first announced 11 years previously.

Speculation was rife amongst the specialist motor-sport press that 1991 would be the year the other Japanese manufacturers would finally see off the Lancia challenge. After all, they reasoned, the 16v integrale was heading into it's second consecutive season with no development or modifications, whilst Toyota and Mitsubishi had more modern cars with plenty of scope for evolution.

Monte Carlo Rally 1991

Most thought their predictions were vindicated when, half-way through January's Monte Carlo event the Lancias were clearly struggling, over two minutes behind Sainz' Toyota.

But the main threat to the establishment came from far nearer home than Japan. Ford had finally brought an effective rally car to the start of a World Championship event after some years of struggling. The Sierra Cosworth 4×4 was proving extremely quick in the hands of Francois Delecour and took the lead from Sainz.

From Turin, in addition to two new Martini cars for Biasion and Kankunnen, there was a Jolly Club car for Auriol, a Fina car that won the previous year's French championship, a car for Saby and Biasion's 1990 RAC car for Loubet. The only technical development being the addition of a rear anti-roll bar adjustable from inside the cockpit.

Were Lancia about to experience the end of their Monte Carlo run of success? The fight soon resolved itself as being between Toyota and Ford.

Lancia rather shot itself in the foot when Saby was proving himself to be the fastest of all their entries and was drawing away from Biasion. With a 17s lead over the Italian they called him in for a works turbo change, which promptly broke on the next stage undoing all his hard work.

One crew suffered a tragi-comic accident when they read their pace-notes for one corner as saying, 'brake at the broken telegraph pole'. Unfortunately someone had been along and repaired the pole in the meantime and they missed their braking point.

Even Toyota was outpaced by the Ford and was relieved when it failed on the last stage. Lancia were second by some five minutes with Biasion, and Auriol had retired with engine trouble.

Portugal Rally 1991

The Lancia team made a concerted effort in Portugal in March to try to reverse what were seemingly waning fortunes, and Auriol with the Fina-sponsored car was the man who took the fight to the Toyotas. He fought for the lead with Sainz and looked as if he might pull off a victory, but settled for second place after a big moment involving some rocks on the track. He decided that he was 'driving too hard' and duly finished behind Sainz who won again. Behind came Biasion and Kankunnen with no retirements.

The situation may have become somewhat precarious for Lancia on the international rally scene, but back in the real world, the integrale

Fina sponsored some works built cars in national and international rally championships. This car was run by the semi-works Jolly Club team in 1990 and Didier Auriol won in it on Corsica and at San Remo.

was still proving itself to be top of the heap on the public roads. VW introduced a limited edition 16-valve supercharged four-wheel drive Golf in 1991 and Tiff Needell of *Autosport* magazine was able to test one back-to-back against an integrale. The answer to the question, 'Would the 4WD Golf lead the field as the front-wheel drive version has done?' was 'No'. Needell concluded that the Golf G60 limited would make a fine collector's item, but that the integrale would astill go out and do the job of rally winning.

Safari Rally 1991

Needell's words were prophetic, for the first time since 1990's San Remo, a Martini car, with Kankunnen at the wheel, beat off rough, tough conditions and the massed ranks of Japanese machinery to take a much-needed win on the Safari rally.

Pressure from the Japanese was immense, with competition from Toyota and Mitsubishi as usual, but joined for the first time by Nissan. Lancia had tested hard for months prior to the event, as in the past, and some innovations were to be found on the cars brought for Biasion, Kankunnen and Recalde. For the first time the team was confident enough to utilize the 16-valve engines in Africa, but the changes went considerably deeper than that. The extremely rough and muddy conditions prompted Lancia's engineers to spend much time setting the very best ride-height commensurate with ride comfort. The suspension, as always, would be under immense pressure so, to relieve some of the stresses, the front suspension struts featured water-cooling. Externally, to protect the engine and intercooler from damage, the front protective roll-bar was strengthened. To avoid damage at the rear, the bumper was reinforced as, to avoid getting stuck in deep mud holes, it was sometimes necessary for the cars to be pushed through by a service vehicle. Extra large fuel tanks of 160ltr (9,765cu. in) capacity were fitted for the long distances involved and, just to be certain, Kevlar boards were added to the bottom of the doors to stop water coming in when fording rivers.

Bizarrely, Biasion was to retire from the effects of a road-traffic accident with his car

An Italian integrale club meeting gathers on the disused backstretch of the old Monza circuit for some driving tests.

under the back of a truck. Meanwhile Kankunnen took the lead when Sainz' engine broke and, after suffering two flat tyres, which were supposedly puncture proof, Recalde finished third.

In addition to it being the first time that Lancia had won a World Championship Rally since San Remo the previous October, the result, most crucially, rocketed them and Kankunnen, to a closely competitive position at the head of the points races for the two series' leads. The roads and the tempo were set to dramatically change though, as next was Corsica with its high-speed twists and turns. Could Lancia maintain their new-found momentum?

Corsica Rally 1991

Development was definitely not at a standstill. The traditional appearance of Martini Deltas on the annual Costa Smeralda rally in Sardinia in April, resulted in 16v integrales finishing in first through to eighth places, and Lancia had taken the opportunity to go public with a new electronically controlled central differential, where the level of traction at each end of the cars could be adjusted according to the drivers' preferences. Kankunnen had won the rally, commenting along the way that he thought the 16v car was now at its best 'using all four tyres, all the time'. As an indication of driving styles, Kankunnen and Deila, who was also driving a factory car fitted with the new equipment, were both totally unhappy with each other's settings.

A mixed bunch of Lancias were present for the Corsica race with a new Fina-sponsored car for Auriol and a Martini-liveried car for Loubet, both built and serviced by Abarth. A French-built car was sent for Saby, also in Fina colours, whilst Astra from Bra near Turin entered a Group N 16v for Sillankorva.

Martini were seriously worried about keeping both the cars and their occupants cool on the long stages, and water-cooling, on a total loss basis, was being utilized for the one-piece front brake calipers. In order to keep the crews cool, an aerodynamically shaped scoop was fitted above the windscreens and tubing directed the air to adjustable nozzles in the car.

Despite not being the quickest car on the island, Didier Auriol kept his Jolly Club machine in touch until the very end and finished second. Almost neck and neck with the winner, Sainz, until the last long stage, he was let down when his Michelin tyres started to lose their efficacy half-way through. Back at home, the development of the electronically controlled centre differential moved up a gear. Whilst the original arrangement, introduced with the HF4WD, involving a Ferguson viscous coupling, had been innovative in 1986 and proved capable of coping with power increases since then, by 1991 it was proving to be an increasingly weak link in the Delta's transmission system, as newer cars from Japan benefited from the improved technology of controllable, variable, torque distribution front to rear.

Kankunnen related in an interview that he felt the new equipment 'was the way ahead'. He also provided an insight into driving the Martini integrales, 'they require a different driving style than the others…it took me a long time to get used to driving the Lancia again' (having spent a year at Toyota). As a pointer to the future, he also said that lots of space was needed in all the new cars for suspension and tyres, everything needed to be built larger right from the start. Prophetic words indeed, but then he must have known what was going on back at Corso Marche.

In addition to technical developments, a merry-go-round of personnel changes was taking place at Abarth. Failing Ferrari fortunes in the Formula One scene had prompted the sacking of Cesare Fiorio, the team manager. Totally unexpectedly, Lancia's rally man Claudio Lombardi was chosen to fill the vacancy at Maranello. In turn, this meant there was then a job on offer at Abarth and the man to fill it was Mario Petronio, formerly with the Fiat Technical Centre, who joined to head-up the Abarth competitions department. That was not all though, for the vastly experienced and multi-talented Giorgio Pianta rejoined Martini and Abarth once again and took up the position of on-event manager, starting with the Acropolis, the next world rally.

Acropolis Rally 1991

The new electronic differential was entrusted to Biasion on the rough roads of Greece 'to see if it could stand the pace'. It could, so Biasion brought his car with the new device home in third place. Another innovation being tried was a hydraulically operated radiator cooling

Many have modified their cars for even more exhilarating performance. This is a 16v on the track.

In the UK the Lancia Motor Club's annual track day at Goodwood is a great place to explore a 16v's limits.

system, previously tried by Liatti on the 1990 San Remo, and water-cooling was once again used for the shock absorbers.

Kankunnen took the overall win without being quickest at all times. The very rough conditions allowed a new Mitsubishi to prove quick, but its challenge was thwarted by navigational errors. Meanwhile Sainz' Toyota and Auriol's Lancia slugged it out at the head of the rally only to suffer problems – in particular punctures. Auriol was extremely angry when one of his 'run-flat' tyres exploded.

Before he left for Ferrari, Lombardi had said to Pianta that he considered the integrale was no longer competitive, so some tests were carried out whilst the team was in Greece. The conclusion was that Pianta reckoned that the basic problem was one of tyres. "On my return to Turin, I contacted Michelin and arranged a meeting with Dupasquier the competitions tyre manager. Fiat provided me with a private plane to fly me to Clermont Ferrand and there we discussed the problem coming to a solution that would require Martini Lancia to find another 2 million Lire budget. So, I rang Mr. Cantarella for this extra money. 'Pianta', he said, 'if you think you can win I will make the money available.' We went on to win our fifth World Championship that year."

New Zealand Rally 1991

Lancia felt they were back in the hunt for World Championship honours in both the drivers' and manufacturers' series, but it was not immediately apparent. Kankunnen headed off to New Zealand at the end of June with his Portugal rally car and Auriol had his Jolly Club machine, but neither were able to stop Sainz winning, although the Martini cars used did not incorporate anything new. Both drivers had signed for a further year with the Lancia team. The new car was due to appear in the 1992 Monte Carlo, so they would have had inside knowledge of what was to come as it had been under development for six months.

Argentina Rally 1991

Sainz beat them again in Argentina, although Biasion was only 8s behind but, again, no new technical innovations were tried. Biasion tried hard throughout the rally and this was Lancia's biggest effort of the season so far. Minna Sillankorva, who used Biasion's training car to win the Ladies Cup and put herself into a substantial lead in the FIA Lady Drivers championship, provided small comfort.

By August Toyota was showing its hand for 1992 by testing its latest development Celica coupé contender, whilst no less than Biasion was in the process of deciding whether to stay with Lancia or to defect to another team.

1000 Lakes Rally 1991

Flat-out motoring returned to the menu with the 1000 Lakes rally the same month. Markku Alen's Subaru was reported as being absolutely flat-out for up to 10s at a time, as the great Finn was not even lifting the throttle when taking off over the jumps. Both Lancia and Toyota were trying ever more exotic fuel brews, with the former's mechanics being seen with tears in their eyes at the service points.

Nobody at Lancia needed to cry this time though as the cards all fell the way of Turin. No new technical advances were tried, the electronic differential not having reappeared since Biasion had tried it in Greece. This had always been local ace Kankunnen's demon event and slowly he got the measure of Sainz. The Martini team, using every advantage they could think of, helped him on his way. Only the smallest amount of fuel was added at stops in order to keep the car's weight down.

Sainz obliged Lancia by putting his car off the road far enough to drop to fifth. So Kankunnen was able to lead Auriol home for a now less-common integrale 1–2. Was the intensity of attempting to win a second World Drivers Championship getting to Sainz?

Only two weeks later it all went wrong again for the Spaniard who was clearly displaying the effects of the pressure of the expectations the team had of him. Kankunnen, in contrast, was thoroughly enjoying himself and was only having problems with team-mate Auriol, who was potentially in line to take the Jolly Club's first ever world-championship win until, with no warning, his engine blew up. Kankunnen's win put him only two points behind Sainz and Lancia overtook the Japanese to gain the lead in their much coveted manufacturer's series.

But if you are going to drive them hard, try an integrale driving course first so that you do not get any nasty surprises.

With these championship positions so finely balanced, Lancia announced a blitzkreig plan for San Remo, entering no fewer than seven cars in an attempt to steam-roller Sainz out of the top positions.

The New HF integrale

The press meanwhile had had a preview of what the Lancia team drivers would have at their disposal in 1992. The New HF integrale made its bow.

above *The interior was a vast improvement and air conditioning was an option.*

below *The first sight of the Evoluzione HF integrale in September 1991 brought gasps from even the press.*

The Fiat group was, for the moment, quite happy for the model to continue its development. The rally success was continuing to produce unprecedented parallel interest in the showrooms and so far, 30,000 total-traction Deltas had been sold as road cars. Not bad when one considers that as a homologation expediency, Lancia need only have actually sold half that number. In comparison, as examples of other manufacturers' then-current homologation road cars, BMWs M3 first-series car only sold 18,000 units and Toyota saw 26,000 GT-Four Celicas head out of showrooms to new owners.

Lancia's New Delta HF integrale, as it was officially called, received immediate praise from the pundits. Front and rear track had been increased by 2in (5cm), thus accounting for the considerably increased size of the wheelarches seen on the prototypes. In fact, this much-needed new body style had first been created over a weekend back in late 1990 at Fiat's Stabilimento Pilotta pre-production works in Turin.

Both front and rear suspension had been revised and reviewed and improved with stronger and reinforced parts and, in particular, larger diameter dampers with longer travel in an attempt to rectify probably the one serious flaw

Auto Italia *magazine was able to test Didier Auriol's semi-works Jolly Club Fina 16-valve car in 1994.*

The Jolly Club run cars were always built by Abarth at their Corso Marche Turin premises.

in the integrale's armoury. The power steering unit was fitted with equipment to cool the fluid and *Autosport* magazine reported that all these revisions led to a car that 'drives with remarkable refinement and poise...a real cracker, steering and cornering with stunning dexterity'.

It was suggested that rivals had a lot to worry about for the 1992 season, as production of the new car was well advanced with the necessary 5,000 being built well before the car's expected Monte Carlo rally debut.

San Remo Rally 1991

There was still unfinished business on the special stages to be dealt with before the end of 1991 and the luck that had run with Kankunnen during the previous two events abruptly departed when he hit a rock on only the second stage of San Remo and retired. So those seven entered cars became six, but Lancia could still breathe easily as an inspired Auriol was powering away to lead by as much as one and a half minutes. Sainz suffered a blow when his steering's power assistance failed, dropping him down the leaderboard.

Team manager Giorgio Pianta was a happy man, however, with five integrales finishing in the top ten – just like the old days. A one, two, three, flourish that few could answer. The Lancia team's ability to recover from the edge of an abyss was becoming remarkable. In addition, this was at the end of the 16v car's life-cycle. After its death-knell had been tentatively sounded, it appeared as if the iconic myth status that the Delta had created was in danger itself of being upstaged once again.

Lancia had achieved yet another manufacturers' rally title but the drivers' award was still the subject of dispute between Sainz and Kankunnen.

Catalunya Rally 1991

Toyota's situation was not helped when, at the new Catalunya rally in Spain, Sainz' engine failed to start leaving Kankunnen to take second place and more points. This also meant that Lancia would have to take part in the UKs RAC Rally, as there was now a possibility that Turin could grab both titles.

On Catalunya, the integrale entry details were particularly complex. Kankunnen's car was the one he had used on the 1000 Lakes rally, whilst Aghini and Trelles had been entered under the Jolly Club banner. Aghini's entry was Auriol's San Remo car and had originally been prepared for the Frenchman to run in Spain. Because of this, the car that Aghini was originally due to drive was handed over to Trelles. Recalde also ran in this rally with a private car run under the ART banner but rented from Abarth. Jesus Puras tried an ex-works car, which had been used by Loubet in the Monte Carlo and was run by the Nocentini team, whilst the Grifone team looked after Monzon and his car was in Marlboro colours.

In order to win the FISA Ladies Cup, Minna Sillankorva and Michela Marangoni merely had to start in their integrale. This they did and promptly retired on the first special stage with their mission accomplished.

RAC Rally 1991

Two Martini integrales arrived in the UK for the RAC Rally in November and their mission

Fina also sponsored the European rally championship winning 16v car of the Belgian Droogmans in 1990.

By the 1990s the top professional co-drivers had computerized equipment at their disposal in the cockpit.

was to make a last-minute snatch for the driver's crown, and thus grab both top FISA awards.

Many changes were to take place over the coming winter and it was expected that the new, updated integrale would be ready for Monte Carlo in 1992. So the RAC was to be the swansong of the model in its current state. Would Kankunnen allow it to bow out in style, and had Biasion learnt from his previous RAC experience for this, his last appearance for the Turin team, as he had decided to move over to Ford for the next season? Sainz, for Toyota, admitted that it was difficult staying ahead of the Lancias and '...the company had injected so much new speed into their Deltas...'.

Unexpectedly, it was Didier Auriol who translated this speed into serious action. It should have been either Kankunnen or Sainz, but from the rally half-way stage, the Frenchman started to fly, leaving them both behind. This speed was being achieved in the Jolly Club-entered car that Didier had driven in Australia, whilst Juha was in the car with which he won that rally and Miki's was his mount from San Remo. The latter was not destined to finish the RAC, with retirement following a three-times end-over-end accident

Ing. Sergio Limone was present for the very first runs of the Abarth built Martini Evoluzione integrales with the initial testing being conducted by new driver Philippe Bugalski.

The wider wheelarches allowed the use of bigger wheels and tyres. Note that four-stud fixing was still being used, although the road car was announced with five-studs.

on the final stage on the Monday. Sadly for Toyota, their efforts came to naught when Sainz suffered a small accident, which was enough to cause cooling difficulties and eventually a blown head-gasket. He continued to finish third, whilst Auriol had an off, after which he elected to help Juha by following him closely. This was only possible by checking in 19min and 30s late at one point, putting him out of contention for a top ten finishing spot.

Kankunnen switched to 'Tourismo' mode in his own words and won overall by nearly three minutes.

So the Lancia Delta integrale 16v finished its factory career in the best way possible and, to prove to the world that they had no intention of resting on their laurels, a week after the RAC, pictures were published in *Autosport* magazine of Philippe Bugalski testing the new updated model. To rub it in, Mario Petronio, Abarth's general manager admitted when asked, that the new car was lighter, stronger and faster than the out-going model. Bad news for Toyota, Ford and Nissan.

Official Factory Lancia Integrale Works Cars 1989–90 (Abarth SE 045)

1989	1990–91
TO 66486F Converted from HF4WD	
	TO 36175N
TO 01768G Converted from HF4WD	
	TO 36176N
TO 74227G Converted from HF4WD	
	TO 36177N
TO 34164H	TO 51887N
TO 34165H	TO 51889N
TO 34166H	TO 51890N
TO 54902H	TO 51891N
TO 54904H	TO 54910N
TO 66643H	TO 54911N
TO 66644H	TO 85046N
TO 66645H	TO 85047N
TO 89092H	TO 95238N
TO 89093H	TO 95239N
TO 89094H	TO 95240N
TO 89095H	TO 23901P
TO 70780L	TO 23902P
TO 70781L	TO 23903P
TO 74782L	TO 23904P
TO 74783L	TO 23905P
TO 74784L	TO 23906P
TO 74785L	TO 40001P
TO 74786L	TO 40002P
TO 74787L	TO 56249P
TO 78557L	TO 56250P
TO 16989M	TO 56251P
TO 16990M	TO 22602R
TO 33820M	TO 44774R
TO 33821M	TO 55235R
TO 33822M	TO 55239R
TO 62124M	TO 71981R
TO 62125M	TO 76853R
TO 62126M	TO 76854R
TO 86305M	TO 76855R
	TO 76856R
	TO 99926R
	TO 99927R
	TO 99928R

Just how many more lives did the integrale still have up its sleeve?

Lancia won both the 1991 World Rally Championships for Drivers and Manufacturers with Juha Kankunnen.

6 1992 – Piling Up the Trophies

What was to prove to be the last major change in a distinguished line of four-wheel drive Lancia Deltas had first been introduced to the UK public as a road car in *Autosport* on 5 October 1991. No-one could have failed to have been impressed.

On the threshold of clinching a fifth World Rally Championship in a row, Lancia were also very satisfied that their baby had now notched up over 30,000 road going car sales up to this point, of which just under five hundred had found their way to the UK. This relatively low number was not surprising as apathy and prejudice regarding the Lancia marque was a feature of the UKs conservative car-buying public. They were the losers, as one look at the new car was enough to shock and the new shape left the viewer with no mistake about the purpose of the machine. Ever larger wheelarches were the most spectacular change to the external look of this latest integrale update.

Why did it need them? The engineers at Abarth in Turin accepted that the 16v car's limitations were mostly centred on restricted wheel travel and suspension. Ing. Sergio Limone:

> The Deltona or large Delta [referred to as Abarth SE 050 Lancia Delta integrale 16V Group A Evoluzione/Allargata on the competition department's list of 'Abarths'] started off as a sketch pencilled in on a photocopy of the red Martini liveried San Remo car in 1990. It was a newspaper advertisement from after the team had won. The sketch was just that, entirely hand drawn, and Ing. Crea was made responsible for the final project. The big rear wings were initially added because we thought that the car would need four-wheel steering.

In fact, in typically thorough fashion, a test car was built and fitted with this facility and the project carried the Abarth number SE 049, but with time-constraints forced on the development team by the pressure of competition requirements, it was too late to be included on the production car.

So how did the car evolve from this point onwards? Let Ing. Rodolfo Gaffino, responsible later for the one-off Agnelli Cabriolet integrale, take up the tale and recount how the first prototype Evoluzione came about:

> We were called up one Friday [in late 1990] and told that we had one weekend in which to create a new body for the integrale Evoluzione. We all met on Saturday morning and tried to decide what to do. The group consisted of Cesare Fiorio, Ing. Sculari who was responsible for Fiat Design, Ing. Pianta Director of Fiat Production, Ing. Maioli from Centro Stile Fiat, Claudio Lombardi, Abarth's Technical Director and myself. The engineers told us what sort of dimensions they needed, so we made up the patterns for the bigger wheelarches from paper and started from there. The front wings were done by eye around the pattern of the Fiat Ducato van. By the end of the weekend we had come up with the Evolution HF integrale shape and had created a chassis totally hand finished.

Those big arches and wider track are an unmistakeable feature of the Evoluzione.

The model was to become known colloquially as the Deltona, or big Delta. Development was to take up the majority of 1991.

The New Delta HF Integrale – Introduction and Features

For the first time since its introduction, considerable changes had taken place to the design and shape of the integrale. These can be summarized as:

Changes to the engineering:
- an increase in the width of the front and rear tracks
- new front suspension
- new rear suspension arms and anti-roll bar.
- more powerful brakes
- new and larger exhaust piping.
- altered power steering with the addition of an oil-cooler.
- wider wheels.

Changes to the styling:
- new design of bonnet, front and rear wings, side skirts and bumpers
- new front light clusters
- addition of a spoiler to the top of the tailgate this was the first time one had been fitted, no previous total traction delta had utilised any rear aerodynamic bodywork attachment
- new design of light alloy wheel
- new colour range
- new graphics for the instrumentation, new steering wheel, new grip for gear lever knob.

The engine did not need too much work, although an increase on paper to 210bhp at 5,750rpm with a peak torque of 220lbs ft (3.6kg m) at 3,500rpm belied the fact that management and exhaust systems had been developed to allow different power-band characteristics. The exhaust had been increased in diameter from 54mm (2.13in) on the outgoing 16v car, to 60mm (2.36in) on the new model. This enlargement had had a major part to play in the increase in power over the previous 16v car. The weekend redesign and development had allowed new, segmented, bigger dampers having a top mounting 12.5mm (0.49in) higher than on the 16v, the front and rear track being increased by 54mm (2.13in) and 60mm (2.36in), respectively, so giving the car much more confidence-inspiring stability on the road but also, crucially, allowing the rally cars' wheels more freedom of movement. A strut-brace under the bonnet connected the tops of the two strut towers, contributing still further towards increased overall stiffness and strength. At the rear, replacement stronger transverse arms and uprated springs and dampers with longer travel joined a newly arranged anti-roll bar and stronger uprights. Improved design 15in wheels, with five-stud fixing instead of the previous four, were fitted with rim width increased to 7.5in, although tyre size for the road cars remained the same as before at 205/50 ZR 15 but this necessitated the substitution of the spare wheel by a 16in diameter space-saver wheel carrying a 115/70 R 16 tyre. The power steering, which was now controlled by the use of a chunky leather covered three-spoke Momo steering wheel, was subtly altered and also received and benefited from the addition of its own oil-cooler.

The brakes were redesigned with self-ventilating discs at the front of 281mm (11.1in) by 26mm (1.02in) thick with two pot callipers of 44mm (1.73in) and 38mm (1.50in). Those on the 16v had only one-pot callipers of 50mm (1.97in) and discs of 284mm (11.2in) by 22mm (0.87in) thick. Larger discs at the rear were now up from 227mm (8.94in) to 251mm (9.88in). Assistance came from an 8-inch brake servo unit that was one inch bigger than before.

The bonnet was wider, with a larger bulge and with new lateral air intake grilles and the bumpers were redesigned to take account of the extra air-intake area provided at the front end. The headlights were of a new design, smaller, but of greater efficiency and intensity. Windscreen wipers were up two inches in length – to 20in (508mm) – and those new wheelarches were not just bigger than before, they also contributed to structural integrity as they were pressed to that shape instead of being metal sheet add-ons. Lancia claimed that the new roof spoiler marginally improved the new car's Cd by half a point and that this was enough to counteract the increased frontal area taken up by the wider wings.

The bulges on the bonnet were even larger than those on the outgoing 16v model and extra lateral grilles were provided.

History tells us that the conversion of a competition car into a road car normally results in a compromise at best and a coarse, uncivilized machine at worst, but Lancia had turned a road car into a rally car back in 1986 and was now proving for the third time that reversing that policy could be a resounding success on the road.

Standard trim for road cars was grey Alcantara and a sunroof was fitted. Lancia initially listed seven production colours these being: Monza red, white, Lancia blue, Derby green metallescente, Madras blue metallescente, black metallescente and Winner red micalizzato. UK deliveries started early in 1992.

Lancia was at pains to point out that the new car's top-end performance had changed little compared to the outgoing 16v; what they had achieved was a car that was capable of point-to-point average speeds much higher than before. 'Simply the best...the definitive example of a pedigree classic car that just happens to be in production' said Jeremy Walton of *Motor Sport* magazine.

Lancia Leaves Rallying

It was suggested by *Autosport* magazine that on the basis of the startling new look alone, rival manufacturers were likely to be trailing the factory-Lancias by some distance. Maybe, but a news bombshell burst just before Christmas: Lancia was to disengage from rallying.

On 18 December 1991, a press release from Turin stated: 'Lancia ... suspends competitive activities'. The decision had been

Bigger wheels and deeper bumpers were also built in to the Evoluzione specification to give Abarth every chance possible of cramming more improvements into the 1992 Martini cars.

taken by Mr. Cantarella, boss of Fiat Auto. What he did not know, though, was that Lombardi had hatched a plan much earlier in the year. Giorgio Pianta:

> At the end of 1991 I went to see Mr. Cantarella and he asks me to stop rallying completely. He said that although Lancia has won five World Championships, it could all be ruined by one bad crash [involving the public]. But, Mr. Cantarella I say, I have already got thirty Deltonas ready for next season! [Lombardi had it all planned.] No, stop, said Mr. Cantarella, rallying is far too expensive. He wanted to know how many people were in the competition departments, so I told him that there were 100 at Alfa Romeo and 350 at Abarth. The budget was cut and I was blamed as if it was my fault and I only wanted circuit racing [for Alfa]. So Mr. Cantarella spoke to me again and said that if we were to hand over the team, it would be much better. So I created the Jolly Club Martini Racing Team. This was with top people and Lancia gave them all the engines and spare parts. For Martini this was very good and they doubled their sponsorship.

From then on it was the beginning of the end for Abarth and Corso Marche, as far as rally cars were concerned; they were reduced to the role of building and selling them only to private owners and teams. The racing was to continue, but not out of Corso Marche. Meanwhile, Lancia were at pains to make it clear that the competition days of the integrale were far from over. The responsibilities for World Rally Championship Lancia presence were handed over entirely to Martini who, in turn, contracted Jolly Club to do the work. Thus bizarrely, in Didier Auriol's case, he was leaving Jolly Club at the end of 1991 to join… the Jolly Club!!

The Abarth team personnel were to be integrated as far as possible into the new team, which was to be run by Claudio Bortoletto, boss of Jolly Club. The first-division drivers were to be Juha Kankunnen and Didier Auriol, with the 'second division' – the equivalent of previous years Jolly Club teams – made up of Frenchman Phillippe Bugalski and Italian Andrea Aghini. Giorgio Pianta was to take on overall team management responsibilities, as Mario Petronio, who had only joined in May on the departure of Lombardi, was recalled to the Fiat Technical Centre.

Giorgio, with the initial cooperation of Lombardi, had already had the necessary cars built and tested. In their press release, Lancia stated that it would 'hand over [these] vehicles to the Jolly Club organization, ART and Grifone, who would race them under their own organizations'.

So Paolo Cantarella had effectively been presented with a fait accompli – all Giorgio Pianta and the team had to do was win a sixth World Rally Championship.

The New HF Integrale Rally Car

Monte Carlo was imminent and the new factory competition cars were displayed to the press in Nice in early January 1992.

LANCIA DELTA HF integrale

Specification

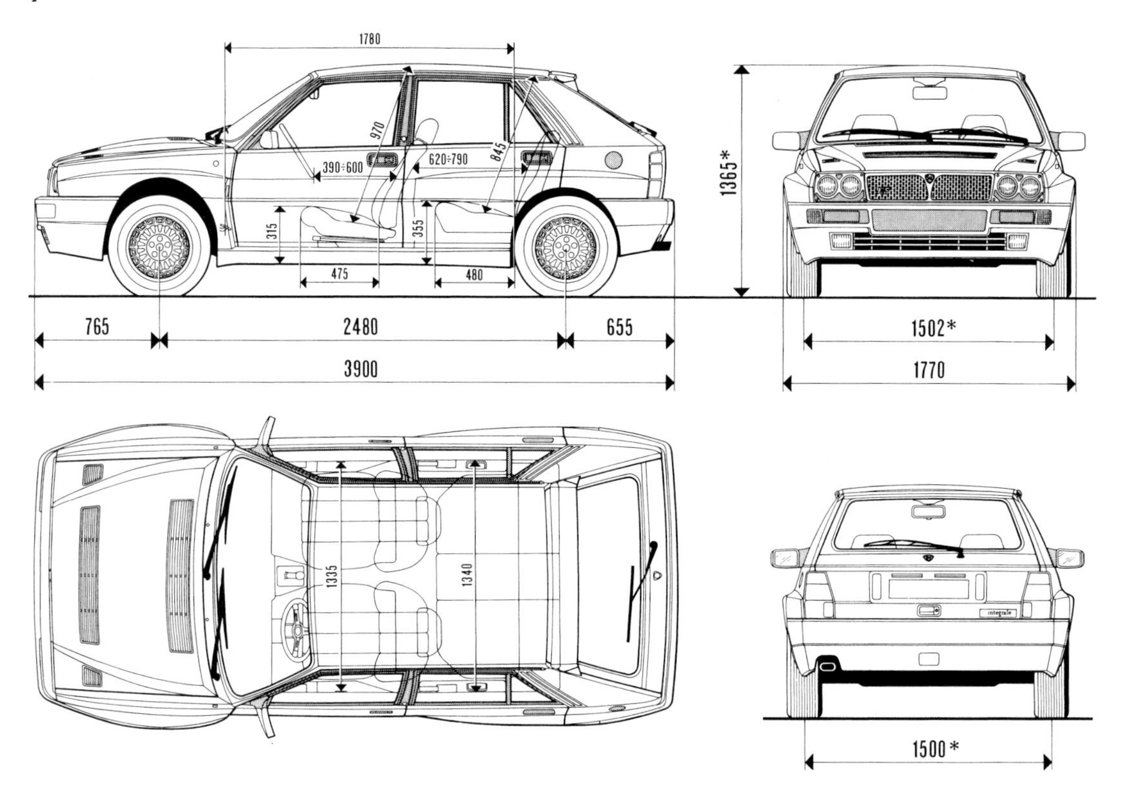

Luggage compartment capacity: 200 dm^3; with back seat folded down: 940 dm^3 * unladen

ENGINE

Main features	
No. cylinders	4, in line
Cycle-stroke	Otto-4
Bore × stroke	84 × 90 mm
Displacement	1995 cc
Compression ratio	8:1
Max. power output DIN	210 bhp (151 kW - EEC)
at	5750 rpm
Peak torque DIN	31 mkg (298 Nm - EEC)
at	3500 rpm
Fuel	leaded or unleaded petrol (RON 95)

Construction	
Layout	front transverse
Cylinder block	cast iron with counter-rotating balancer shafts
Cylinder spacings	91 mm
No. of main bearings	5
Cylinder head	light alloy

Timing	
Valve arrangement	at V (65°)
Timing	DOHC

Timing control	toothed belt
Timing	0.8 mm timing control tolerance
Inlet: Opens	8° BTDC
Inlet: Closes	35° ABDC
Exhaust: Opens	30° BBDC
Exhaust: Closes	0° ATDC
Counter-rotating balancer shafts	2 in the cylinder block
Control	by toothed belt
Ignition	
Type	electronic with mapped advance and knock sensor, combined with the injection
Firing order	1-3-4-2
Spark plugs	Bosch WR6DTC
Fuel feed	
Type	supercharging by turbocharger and air/air heat exchanger on intake and overboost (automatically engaged at full revs)
Fuel pump	electric
Injection	electronic IAW Weber combined with the ignition
Air cleaner	dry-type, with paper cartridge
Turboblower: type	water-cooled Garrett T3
Max supercharging pressure	1 bar
Lubrication	
Type	forced feed with gear pump and oil radiator
Oil filter	cartridge
Engine cooling	
Type	water-forced by pump with radiator and additional expansion tank
Control	thermostat
Fan	electric, controlled from a thermostatic switch on the radiator

TRANSMISSION

Power drive: type	permanent 4 wheel drive with centre differential, epicyclic torque converter and Ferguson viscous joint; Torsen-type rear differential with 5 to 1 wheel torque ratio
Clutch	dry, single plate, hydraulically controlled
Friction ring diameter (o.d. × i.d.)	230 × 155 mm
Transmission ratios	
Gearbox	
1st	3.500:1
2nd	2.176:1
3rd	1.523:1
4th	1.156:1
5th	0.916:1
Reverse	3.545:1
Final drive ratio	3.111:1 (18/56)
Bevel gear front/rear	2.263:1 (19/43)
Torque splitter	front: 47% rear: 53%

CHASSIS

Body	self-bearing structure
Braking system	front and rear discs with double cylinder front and rear floating calipers, diagonal-split type hydraulic brake circuit with vacuum servo and brake effort proportioning valve acting on the rear wheels. Optionally available: ABS
Front discs	
– diameter	281 mm (self-ventilating)
– total front brake linings	$54 \times 4 = 216$ cm^2

Rear discs	
— diameter	251 mm
— total rear brake linings	$35 \times 4 = 140$ cm^2
Parking brake	acting on the rear brake discs
Front suspension	independent MacPherson-type struts, lower wishbones, anti-roll bar, and double-acting gas-type hydraulic telescopic dampers
Flexibility at the wheel	0.50 mm/kg
Wheel wobble { upper	60 mm
Wheel wobble { lower	103 mm
Wheel position (unladen)	
— camber	$-1° \pm 30'$
— caster	$3°10' \pm 30'$
— toe-in	$-2 - +1$ mm
Rear suspension	independent MacPherson-type struts, transverse links, longitudinal reaction rods, anti-roll bar and double - acting gas-type hydraulic telescopic dampers
Flexibility at the wheel	0.51 mm/kg
Wheel wobble { upper	60 mm
Wheel wobble { lower	125 mm
Wheel position (unladen)	
— camber	$-1°30' \pm 30'$
— caster	$2°30' \pm 30'$
— toe-in	3 - 5 mm
Steering	rack and pinion power steering
Turning circle	10.4 m
Steering wheel turns lock to lock	2.8
Road wheels	
Rims	light alloy: 7½ J × 15″
Tyres	205/50 ZR 15
Inflation pressure	
— front	2.2 bar (2.5 bar**)
— rear	2.2 bar (2.5 bar**)
Spare wheel	
Rim	light alloy: 3½ B × 16″ H2-37
Tyre	T115/70 R 16
Inflation pressure	4.2 bar (front and rear)
Top speed permitted	80 km/h

(**) at high constant speed, fully laden

Electrical equipment	
Voltage	12 V
Alternator with built-in electronic voltage regulator	65 A
Starter motor	1.1 kW
Battery capacity	45 Ah (service free)

WEIGHTS

Kerb weight (DIN)*	1300 kg
Distribution { front	62.4%
Distribution { rear	37.6%
Laden weight	1750 kg
Max. weight permitted { front	1030 kg
Max. weight permitted { rear	1030 kg
Maximum payload	450 kg
Max towing weight	1300 kg
No. of seats	5

(*) Inclusive of fuel, water, spare wheel, and accessories.

PERFORMANCE

Top speed (in 5th)	220 km/h
Max gradient climbable (laden)	58%
Speed at 1,000 rpm { in 4th	30.3
Speed at 1,000 rpm { in 5th	38.2
Power/weight ratio { kg/bhp-DIN	6.19
Power/weight ratio { kg/kW-EEC	8.6

Acceleration (2 adults + 20 kg) (secs)

0-100 km/h	5.7
0-1000 m	26.1

Pickup from 40 km/h (in 4th)
(2 adults + 20 kg) (secs)

over 1000 m	30.5

Conventional fuel consumption (l/100 km)

at 90 km/h	7.9
at 120 km/h	10.5
urban cycle	11.2
ECE average	9

SUPPLIES

	dm^3 (l)	kg
Fuel tank capacity	57	—
including a reserve of:	6 to 9	—
Engine radiator, expansion tank, and heating system liquid	6.2	—
Oil Sump	4.9	4.4
Total capacity of Sump filter, radiator and ducting oil	5.8	5.2
Gearbox and differential, oil	3.8	3.4
Rear differential	1.1	1
Power-steering box	0.75	—
Hydraulic brake circuits liquid	0.40	—
Wind-screen and rear screen washer bottle	2	—

CHARACTERISTIC ENGINE CURVES (EEC)

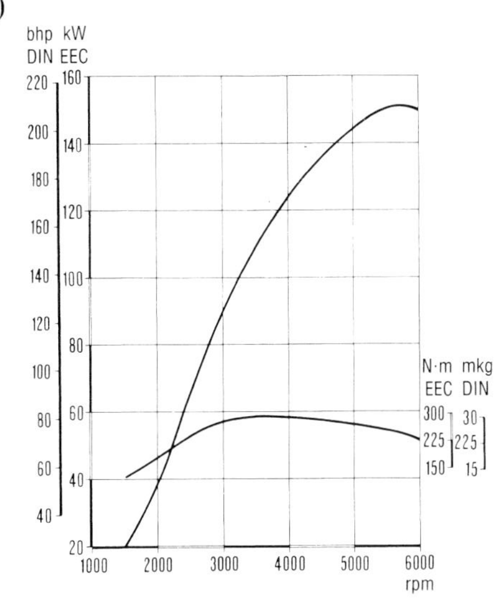

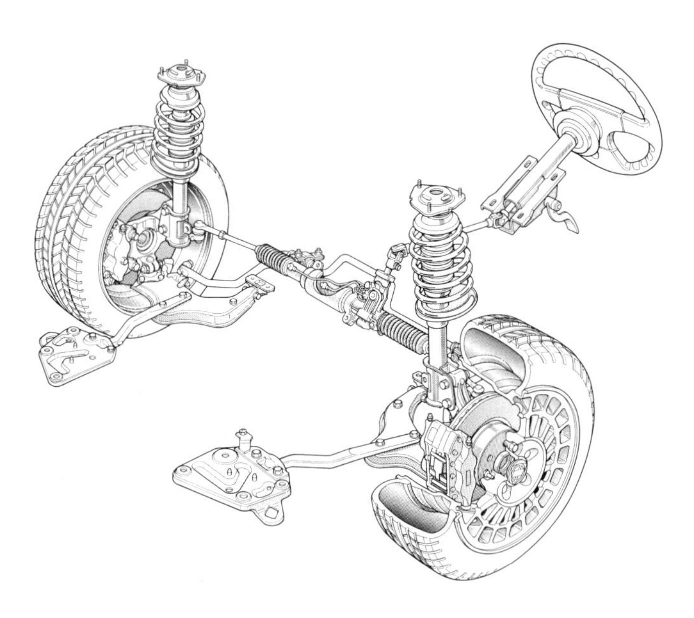

The big new wheelarches of the Evoluzione, thrashed out over a weekend's work in Turin, gave the integrale a new lease of life and allowed yet more suspension travel and better location as well as bigger wheels.

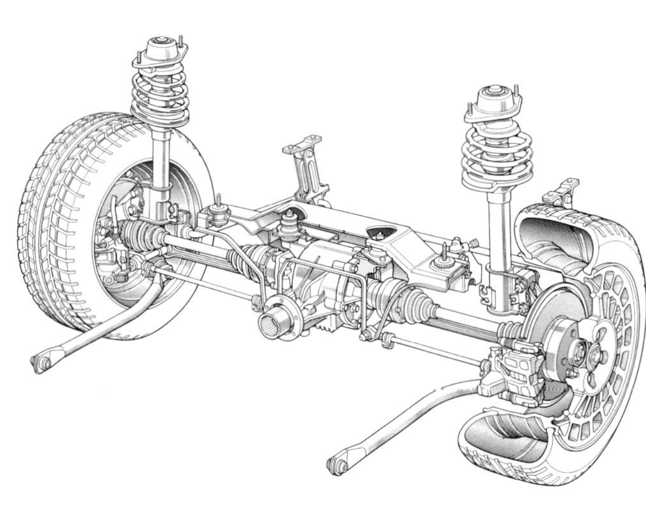

The ultimate reason for the size of the rear wheel arches was the adoption of rear wheel steering. In fact this never happened as it was developed too late, but at least the suspension took advantage of all that extra space.

From the front of the competition cars moving back, it was clear that much attention had been paid to increasing the throughput of cooling air with extra grilles and slots allowing approximately 25 per cent more air through the engine bay. The engines of all World Rally Championship cars for 1992 were subject to new turbo air-restrictor rules, the figure settled on being 38mm (1.50in), and as always in the fast evolving world of motor sport, the Abarth engineers did not consider it would take long to catch up to 1991 output figures and beyond. Give the engineers a new rule and see how quickly they can find a way of nullifying its effect.

Those big new wheelarches were the outward indications that the shock absorbers had an extra 25mm (0.98in) of travel and tyre diameter could be increased by about 10mm (0.39in) to 620mm (24.4in) for asphalt and up to 670mm (26.4in) for gravel.

The rear of the new car displayed one of its most obvious features: the new wing that was adjustable in three positions. Under all normal circumstances, it would be flat, almost as a continuation of the roof. This is how it appeared as fitted to a new road car. Two alternative fixing bolts and holes could be used to turn the incidence of wing upwards for more down force on gravel. For ultimate grip on asphalt stages an extra bracket could be fitted which allowed the wing to sit almost vertically across the rear of the roof.

'It is very good,' said Claudio Bortoletto, of the Jolly Club 'over 80km/h [49.7mph] it is possible to feel the back end of the car really sit down'. In his opinion, it was on asphalt surfaces that he considered the car would be most improved as its forbears were 'very nervous on that surface, but now it is much more stable'.

Monte Carlo Rally 1992

In its report on the Monte Carlo rally, *Autosport* magazine described the new HF integrale as 'fearsomely quick and effective'.

Handling and steering of the New HF integrale were considered beyond praise by UK magazines.

The drivers of the new cars on this first outing were Juha Kankunnen, Didier Auriol and new boy Phillipe Bugalski.

Didier Auriol was clearly the hare of the Martini team, able to cope with Sainz' new Toyota except for one short section of 1.2km (0.75 miles) on the Sisteron stage, which nearly spelt disaster for all the integrales.

It is surprising to find out that, not only on dry asphalt but also on ice-covered tarmac, slick tyres are used. They work in the same way as your hand sticks to freezing surfaces, so they actually obtain good standards of grip.

The problem here though was that a layer of snow had fallen on top of the ice and for once this was a combination that completely fooled the four-wheel drive system. Auriol is quoted as saying, '... we sat there, with all four wheels spinning and gradually the car was moving closer and closer to the edge...'. Luckily this did not give them a permanent loss of time, but it did put them back behind Sainz.

An indication of the effectiveness of the new HF integrale was that Auriol was easily able to make up the lost time and he retook the lead and went on to win, saying at the end that the new car was much softer and easier to drive than previous models. Not what the opposition wanted to hear. Sainz said that '...[the Lancias] had had it easy here. We shall have to make it harder for them next time'. Would they? Could they?

Portugal Rally 1992

It was not Sainz who caused the integrales problems in Portugal, next rally on the schedule, it was Ford, with Francois Delecour who set a tremendous pace on tarmac after Auriol retired from the lead with a blown engine.

Delecour later suffered mechanical problems and Kankunnen put his gravel driving experience to good use on the latter part of the event to finish a clear 1.5min ahead of Biasion. The three Martini cars were all new for Kankunnen, Auriol and Aghini. The latter went off and had an accident in fog but Carlos

Juha Kankunnen finished first in this Evoluzione on the 1992 Portugal rally nearly one and a half minutes ahead of Biasion who had defected to Ford.

Menem, the son of the Argentinian president, taking the Group N version of the new car to an overall category win, heartened Lancia. Despite two out of three of the Martini cars failing to finish, it was clear from the car's performances that Toyota and Ford had much work to do if they were to topple the once again seemingly invincible Turin team.

Safari Rally 1992

Toyota was given a glimmer of encouragement on the Safari rally when Sainz took their new Celica to a win but this African marathon of a rally was a world apart from the other events that constituted the World Rally Championship. The terrain, the speeds and the sheer torture dealt out to all the components on the cars were different in almost every way to that experienced on other rallies.

Martini had added veteran driver Bjorn Waldegaard to their team on the basis of experience. Sadly he encountered the sort that nobody wanted. During a short refuelling stop it is believed that some of the liquid was spilt.

By this time in 1994 the car had moved to the Astra team who ran ex-works cars for up and coming drivers in national and international events.

This ignited and in the ensuing confusion the fire took hold. The car was completely burnt out and it was only a very quick thinking Bjorn who saved his co-driver, Fred Gallagher, from very serious injury by pulling him out of the driver's side of the car.

Kankunnen finished second with an unexpected problem: the rear shock absorbers on all the integrales failed and leaked and, in addition, their Michelin tyres were subject to many punctures, all brought on by the high speeds and constant pounding on the rough terrain. The punctures were largely a result of Michelin not being able to fit their run-flat foam tyre inserts, due to the much higher speeds the cars were achieving on the new, longer stages.

Corsica Rally 1992

The previous shorter stages were what had always characterized the roads of Corsica and the Mediterranean French Island event had always been a love/hate hunting ground for Lancia The 1992 event was no exception.

Seventeen-inch wheels were being used for the first time and this meant that the drivers were able to make use of better traction and braking, and tyre longevity. It also meant that softer compounds could be employed which, with the return of Michelin's run-flat inserts, allowed Martini to run their integrales without spare wheels. This, in turn, meant that the cars came to the stage starts weighing less than ever before, which probably meant that these were the lightest Group A cars the public would ever see, as the FIA was raising minimum weight limits from 1 January 1993.

The Martini team said that they had already managed to develop their engines to produce as much power with the new 38mm (1.49in) restrictors as they had when they were using 40mm (1.57in).

For the first time in 1992 Martini arrived with previously rallied cars, although Auriol's was new. Bugalski used Kankunnen's Monte Carlo car, Aghini had Bugalski's Monte mount, whilst the first factory car had cascaded down to private team ART so that their driver, Liatti, was able to enjoy the use of Auriol's winning Monte Carlo machine. With this, he was able to finish eighth overall, whilst its previous driver was running away with the event, leading from start to finish with virtually no competition, although Ford's Francois Delecour tried hard to keep up over the first day.

The new, bigger, wheels allowed a new gearbox with lower ratio top cog in the integrales and Auriol used the car to sweep to a very conclusive win, Bugalski bringing his home in third. Auriol later told Martin Holmes that 'driving [the new] car, was a holiday compared to previous Lancias!'.

Martini had already built up a fourteen-point lead in the World Rally Championship, but it seemed as if it all might be a rather futile effort. It was reported that Martini, who effectively employed Jolly Club to run the cars for them, had intimated that there might not be a budget available for 1993. After six years of success did this mean that the world would be watching the integrales for the last time? There was a mixed reaction to the news but Claudio Bortoletto of the Jolly Club was not acting in a confident manner.

From someone in the Martini organization came the comment, 'We must put pressure on Lancia to continue development of the Delta'. Would they listen?

Unlikely, as Cantarella had made it clear before the 1992 season started that he was

The Martini cars were virtually unbeatable in the World Rally Championship during 1992.

unwilling to pour any more Fiat money into the project, so the chances of continuing into 1993 seemed very slim.

Acropolis Rally 1992

The team though, Auriol in particular, were continuing to do a very convincing job of winning rallies. The Acropolis, with its combination of heat, dust and rough tracks, fell to the Frenchman when he remarkably led from start to finish. The season was increasingly falling his and Martini's way. This was the second consecutive ramp to flag win for the team, Auriol's first on an all-gravel event and his third win of the year.

Martini had brought along two more of Giorgio Pianta's new integrales and these had been to the same specification as their Safari cars. As Illka Kivimaki, Markku Alen's Toyota co-driver said, after the event, 'For us winning [the title] is not impossible, it's just even more difficult'.

Meanwhile, the HF integrale was receiving rave reviews from all who tried it. Cars were now becoming available to the press and in the UK, both *Motor Sport* and *Autosport* magazines were able to try one. 'Only the Escort Cosworth can hold a candle to it' said *Autosport.* Precise handling and superb power-steering were considered beyond praise by both and later, *Auto Italia* magazine's test driver commented that it was so good that the car 'could be placed so precisely that [he] found himself easily changing lanes without hitting a single cat's eye'.

The instrumentation had been revised to give it a 'more modern' look, but it actually had not changed much over the years – why should it, it did not win rallies. It came in for some criticism, *Motor Sport* suggesting, 'The Veglia instruments should be renamed Vaguely', and Quentin Willson of television fame suggested it was 'gimcrack'.

'For long cross-country journeys or scampering around city streets, it's a tough act to follow,' said Roberto Giordanelli in Auto Italia – Toyota, Subaru and Ford were finding out just how true those words were.

New Zealand Rally 1992

The New Zealand rally had been given a miss by Martini, so Toyota was hoping to make up for its earlier disappointments. To an extent it

Motor Sport *magazine suggested we should all be grateful that the rules of rallying had made Lancia produce the Evoluzione for anyone to buy.*

did so, Sainz winning the event but, to their surprise, Pierro Liatti who normally only competed in the European Rally Championship, took a solid second overall. Even more surprising was that he achieved this in a privately run car (TO55239R) from ART that had been converted from an earlier 16-valve integrale into the new wide-tracked specification.

Argentina Rally 1992

Nobody was particularly keen to go to the next round in Argentina, due to the distance and the cost, but the rules stated that at least one non-European event had to be started by all World Rally Championship contenders, virtually forcing Martini to send Didier Auriol.

It was a strange event with organizational and spectator problems. At one point a crowd attacked the Martini integrale, breaking its windscreen and pushing a burning log through the roof ventilator. This prompted Didier to let out the clutch and make off for two kilometres until they felt safe. The organizers generously allowed replacement of the screen in parc ferme.

Musical chairs were again played with the various integrales entered. Auriol's was new in that it had been planned to run the car on the Acropolis for Bugalski but it had been withdrawn before that event. The car that Auriol had used in Greece was brought for, and used by, Jorge Recalde, whilst a third, training car was reprepared after practising for Trelles to use on the event. Fiorio had to make do with his own ex-Acropolis car prepared by Astra.

Yet another win for Auriol then, as Martini continued to stamp its authority on the 1992 series. Would Toyota come good during the second half of the season? When was the new Escort Cosworth from Ford going to enter the arena?

It already had, as a road car and *Autocar* had pitched it against Turin's inspired son. In some areas the newcomer beat the integrale but a peaky on–off engine power delivery and less communicative chassis handed the win to the Lancia, which was described as 'a consummate all-rounder'.

Not surprising then that after winning the next world championship counter in Finland, Auriol said, 'If I had been driving last year's car at these speeds, I would have been going end-over-end down the road all the time'.

1000 Lakes Rally 1992

The 1000 Lakes is very fast and has considerable jumps. The ease with which the new integrale could take these was the deciding factor in the results. The real surprise was that Frenchman Auriol was consistently quicker than team-mate and local, Kankunnen.

The result wrapped up yet another World Rally Championship for Lancia, a record-breaking sixth in a row. It was enough to cause Giorgio Pianta to send a message from Turin: 'Yet another success for the Delta integrale, a car that has stopped time…'.

Uncertain Future

Giorgio's foresight in preparing so many cars well in advance of the season had paid off handsomely. In Finland, three more new cars had been provided to make sure of the result but in Turin conflicting stories were emerging of the future. In August, Cantarella intimated that the superb results being achieved by the team should not be wasted and that the development of the integrale should continue into 1993. Later, the opposite emerged.

Claudio Bortoletto was becoming extremely impatient with the delays to the making of a decision, as he had to start making plans for 1993 very quickly, if the team was to maintain its winning record. It was unlikely that Auriol would stay anyway and Kankunnen was suggesting that the delay would probably mean that he would leave also. Was it possible that the

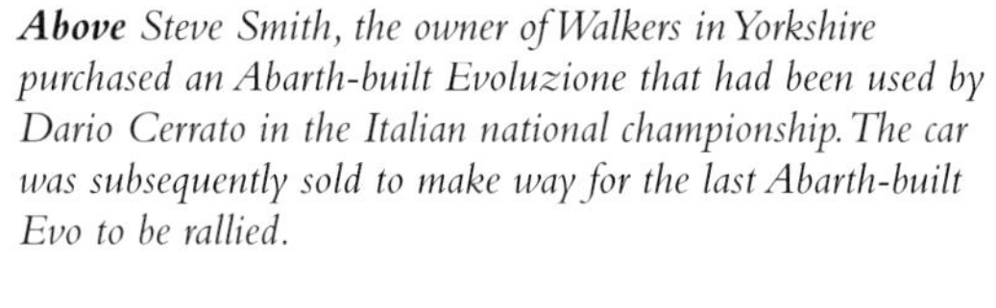

__Above__ Steve Smith, the owner of Walkers in Yorkshire purchased an Abarth-built Evoluzione that had been used by Dario Cerrato in the Italian national championship. The car was subsequently sold to make way for the last Abarth-built Evo to be rallied.

__Left__ Steve was privileged to compete on British national events in a cockpit most could only dream of!

__Bottom left__ Steve in action on the Sunseeker Stages rally, part of the British national rally championship.

__Below__ Traditional-style Turinese numberplate as applied to the front bumper of Steve's Evo.

most successful rally car and team ever, would finish its career due to indecision?

The team itself was working towards the possibility of continuing into 1993 and tested near San Remo with the cars weighing-in at 1,200kg (2,646lb), as would be required by the new rules for the next season. The extra 50kg (110lb) was found to make little difference to stage times. On tarmac the car was only 0.2s slower per kilometre.

Rally Australia 1992

Meanwhile, in Australia, Claudio Bortoletto, boss of Jolly Club Martini Lancia, openly criticized the men at the top back in Turin for their inability to come to any decision over 1993.

The cars used on the Rally Australia had already seen service on the 1000 Lakes rally. Bortoletto stated he had 'forty mechanics waiting to hear whether the team was to continue into 1993 or not'. They were good men, he said, who had completely rebuilt the cars in four days from arrival from Finland to departure for Australia.

New cars or used cars, the result was the same. Didier Auriol won for the sixth time in 1992. Interestingly, the cars' scrutineering weights were both over 1,200kg (2,646lb), as required for the new rules, but, as the team had found in their earlier tests, this seemed to make no difference whatsoever, giving Bortoletto confidence for the future.

Finally, at the beginning of October, Fiat officially announced that everything they had relevant to the rallying integrales would be handed over to the Jolly Club. On the face of it this was a generous gesture, but it meant that Bortoletto was now responsible for obtaining the necessary budget to run everything and if they failed, it would be their fault. Lancia had washed their hands of the integrale in motor sport when it was at the height of its powers; if success crumbled, they could now put up their hands and say that it was nothing to do with them.

Another Evoluzione was built up for David Scialom and he used it to good effect on British club rallies.

David Scialom in action on Salisbury Plain in 1996.

San Remo Rally 1992

There were still three rounds of the 1992 World Rally Championship to go though and at the annual pre-San Remo Rally press conference, the Jolly Club announced that Kankunnen and Aghini were their preferred drivers for 1993. Auriol confirmed his departure at the end of the year, to Toyota.

An omen? Possibly he spoke too soon, as the Italian gods decreed that Didier's run of wins would now cease. During the rally some wheel nuts sheared and, with only three wheels, the car went off the road. It was the end of the rally for the championship leader. There was some conspiracy theory muttering from the press but Jolly Club mechanics soon put them right.

Andrea Aghini, future hope for the team, then took the lead and, displaying serious speed, held it to the end, beating Kankunnen by 40s. Six of the cars in the top eight finishers were integrales. It was beginning to look as if nothing would ever happen to stop the integrale. No one could have believed that its fall from grace was so imminent.

Martini had entered four cars for San Remo, with all of them back to their normal 1992 weights of approximately 1,165kg (2,569lb), as opposed to the over 1,200kg (2,646lb) in Australia. Three were for Auriol, Kankunnen and Aghini but a fourth was entered for Giorgio Faletti. Who? He was an Italian comedian and it was a publicity stunt to boost rallying on television. He brought the car to the finish though, in fifteenth place, joking that he was showing 'how slowly' the integrale could be driven.

Catalunya Rally 1992

Six integrales again finished in the top eight at the Catalunya rally but the big news was that the winner was Sainz in his Toyota and not an integrale at all. Auriol had summoned up evil spirits again and had problems, crashing out of the top positions leaving the World Rally Drivers' Championship on a knife-edge.

Perhaps the most sensational news however, was that Sainz might be moving to Lancia for 1993. Due to sponsorship and contractual difficulties he was certainly unlikely to stay with Toyota.

Martini was running three cars in Spain and by now the new ones seemed to have run out. Auriol was in his Australia winner, Kankunnen had his second-placed San Remo car and Aghini was reunited with his San Remo winner.

RAC Rally 1992

Australia was to prove the last Lancia win Auriol took during 1992. The RAC rally was the drivers' title showdown and Martini brought three cars again that had all been previously seen; Kankunnen had his Australian machine, Auriol was in the car that had lost a wheel at San Remo and Aghini was trying Auriol's Argentina winning car.

How long ago those golden days of summer must have seemed to the team as they worked

Perhaps the ultimate contemporary driving pleasure available today. An Evoluzione integrale and an open country road.

in typically cold, miserable, RAC weather to no avail. Auriol retired and with the retirement went all chance of the drivers' championship that seemed his for the taking earlier in the year. Still active in the World Rally Championship and speaking recently, he still recalls the year with good feelings and considers it was probably his best.

The question now was, with Auriol leaving Jolly Club in 1993, would Bortoletto and his men have the ability and resources to further develop the integrale in order to counteract Toyota's rising Celica and attract a top driver. At the end of the RAC they did not even have a number one. It seemed inconceivable that the car, which had swept all before it in world rallying, was about to bow out with a whimper.

By 1995, production of the Delta's replacement – the 'New' Delta – was well under way. Here one is being compared to the legendary Evo.

right *Whilst the new car was never going to be as good as its predecessor being only front-wheel drive, the top of the range HPE could keep up well on straighter roads*

Early in December the musical chairs were resolved as Sainz' personal Repsol sponsorship precluded him driving a Castrol sponsored Toyota. He therefore chose Jolly Club Lancia for 1993 and Kankunnen left to replace him at Toyota.

End of the Martini Integrales

It was all change as, at the same time, Martini announced that their support of the team was over. The legendary Martini integrales would never be seen again.

P887 XOU

AG·227 TD

Claudio Bortoletto, however, remained upbeat, as Abarth had agreed to prepare next year's cars to the 1993 specification before they were to close their doors finally and leave Jolly Club to run their own team. Bortoletto was also happy as Repsol was to provide the total budget for Sainz' programme and the Commission Sportive Automobili Italia was to pay for Aghini's seat.

All was revealed to the press when Sainz went testing with the Jolly Club for the first time around the middle of December. It was strange to see an integrale in the colours of the Spanish national oil company. The regulations for 1993 required smaller tyres but Carlos seemed happy with the car. Others extremely happy with their integrales during 1992 were Atakan, Deila, 'Jigger' and Puras, who had each won their national rally championships.

In retrospect, maybe it should all have ended there. The integrale had delivered record results and boosted Lancia's image by a huge margin, helping to make the Delta Lancia's best-ever seller. The brand-new restyled model, front-drive only, had now made its debut, so perhaps a further season in 1993 was extending the sell-by date a little too far.

For whatever reason, Paulo Cantarella certainly thought so. Giorgio Pianta:

> I had a meeting with Mr. Cantarella towards the end of the season and he asked me how much equipment existed in connection with the Martini rallying integrales. I told him and he said give it all, free of charge, to the Jolly Club. I do not want to see any more rally cars in our colours. After all the years of work and success you can imagine how I felt.

Official Factory Works Built Lancia Delta HF Integrales Used in World Championship Rounds During 1992 Season (Abarth SE 050)

TO 45701S
TO 45702S
TO 45703S
TO 53226S
TO 53227S
TO 53228S
TO 53229S
TO 53230S
TO 53231S
TO 76570S
TO 76571S
TO 76572S
TO 76573S
TO 13717T
TO 13718T
TO 13719T
TO 13720T
TO 13721T

Whatever was being said at the top, Lancia won the 1992 World Rally Championship for Manufacturers and in addition won the National Rally Championships of: Greece, Hungary, Italy, Spain (both gravel and tarmac) and Turkey.

7 Final Act – The King is Dead! Long Live the King!

So at the end of 1991, Fiat had tried to wash its hands of the integrale in motor sport. Now came the divorce.

Giorgio Pianta:

> 1993 was a terrible year. There had been no forward tyre testing and Jolly Club's budget just wasn't big enough, so there was no serious car testing. Mr Cantarella said to me before the season started that if I was seen at all at any rally during the year, I would be immediately sacked from the Fiat group. It would have been very difficult anyway to run the Deltonas as I had only 200 people in Fiat Auto Corse and Alfa Corse, of which 100 were full-time on the big Alfa Romeo expansion into the Deutsche Tourenwagen Meisterschaft and the others had to maintain new Alfa Touring Cars all over Europe. On two or three weekends we had 20-30 cars out racing.

The closure of the Fiat Group competitions department in Corso Marche, Turin, was the decree nisi. Activities moved to a factory at Chivasso under the name of Fiat Auto Corse; this building has since become the home of N Technology. Ironically, standing in the main reception area there is none other than the very last Abarth-built Martini Deltona, which has never turned a wheel in anger. Whilst the agreement had been that Abarth would build the new cars for Bortoletto to the 1993 specifications, these would be the last actions they would take to help the Jolly Club.

Fiat was divesting itself of the production problems associated with the integrale as well. Well-established Turinese car producers and coach-builder Maggiora had bought part of the old Lancia plant at Chivasso and contracted with Fiat to build the New HF integrales there on their behalf. This suited both parties well, as Fiat wanted Maggiora to do the work, as the latter now had more suitable plant and, as Alessandro Sopetti, who was then a director of Maggiora, said, 'The focus could be only on the integrale and we all worked hard to improve the quality of the cars. The workers became very proud of making them'.

These new Maggiora-built integrales were painted by Bertone and there is a stamp under the front bumper to prove it. After initial assembly at Chivasso, the shells were trucked to the Bertone factory in Turin before returning for final completion.

Some testing of the competition cars had continued over the winter, before the final break with Abarth, so that Sainz could get used to how his new mount behaved. It did not help when a tyre came off a rim and the Spaniard's car rolled, but he was uninjured. The public could perhaps see that 1993 was not going to be easy for the new team, as most bets were being placed on Auriol in a Toyota to win the first rally of the year, as always the traditional Monte Carlo.

Monte Carlo Rally 1993

Jolly Club entered two cars for Sainz and Aghini, the former in Repsol livery, the latter in

Totip cigarette colours. Nothing was proved as both cars suffered serious accidents. Aghini's was enough to cause retirement, whilst Carlos managed to continue, albeit dropping to seventy-sixth overall at one point. There were flashes of speed, with a few fastest stage times, but in general it was a disappointing and unsatisfactory start to the new season.

Swedish Rally 1993

A name to note for the future made a successful return to the driving seat of a Lancia, when later world champion Tommi Makinen took part in the Swedish rally in an integrale run by the Astra team. This was TO 53226S, which had been Kankunnen's winning car on the

Maggiora

The company was established in Turin in 1925 by Cav. Arturo Maggiora and was soon engaged in sub-contract work for many of the fast-developing automotive businesses in that city. By 1936 they were building their own complete bodies and, in particular, Viotti's Fiat 1500 based Cabriolets.

In 1949, Vincenzo, Arturo's son, joined the company after an apprenticeship with Fiat and the connection with Viotti continued with a new Cabriolet. Production of Lancia-based light commercial vehicles started and a Giardiniera version of Fiat's new 1100/103 was introduced in 1953. Many bodies were built for other companies, such as 2000 Touring spiders for Alfa Romeo, Maserati 5000 GT Touring coupé, Maserati Mistral in 1967 and later the Bitter CD. They also produce one-offs for prototype work and built a Dedra integrale-based Punto purely for show. The quality of their work has always been appreciated by Fiat and so in the last few years they have built the Lancia Kappa coupés in addition to the New HF integrales.

Main emphasis recently has been on the Fiat Barchetta, which is produced at their Chivasso factory, which is approximately 20km north-east of Turin. They also run another plant at Moncalieri on the southern outskirts of that city where they produce commercial vehicles based on smaller Fiats.

Maggiora, builder of the Evo integrales, also made one-offs. This little machine is the Grama 2 and consists of a Punto body stretched over a Dedra four-wheel drive floor-pan. They nicknamed it the Puntegrale.

TO 53226S at the Chivasso Delta Day in 1994. This car was a Martini works car during 1992 before being taken over by Astra. In 1993 it was used by Tommi Makinen to gain some good World Championship results and also by Pier Cesar Baroni to help him win the European rally championship the same year.

previous year's Portugal Rally. He finished fourth. His first World Championship rally in a Lancia had been the 1987 1000 Lakes in Finland, when he crashed and failed to finish in a Delta HF4WD.

Portugal Rally 1993

Matters did not improve for Jolly Club in Portugal when Carlos rolled for the third time in the year – this time it was in a brand-new car fitted with differently shaped rear wheels, so that bigger rear brakes could be fitted. Aghini persevered and was rewarded with third overall at the end. This turned out to be best of the rest, as Ford's new Escort Cosworths had dominated the event. Although Carlos' car was new, Aghini's had been Kankunnen's 1992 San Remo machine.

Tour de Corse 1993

Significantly, Aghini was the only man to match the Cosworths on the longest stage of the Tour de Corse. But it was with Pirelli tyres instead of Sainz' Michelins. Was it just a matter of tyres that was causing the integrales to rapidly look more and more like yesterday's cars? Bortoletto is on record as saying, 'Judge the reason for yourselves', referring to the fact that the Pirelli shod car was decisively quicker than that with Michelins.

New cars had again been built and Sainz was able to finish again, albeit down in fourth place nearly four minutes behind the leaders. 'I am doing my utmost best,' said Sainz, 'I cannot go any faster.'

Acropolis Rally 1993

The rough tracks of the Acropolis proved little as Aghini stuck with Pirelli and Sainz remained on Michelins, but the world champion seemed to be back on form at last and finished an encouraging second. Interestingly Alfa Corse's 155 touring cars were using engines that were substantially similar to the integrale unit and developments on these engines had enabled some help to filter down to the Jolly Club rally cars. This was not a case of the decision to withdraw Abarth support being reversed, as Alfa Corse was an entirely separate and circuit-racing orientated set-up within Fiat. After the event, looking down the results list it seemed like the old days, as seven integrales finished in the top ten cars. Tommi Makinen in another of the Astra cars again showed well and was hoping for a top three finish before two punctures forced him down to sixth.

Sainz was using his Monte Carlo car rebuilt, whilst Aghini's was another Sainz rebuild from Portugal. Jolly Club had also sent a second Repsol car for Gustavo Trelles. They desperately needed more results in this vein but the signals were confusing. To confuse matters further, the team was also running a car in the Italian national championship with, ironically, Martini sponsorship and, driven by Cerrato, it was proving to be virtually as quick as the Escort Cosworths.

The last time an integrale was to appear at the London Motor Show on the official Lancia stand was in 1994. The official title of the Evo 2 was unchanged from the Evo.

Argentina Rally 1993

The long journey down to Argentina produced heartbreak in the form of first-stage engine failure for Carlos in his Abarth built car, Aghini did not go and so Jolly Club ran Trelles instead.

The Lancia Delta HF Integrale Evoluzione 2 – Introduction and Features

By this time, in the middle of the year, better news for consumers was forthcoming from Italy in the shape of another new road version of the integrale. Maggiora had developed the ultimate and last road-going integrale, which has become known as the Evo 2. The titles of these post-16v cars have always been a matter of discussion and sometimes controversy. The

Note the Montecarlo badge, which was fitted to all official Lancia UK imported and sold Evoluzione 2 integrales.

first wide-tracked big-winged car, introduced in October 1991, was officially called the Lancia Delta HF integrale. At Abarth and at Maggiora it was known as the Evoluzione or simply Evo. Thus when the new, updated road car arrived, it naturally took on the unofficial title of Evo 2. All these cars were also known colloquially as Deltonas, or big Deltas and it is important to note that this latest and last model had no effect on rally car specifications and was therefore the only new model integrale to be introduced for road-car purposes only. There is therefore, in Italy, even unofficially, no such car as an Evo 3.

Once the Evoluzione 2 was introduced, first UK deliveries started arriving in August. Although basic engine structure stayed the same and there were no chassis changes, the most important news was that the car was now environmentally friendly as a three-way catalytic converter was a standard item and power was officially up to 215bhp with improved torque. Because of the catalyser, Marelli had come up with a new version of their IAW-integrated engine control system called the P8, which included other tweaks such as remapped ignition, an anti-evaporation system optimized for the turbo engine and a new Garrett turbocharger, water-cooled with boost controlled by feedback from the ECU to improve mid-range torque delivery, providing better response to throttle inputs. The camshaft cover was painted red, a body colour roof-moulding was added and different Solarcontrol glass was fitted, but there were now only three standard colours available: red, Lancia blue and white, the latter being the least popular.

Wheels were of the same design as the Evo 1 but were up 1in in diameter to 16in. These now carried 205/45 ZR 16 tyres. No sunroof was now available as all cars were fitted with air-conditioning as standard and all cars had high-backed front seats in Alcantara unless otherwise specified and a new Momo Corse steering wheel. Effectively Maggiora standardized on the Evo 2 those items that had been optional extras on Evo 1.

Back on the World Rally Scene

An agreement had been reached with Lamborghini for technical assistance, although it was too late to help the team in South America. Engineer Franco Antoniazzi from Sant'Agata was to assist Bortoletto's hard-pressed team. Was it going to help luck to swing in their favour? Perhaps New Zealand's rally would provide some answers, although it was unlikely as only a minor rerouting of cold-air flow to the cars' turbo was tried at first.

Things turned out to be so bad that Carlos was happy just to finish fourth in his Acropolis car, so nothing was proved. Aghini had not gone and so, once again, Trelles was run in the second car.

The team was by now just running out of time. They declined to enter the 1000 Lakes where, running down the entry list, the first integrale could be found in Makinen's hands due to start at number 13. Ignoring superstition,

LANCIA DELTA HF integrale

Technical specification

* unladen

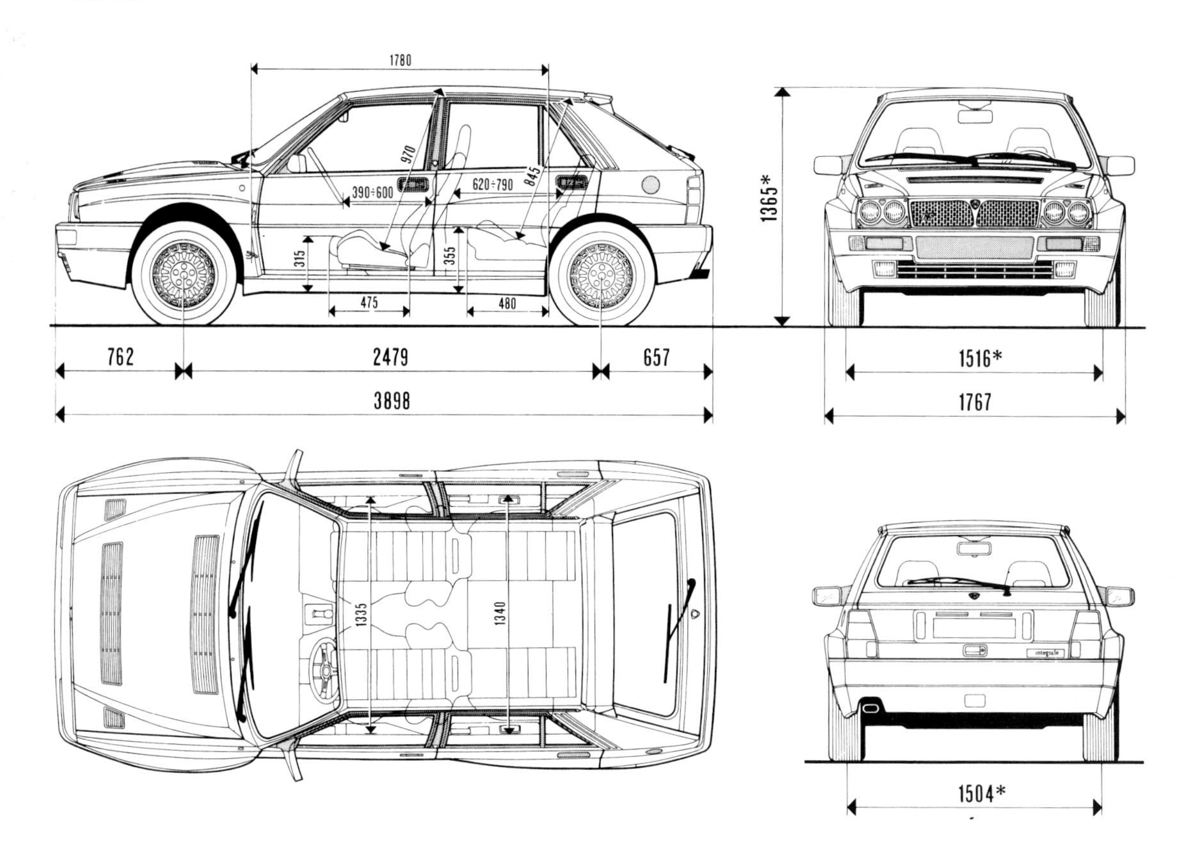

Boot capacity: 200 dm^3; with rear seat folded: 940 dm^3

ENGINE

Main features

No. of cylinders	4, in line
Cycle-stroke	Otto-4
Bore x stroke	84 × 90 mm
Displacement	1995 cc
Compression ratio	8:1
Max power output DIN	215 bhp (155 kW-EEC)
at	5750 rpm
Peak torque DIN	32 mkg (308 Nm-EEC)
at	2500 rpm
Fuel required	unleaded petrol (95 RON)

Structure

Position	front transverse
Cylinder block	cast iron, with counter-rotating shafts
Cylinder spacing	91 mm
Main bearings	5
Cylinder head	light alloy

Timing gear

Position/No. of valves	V (65°)/4 per cylinder
Timing	DOHC
Timing control	toothed belt
Valve gear timing	with tappet play of 0.8 mm
Intake — opens	8° BTDC
Intake — closes	35° ABDC
Exhaust — opens	30° BBDC
Exhaust — closes	0° ATDC
No. of counter-rotating shafts	2 in cylinder block

Ignition

Type	electronic mapped advance, knock sensor, integrated with injection
Fire order	1-3-4-2
Spark plugs	Bosch WR6DTC

Fuel feed	turbocharged with turbocompressor and air/air heat exchanger on intake + overboost (and automatic cut-in with engine at full revs)
Petrol pump	electric
Injection: type	IAW electronic MPI combined with ignition
Air filter	dry-type with paper cartridge
Turbocharger: type	Garrett T3, water cooled
Max. boost pressure	1 bar

Lubrication

Type	forced-feed, geared pump, with oil radiator
Filter	cartridge

Cooling

Type	liquid, with pressurised circuit, radiator pump and supplementary expansion tank
Control	by thermostat
Fan	electric, controlled by a thermostatic switch on the radiator

Emission control	three-way catalytic converter, lambda sensor

TRANSMISSION

Drive: type	permanent four-wheel with central differential, epicyclic torque splitter and Ferguson viscous joint; Torsen rear differential with 5:1 torque ratio between wheels
Clutch	dry, single plate, with hydraulic control
Friction lining dimensions (OD x ID)	230 × 155 mm

Gear ratios

1st	3.500:1
2nd	2.176:1
3rd	1.523:1
4th	1.156:1
5th	0.916:1
Reverse	3.545:1
Final ratio (spur gear pair)	3.111:1 (18/56)
Front and rear bevel gear pair	2.263:1 (19/43)
Torque split	front: 47% rear: 53%

CHASSIS

Body	stress-bearing
Braking system	discs front and rear with double cylinder front calipers and floating calipers at rear. Pedal control, with vacuum servo, two independent diagonally split hydraulic circuits, and load proportioning valve on rear wheels. Standard ABS.
Front discs	self-ventilating
- diameter	281 mm
- total lining area	54 × 4 = 216 sq. cm.
Rear discs	
- diameter	251 mm
- total lining area	35 × 4 = 140 sq. cm.
Parking brake	acting on rear brake discs
Front suspension	independent MacPherson struts with transverse lower wishbones and anti-roll bar
Dampers	dual action hydraulic, gas telescopic
Flexibility at the wheel	0.50 mm/kg
Wheel wobble – upper	60 mm
Wheel wobble – lower	103 mm
Front wheel geometry unladen	
– camber	– 1° ± 30'
– caster	4°10' ± 30'
– toe-in	– 1 ± 1 mm
Rear suspension	MacPherson independent type with trailing arms, longitudinal reaction bars and anti-roll bar
Dampers	dual action hydraulic, gas telescopic
Flexibility at the wheel	0.51 mm/kg
Wheel wobble – upper	60 mm
Wheel wobble – lower	125 mm
Rear wheel geometry unladen	
– camber	– 1°30' ± 30'
– caster	2°30' ± 30'
– toe-in	3 – 5 mm
Steering	rack and pinion, with power steering
Turning circle	10.4 m
Steering wheel turns lock to lock	2.8
Wheels	
Rims	7 1/2 J × 16", light alloy
Tyres	205/45 ZR 16
Inflation pressure	
– front	2.2 bar (2.5 bar*)
– rear	2.2 bar (2.5 bar*)

(*) continuous high speed, fully laden

Spare wheel	
Rim	3 1/2 B × 16" H2-37, light alloy
Tyre	T115/70 R 16
Inflation pressure	4.2 bar (front and rear)
Max. speed permitted	80 km/h
Electrical equipment	
Voltage	12 V
Alternator (with incorporated electronic voltage regulator)	65 A
Starter motor	1.1 kW
Battery: capacity	110Ah

WEIGHTS

Kerb weight (DIN) (*)		1340 kg
Distribution	front	63.3%
	rear	36.7%
Max. permitted weight	front	1020 kg
	rear	1020 kg
	total	1790 kg
Max. payload		450 kg
Max. towing weight		1200 kg
No. of seats		5

(*) Kerb weight (inclusive of fuel, water, spare wheel and accessories)

PERFORMANCE

Max. speed in 5th		220 km/h
Max. gradient (negotiable fully laden)		58%
Speed with engine at 1000 rpm	in 4th	30 km/h
	in 5th	37.9 km/h
Power to weight ratio	kg/bhp-DIN	6.2
	kg/kW-EEC	8.6
Accelerations (2 adults + 20 kg) (secs)		
0 to 100 km/h		5.7
0 to 1000 m		26.1
Pick-up from 40 km/h in 4th (2 adults + 20 kg) (secs)		
1000 m		30.5
Conventional fuel consumption (l/100 km)		
at 90 km/h		8.2
at 120 km/h		10.6
urban cycle		13
ECE average		10.6

CAPACITIES

	dm³ (l)	kg
Fuel tank	57	–
including a reserve of:	6 – 9	–
Radiator, expansion tank and heating system, fluid	6.2	–
Engine sump and filter, oil	4.9	4.4
Total engine sump, filter and circuit, oil	5.8	5.2
Gearbox and differential oil	3.8	3.4
Rear differential	1.1	1
Power steering	0.75	–
Hydraulic brake tank, liquid	0.52	–
Screenwasher and rear window washer bottle	2	–

ENGINE CURVES (EEC)

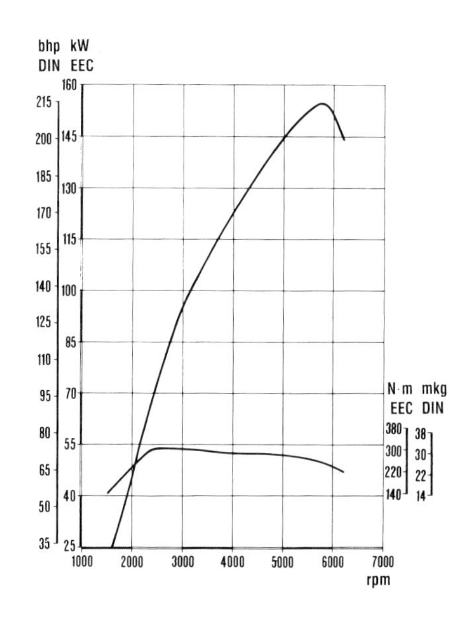

The Italian press could not wait to get to grips with the last of the line Evo 2.

The same Evo 2 shows off its 16 inch wheels.

Reflection of continued glory. Rain or shine, it does not matter to an integrale.

he finished fourth marking the youngster as a man to watch and maybe polishing away just a little of the integrale's tarnish.

The year was unfolding, quite literally, as if a carpet had been pulled out from under the team's feet. So many things were going wrong or not to plan, even when not actually taking part in events. During testing for the San Remo rally, their service van was stolen and then the police arrived and arrested Sainz as they thought the team had not been granted permission to drive a modified competition car on public roads for the test session. He was later released.

Amidst rumours that both their drivers were likely to leave at the end of the year, the Australia result was yet another disaster. Sainz hit a rock and tore a wheel off his ex-New Zealand car. It seemed there was hardly any point in continuing; the team was in despair.

The announcement that it would all end at the Catalunya rally in November came almost as a relief.

Evo 2 interiors featured high-backed seats as standard along with air-conditioning.

San Remo Rally 1993

Despite all this, Sainz was happy at the beginning of San Remo, but the smile soon faded. Aghini crashed his car, which had been converted from Kankunnen's 1991 Monte Carlo winner. Carlos was driving an historic car, his was the last integrale to be built by Abarth and rallied; it was registered TO 81832T. Far too late, work had been completed on development of the engines and both Sainz and Aghini were using Lamborghini-modified units. This involved new cylinder heads with different pistons and exhaust systems. As a link to past glories, Dario Cerrato ran his Italian national championship Martini liveried car, but it did not bring him any luck as the car was retired with electrical problems.

Second for Carlos and a fourth for Pianezzola flattered to deceive, as the Spaniard had been beaten convincingly by the Escort Cosworth of Franco Cunico which was also an Italian national series combination.

It only remained for the circus to travel to Spain for Catalunya.

Catalunya Rally 1993

On his home event, the press mobbed Sainz, not least because he was rumoured to be joining Subaru. Right to the end his luck in a Lancia continued to be bad. After being equal quickest on the opening stage, he suffered a puncture, which led to driveshaft trouble.

Do not do this at home. An Evo needs to be seriously provoked to get into this situation.

Aghini was not even entered. A second Jolly Club car was run for Gustavo Trelles, this being Sainz' from New Zealand. Carlos had his Argentine machine. At last – but too late – the Lamborghini tie-up had borne fruit and they produced engines that allegedly were worth an extra 5–10bhp over previous units. This had been achieved with new camshafts, inlet valve seats and air filters. For the first time also, Pirelli tyres were used by both cars – perhaps that was why Sainz was able to share a fastest time with the new hero, the Escort Cosworth? No one was happy at Lancia's decline. Juha Kankunnen made the point that 'It isn't F1 without Ferrari, it won't be World Championship rallying without Lancia'.

Bad luck stalked the integrale right to the end of the year when the last Abarth-built car, driven by Sainz on San Remo, was wrecked at the Bologna motor show sprint event in December when Cerrato hit a wall.

End of the Road

As a top-flight factory competition car the integrale had reached the end of the road, although many continued to be campaigned in private hands in national status rallies throughout Europe and the Middle East.

Nearly 14,000 Evos were sold by Lancia making it, just, the most popular integrale.

In motor sport all may seem to have been lost, but to the consumer, as late as mid-1994, the Evo 2 was still, in road trim, the all-wheel driven performance car against which all others were considered.

Autocar magazine stacked one up against the Escort Cosworth and new pretender, the Subaru Impreza. Their conclusion? 'Neither of them gets close to dethroning the integrale'. They went on to describe its steering as 'sublime', its handling 'brilliantly neutral', its 'grip prodigious', its 'gear change an indulgence' and its 'seats exquisite'. It 'gives more driving pleasure than any other rival'. Over the hill? They also went on to mention that it was still in production although a new-shape model was expected for 1995.

Back at the Sharp End

At the factory in Chivasso, as 1993 turned into 1994, Alessandro Sopetti described that working with the integrale was like dealing with 'a dead man walking'. The staff had to push all the time just to get simple things done. 'No-one inside Fiat was paying any more attention to it.' Later in 1994 as the last new cars and special editions were moving down the line:

Driving an Evo is a great experience. 'Simply the best' said Motor Sport.

Autocar *1992: 'The integrale remains the consummate all-rounder'.*

above *The crowd's favourite, Markku Alen, at Chivasso in 1994 about to give a demonstration of integrale driving.*

below *At the 1994 Chivasso Delta Day, Roberto Franco proves what* Car *magazine said the same year: 'The integrale is an all-time great'.*

above and opposite top *Markku Alen powerslides TO 51890N round the car-park at Maggiora's Chivasso factory in 1994. Note how the understeering slide turns slowly to oversteer and the back end sits down as weght is transferred for acceleration. The car was a works Martini 16v car that had been converted to Evolution specification.*

It became a real headache because there was an ever-decreasing amount of space and time available in the factory for the production line. This was because the up-coming Fiat Barchetta was about to come on-stream and the new project took priority over the old. All the suppliers knew that the integrale was stopping, so things became a real mess trying to produce the last cars and source the parts. Bumpers and fuel tanks were very difficult and there was much yelling down the telephone. In fact it was a relief to finish, although it was felt that given the resources, the integrale could have gone on until 1998. But Lancias ceased to be 'sporty cars' in the eyes of Fiat, so that was that. It had been a very interesting period.

End of an Era

At the end of 1994, the Chivasso factory of Maggiora, in conjunction with the Italian Delta integrale club, threw a party and organized an open day. It was almost a celebration of the end of an era.

Attending this event revealed the last cars being moved down the production line to make way for the new Barchetta. The integrale had had greatness thrust upon it and had achieved it with distinction as well. At a time when Fiorio and his men needed a quick solution to a big problem, Giugiaro's Lancia saviour had, by sheer coincidence, been there to fulfil exactly the role they wanted. But it was not just a matter of giving a few of Lancia's new cars to the rally drivers and letting them get on with it, it was due to the skills of men like Limone, Pianta, Marascotti and all the Abarth team members that the unassuming looking two-box Delta created for itself the position of icon and will forever carry that accolade throughout time, wherever there are people who appreciate the world's best-ever rally cars.

The 1993 international season was not quite the final chapter of the integrale in international rallying, as its homologation was not actually due to expire until the end of 2000. A few privately entered cars ran on into 1994, most notably on the Monte Carlo rally, but it

Just enjoying an Evoluzione in the best way possible – once again at Goodwood.

was UK enthusiast and specialist, Steve Smith, of Walker's garage in Yorkshire who decided to celebrate the last chance of integrale international eligibility by entering two ex-factory cars on the 2000 Network Q RAC Rally.

Partnered by John Richardson in one of the ex-Sainz Repsol 1993 cars, they finished in a strong position after a trouble-free run. They were backed up by a second entry for integrale stalwart Rodney Bennett, which had been Steve's previous car. This was his ex-Cerrato Italian series car illustrated in previous pages. Their arrival back in Cardiff at the finish really was the final curtain after 14 years of homologation and success.

To a huge number of integrale devotees though, it was the Evoluzione road cars that Maggiora built, which to them signified the word integrale and endowed it with iconoclastic connotations. The number of special editions that emanated from their Chivasso factory is evidence that these feelings were both grasped and encouraged. A highly significant part of the integrale story, we take a look at them next.

Going, but never gone.

Jolly Club Cars Used on World Championship Rounds 1993
TO 92332P
TO 76572S
TO 85302S
TO 13718T
TO 13721T
VA-D 14925
TO 28473T
TO 63022T
TO 73022T
TO 73023T
TO 81821T
TO 81832T

Lancias continued to score wins outside the World Championship. Pier Cesar Baroni used an integrale to take the 1993 European Rally Championship and they were also used to win the National rally Championships of: Croatia, Greece, Hungary, Italy, Portugal and Turkey.

8 Lancia Delta HF Integrale – the Special Editions, Colours, Concepts and Prototypes

It must first be noted that all UK Lancia-dealer ordered and delivered standard Evo 2s were badged 'Montecarlo' on the rear tailgate, the equivalent cars for the German market received 'Sedici' badges. These were not special editions just standard cars with additional badging.

It must also be noted that all cars built for the Swiss market were fitted with catalysers. In the case of 16-valve cars delivered new to that country, these only had an 8-valve engine and are recognizable by the 'kat' badge on the rear. All Evos for Switzerland were detuned to only 165bhp, so beware.

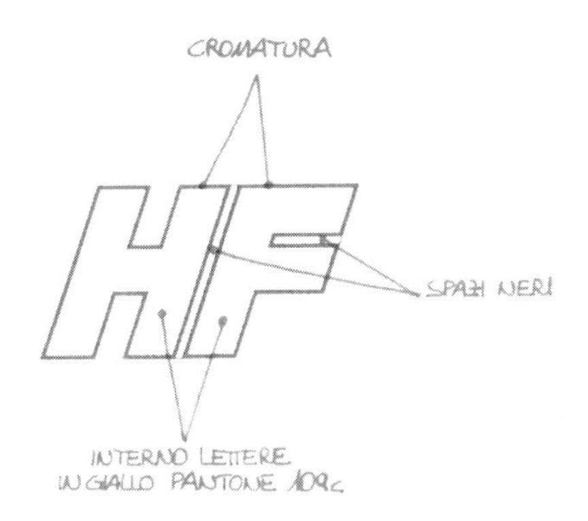

HF for HiFi. The badge displayed exclusivity and competition success. The integrale slotted easily into both categories.

Factory Special Editions

Verde York

These were based on Evo 1s and are occasionally referred to as 'World Rally Champions' due to the special badge on the tailgate. Painted dark green, they came with 15in wheels and beige leather interior with high-backed front seats. In 1994 an exclusive edition was produced at the special request of the French Lan-

cia dealers. Only 22 of these Evo 2-based cars, with 16in wheels and catalytic converter, were made at a price of 262,900 f. each. Total production of the Evo 1-based cars was 580, of which 470 were 16-valve cars and the remainder were 8-valve versions for Switzerland. Breakdown of the former was 360 for Italy, 30 to France, 40 to Belgium, 20 to Spain and 20 to Portugal.

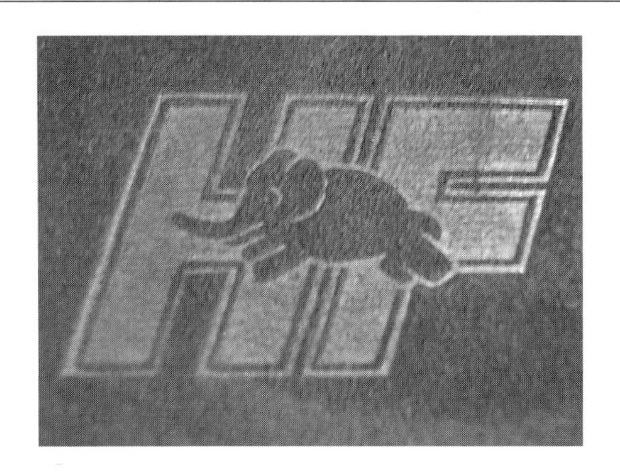

Gialla

These cars were based on Evo 2s and therefore they have 16in wheels, no sunroof and air-conditioning included. They do not carry any special identification badges on the rear or any in the cockpit. The seats are in charcoal Alcantara and those in the front are high-backed and have HF badges embossed on the headrest section. Altogether, 220 were built, of which 20 went to France and 50 to Germany. They were Fiat-marketing inspired after requests from dealers. From June to

October 1992 a further 295 were built, of which 50 went to Germany and these were finished in Gialla Ferrari with either black Alcantara or black leather as upholstery options. Alessandro Sopetti, a director at Maggiora during the whole Evolution integrale period, and intimately involved with the cars, said: 'Giallo was called a special edition but in fact it was always available should anyone want one'.

Dealers Collection

Amongst the last of the integrales to be built, in the latter part of 1994, these cars were painted metallic candy red, which was a General Motors Cadillac Allante optional colour. They were based on Evo 2s, so have 16in wheels and high-backed front seats. Interiors were trimmed in tan leather and on the front passenger-side floor, a footrest was provided. Instead of key/ignition starting, a pushbutton was provided on the dashboard. The instruments were set in a silver-finish dashboard. The same material and colour was

used on the steering-wheel boss around the horn-push. A plaque was applied to each of these cars; these were numbered and fitted below the gearlever. Altogether, 179 were built with deliveries going to Italy, Belgium, France, Holland, Portugal and Switzerland. The latter cars would have had to make do with the 8-valve catalysed engine.

Club Italia

Nowadays the most sought after of all the special versions, these were based on Evo 1s; therefore, they have 15in wheels. Only fifteen were built for members of Club Italia, and all are dark blue with enamelled badges carrying a caricature of a 1958 Pontoon Ferrari Tessa Rossa and the words 'Club Italia' affixed to both front wings. A numbered plaque is fitted below the gearlever. Although fifteen were built, the actual numbers extended to sixteen because Italians are extremely superstitious and there was no number thirteen. An additional plaque, carrying the name of the original owner can be found under the bonnet near to the offside hinge.

Original Owners

01 Patrizio Cantu
02 Renato Pozzetto
03 Dino Morazzoni
04 Guido Avandero
05 Luca Grandori
06 Giuseppe Veronesi
07 Davide Croff
08 Mario Vecchi
09 Luigi Macaluso
010 Edoardo Garrone
011 Umberto Cravetto
012 Renato Della Valle
014 Mauro Forghieri
015 Marco Piccinini
016 Clay Regazzoni

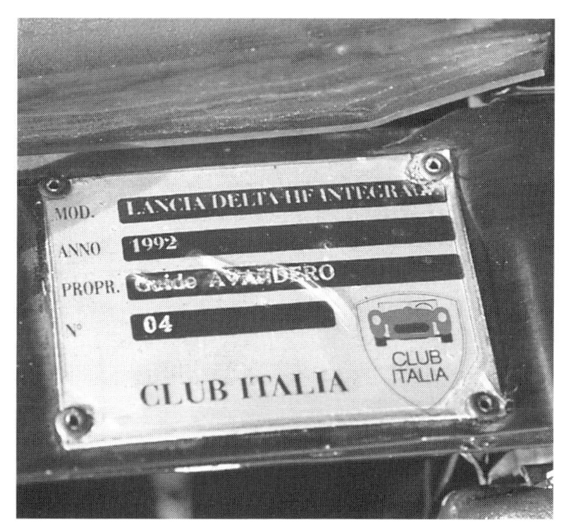

The latter car, number 016, was fitted from new with hand-operated disabled persons controls, as Clay Regazzoni suffers from severe leg injuries caused by a Formula 1 motor-racing accident.

The camshaft covers of Club Italia cars are painted in blue and yellow, mimicking Lancia's Fanalone Fulvias, and their interiors are trimmed in red leather with high-backed front seats. Pushbutton starting is employed. Some cars have 'Club Italia' in white lettering on the rear roof-spoiler and on the bonnet. The cars also normally have drilled pedals.

Every car was in fact slightly different in detail and they were sold new for L.45,850,000.

Blu Lagos

These were based on the Evo 2 and this was another edition that consisted basically of a short-run colour with the addition of a stripe running the length of the car at waist height. They were, again, Fiat-marketing inspired after requests from dealers. The interior was finished in beige

leather with high-backed front seats and, once again, there was a plaque to take the original owners name placed below the gear lever. Altogether, 205 were built during March and April 1994, with 200 sold in Italy and the remaining 5 going to Greece.

Martini 5

These were created to commemorate the fifth consecutive World Constructors' Rally Championship to be won by Martini Lancia at the end of the 1991 season. They are based on Evo 1s but they have black Alcantara interior trim

with red stitching and red seat-belts. The front seats are high-backed. Externally, the cars have 'Martini stripes' running the length of the sides of the car and across the bottom of the tailgate. There is a distinctive 'World Rally Champion' badge at the rear containing the number '5'. The rear roof-spoiler is painted black, as are the grilles on the bonnet. All cars have standard 15in wheels; those fitted to our pictured car are after market. Altogether, 400 were built.

Bianca Perlata
Based on the Evo 2, these were specially painted metallic pearl white, another General Motors Cadillac Allante optional colour, with a thin grey coachline extending down the length of the car at waist height. The Fiat-marketing department were once again responsible after requests from dealers. High-backed front seats and 16in wheels were fitted. The interior was trimmed in blue leather and this extended to the steering wheel. A plaque with the original owner's name was fixed below the gear lever. Altogether, 370 were built.

Martini 6
In a similar way to the '5', Martini Lancia's sixth and final World Constructors' Championship was celebrated, after the end of the 1992 season, by the Martini 6. More decorative than its predecessor, the Martini stripes ran down each side of the car and around the middle of the tailgate. Note that, unlike the '5', the stripes point downwards over each wheel arch. Many people believe these cars to be based on Evo 2s, but the Lancia parts-list show that their exhaust systems are non-catalyser, which technically means they are Evo 1s, although they would have been constructed right at the end

of that run in December 1992, just before the 2s came on-stream.

The legend 'World Rally Champion' is reproduced on both of the lower sides of the car and across the top of the front bumper. A large Lancia logo is on the roof and the rear roof spoiler has 'Martini Racing' applied to it. HF decals are on each rear side-post and a 'World Rally champion' badge containing the appropriate '6' is on the bottom right of the tailgate.

Inside, a carbon-fibre surround fits around the gear lever, which has a numbered plaque below it. The seats are finished in light-blue cloth, the fronts being high-backed. The gear change benefits from Teflon bushes in the linkage, which gives gear-changing a different feel. The wheels are painted white. Altogether, 310 were built with Italy taking 300. The remaining 10 went to various other European outlets.

Lancia Club

The shortest run of all the special editions and sold to members of the factory supported Lancia Club. Alessandro Sopetti said that because the integrale production line at Chivasso post-1992 was relatively small, Maggiora were able to be extremely flexible, which is how such short runs as these were financially viable. 'It was very nice to do these cars although it took lots of meetings to finalise them which became very complicated.'

Only eight were made divided equally between Blu Lancia and Rosso.

Hi Fi

These, as the name suggests, were made for, and sold exclusively to, members of Lancia's Hi-Fi club that exists for long-term Lancia owners who have purchased a minimum of seven new Lancias consecutively. Altogether, twenty-five were built, for L.55,000,000 each, of which eighteen were Blu Lancia and seven Rosso.

FONDO DI ARGENTO
TRATTO IN BLU LANCIA

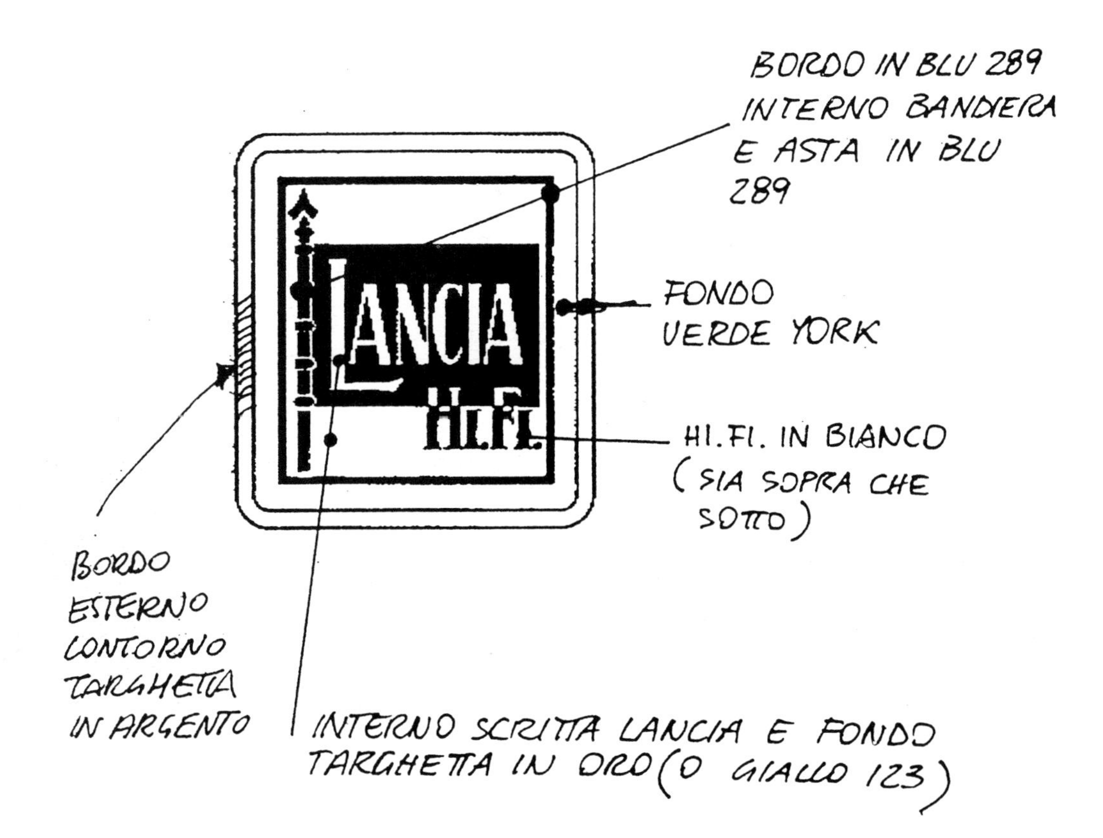

Final Edition

As the name suggests, these were amongst the last integrales to be built. They were intended as being purely for the Japanese market and, therefore, it is unlikely that one will come up for sale in Europe. Specifically requested by Garage Italya, the then importers in Meguro-Ku, Tokyo, there have been false alarms of cars being available outside Japan, but the cars involved have been 'look alikes'.

Alessandro Sopetti:

> The Japanese came to Chivasso and explained what they wanted, then Maggiora finalized what would be on the cars. These cars were the only special editions to have work carried out on them by the factory that would affect their dynamics, as their suspension was lowered by one inch by utilizing specially made Eibach springs. Amongst many different items, we put in footrests for the front-seat passengers. The cars were all painted in a slightly different shade of red to any other integrale. In fact the colour came from the Fiat Ducato van range.

above *This is the last Final Edition made. It is retained at Chivasso and will probably never leave.*

below *This is an example of a German created 'special'.*

A number of right-hand drive Evoluziones were converted in the UK with John Whalley doing most of the work.

They all had a triple yellow/blue/yellow stripe, in the style of 1960s and 1970s works rally cars, running down the length of the car. Pushbutton starting was included and the front grille was of black mesh. They had a unique rear badge stating 'HF integrale', which incorporated the works' style stripe and the seats were covered in half Alcantara and half fabric. In the boot, a rear strut-brace was fitted and 'Kevlar' surrounded the horn-button and the base of the gear lever. The instruments were set in a silver surround and the pedals were drilled. The bonnet louvres were painted black and the wheels were part-painted in grey. Altogether, 250 were built. See the colour centre section for the main pictures of these cars.

In Japan, a very few, very short-run specials were created including the 'Quick Trading Corsa 9', which were all Gialla and incorporated front and rear strut-braces, special dashboard and mirrors, and a quick-shift gear change with shortened lever. The 'Astra integrale' had aftermarket wheels, uprated brakes and suspension, and high-performance exhaust system and the 'Hot integrale' went one step further with engine modifications in addition to the special seats, dashboard and wheels.

In the UK RHD cars were converted by John Whalley and Mike Spence. This is one of their cars' interiors.

The owner of Maggiora's name graces the badge inside the viola car.

One-Off Colours and Specials

Viola

The most important of the unique integrales created at Chivasso, the Viola car carries Maggiora badges and was an in-house project. The title refers to the one-off colour the car was painted, which was a metallic violet/purple.

Developed with the intention of persuading Fiat to put it into production, the engine utilized enhanced electronics to produce 250bhp, whilst the transmission incorporated a viscodrive front differential system developed in Germany. Seventeen-inch Speedline wheels were fitted in the same Monte Carlo pattern as the standard cars' 16in wheels and special interior enhancements included Alcantara in a unique colour. A female member of the PPG paint company suggested the distinctive body colour –Viola.

Alessandro Sopetti said that he '...drove it many times, it was nicer than a standard car and in the wet it was beautiful – a lot of fun! We showed it to Fiat but they said the wheels were too expensive, the transmission hadn't had enough development and wouldn't take the power and there hadn't been enough testing. They simply weren't interested.'

The car is still retained at the factory and a recent run in it with production manager Roberto Franco proved that it was a very serious proposition, being easily controllable – even in very extreme situations. It remains a fascinating might-have-been.

Bianca Perlata and Rosa
Maggiora always made a special effort for the Turin Show and these two colours were produced especially for these shows. The white went on to become a short production run with detail differences (see previous pages), whilst the Rosa Pink remained a one-off. Both of these cars have been retained by the factory.

Other exclusive examples of special colours were: a black Evolution that was finished specially for the Greek

Lancia importer's daughter; another was painted bronze and featured seats in Alcantara Ghiaccio for a test along with the show Bianca Perlata and a car in Blu Lagos. The latter went to the Prince of Denmark and also became the basis of a short production run.

Cabriolet

Just one very special cabriolet-bodied car was built for the personal use of the Agnelli's. Recently restored and back in use with the family, the car was built as a seriously developed project and featured two-door bodywork. It was constructed at Fiat's Stabilimento Pilotta in Orbessano, Turin. This building housed the company's pre-production facility. After the prototype stage had been completed, cars and their production methods were developed here.

The cabriolet was fashioned out of a standard Evolution integrale by a team under the supervision of Ing. Rodolfo Gaffino for whom I am indebted for the pictures, never seen in public previously. It incorporated a special Valeo clutch and the bootlid was a Prisma item. Ing. Gaffino thinks the roof was from a Saab or Maserati. Paintwork was metallic silver grey.

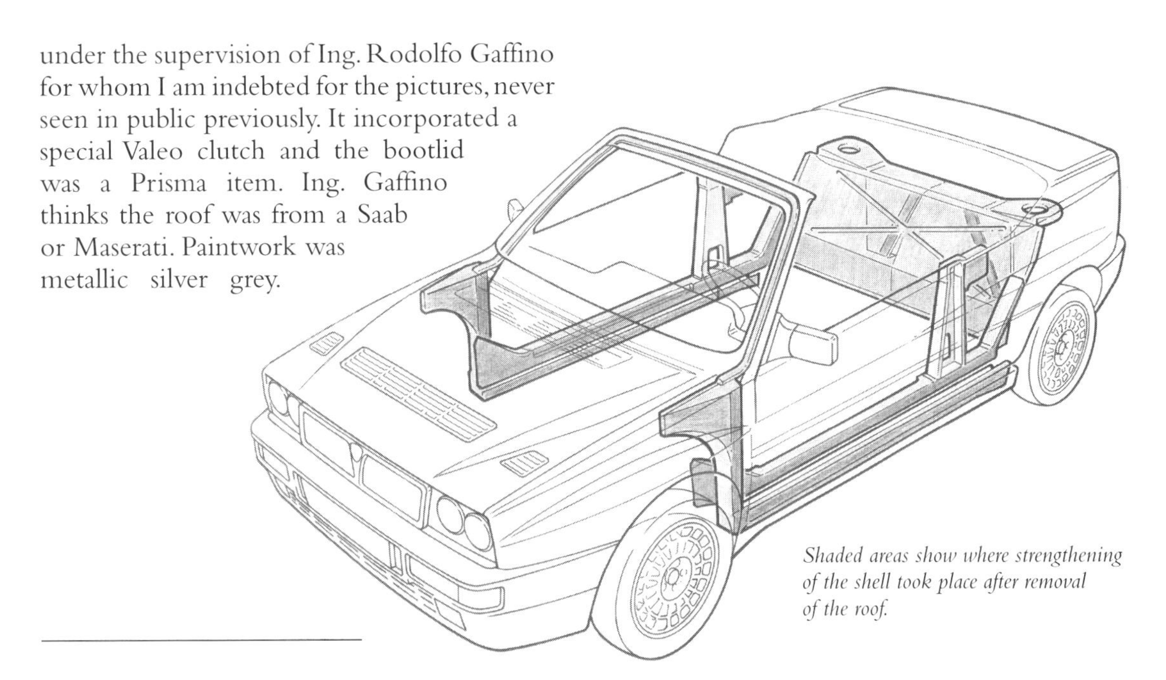

Shaded areas show where strengthening of the shell took place after removal of the roof.

Allegerita

This was just a proposal for a lightened car with more performance that never progressed beyond the concept stage, as it was clear that the whole integrale project was winding down.

Prototypes and Concept Cars

Orca

The world's press had been privileged to try Italdesign's Lancia Delta 4×4 Turbo in the spring of 1982 at La Mandria, but Giugiaro had also completed the design of a concept car on the same chassis and both were introduced to the public at that year's Turin Show in the autumn.

The full title of the concept car was the Lancia Delta 4×4 Turbo Orca. Although it was based on the Delta's chassis, Giugiaro had taken the opportunity to lengthen the wheelbase by 200mm (7.9in). It does not have integrale underpinnings but, as the sister of the pioneer of all the total-traction Deltas, it has a role to play in this book.

It gave Giugiaro the chance to air some of his visions and perhaps allowed him to give automotive manufacturers a prod in the direction in which he felt design should be heading. For instance, he was particularly concerned at the time with dashboard ergonomics. On an earlier design he had fitted all the required pushbuttons to the centre of the steering wheel, but the keyboard was free to turn with the wheel. On the Orca he repeated the concept but this time the keyboard was fixed to the steering wheel boss.

The package was what he considered an effective combination of a spacious passenger

Dashboard design Italdesign style. On the left is an early attempt where the push button pad moves round with the wheel. For the Orca the pad was fixed.

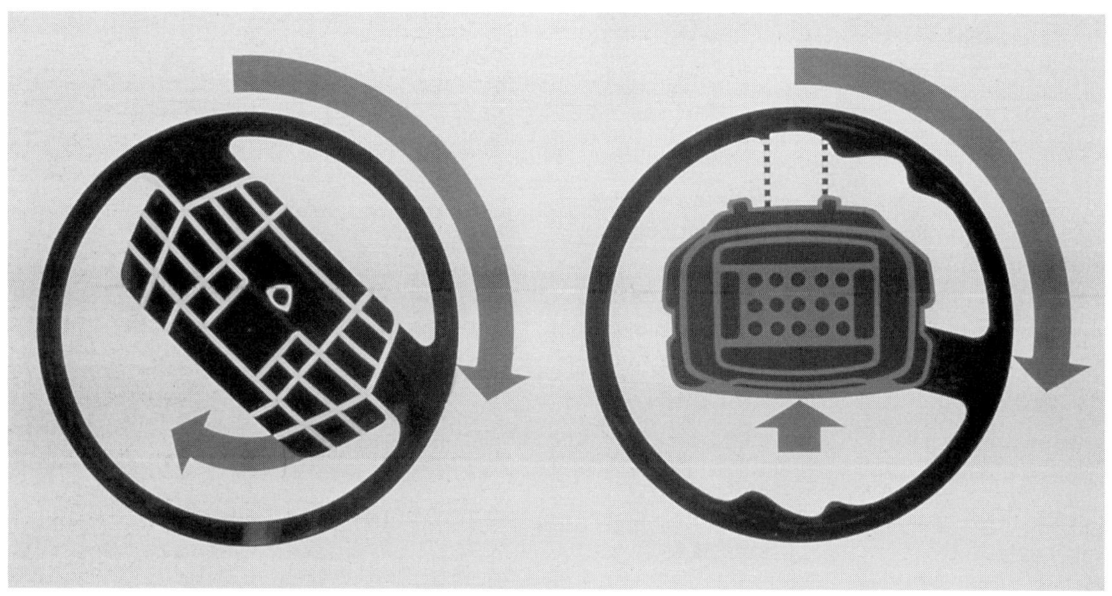

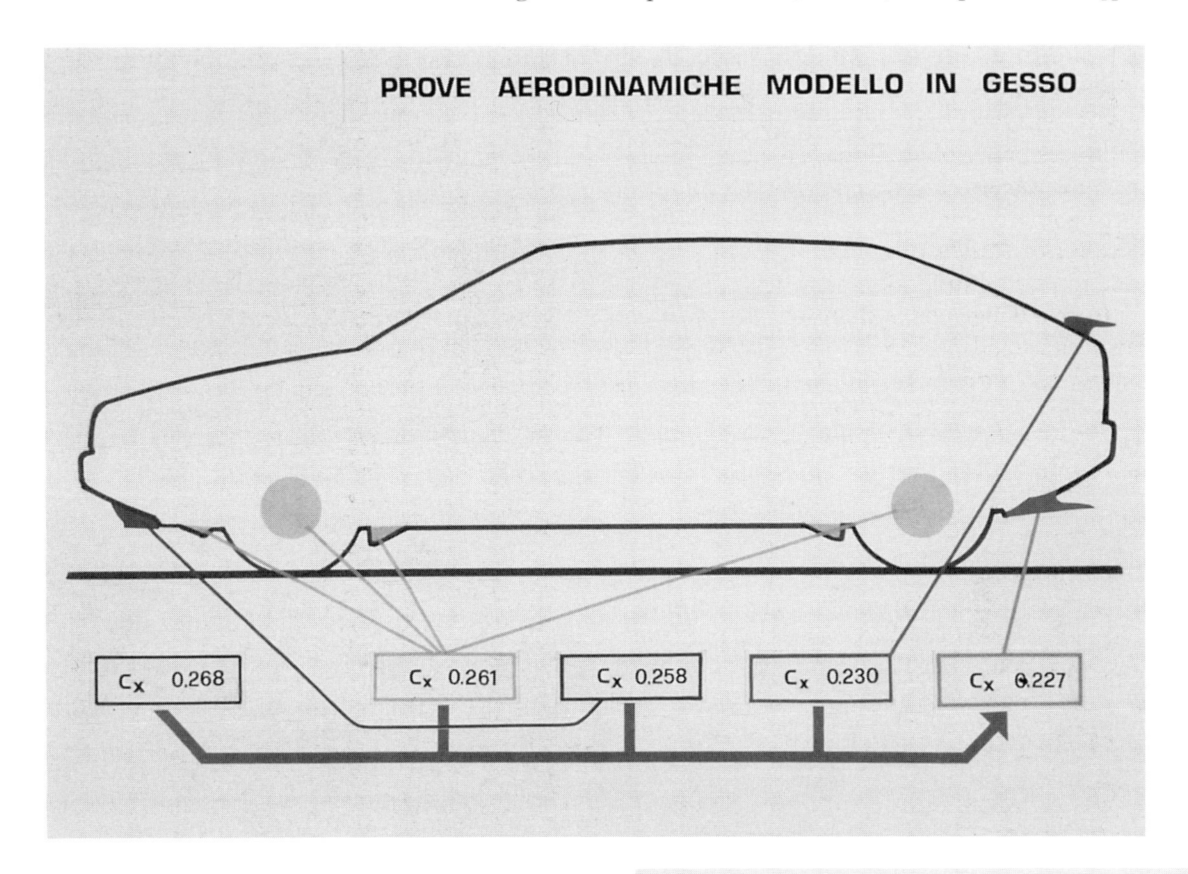

cabin allied to very effective aerodynamics. He asked himself whether it was possible to design a middleweight saloon that would enjoy a very low Cx factor.

He did not make life easy for himself by choosing the Delta as a basis. Its transverse engine stood tall, making it difficult to keep Orca's nose-profile low. Final wind-tunnel tests in November 1981 produced exactly what he wanted – a low Cx figure of 0.245, which figures were actually applied to the rear sides of the car. This was an extremely encouraging figure for a car designed with practicability as a priority and which offered more interior space than his Audi 80 with a virtually identical wheelbase.

Largely forgotten now, Orca was also one of the first practical car designs to utilize a front air dam and rear spoiler as means of reducing aerodynamic drag.

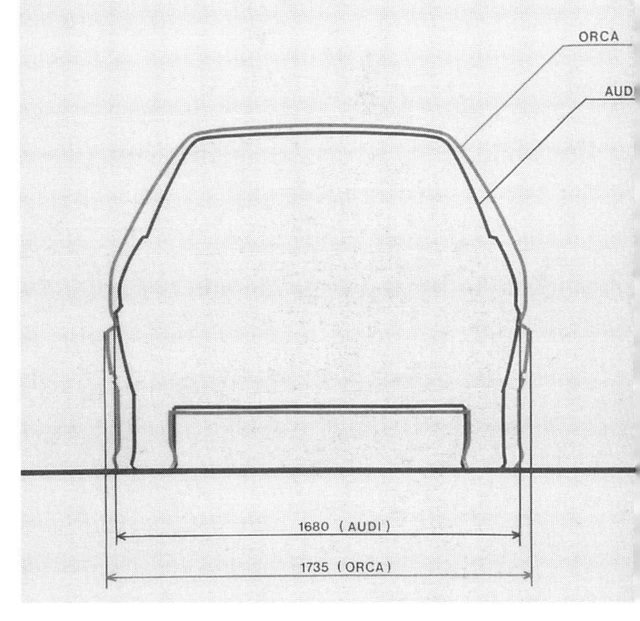

HIT

The HIT was a look by Pininfarina in 1988 into the possible uses and effects of modern composite materials in automotive applications.

According to the Turinese carozzeria it was an attempt to convey something of the flavour of a rally car in the design of a road car. Introduced to the public at the 1988 Turin Show, what better base was there to use than that of an integrale?

The finalized car actually only utilized the engine gearbox and four-wheel drive transmission mechanicals because the chassis was formed from carbon-fibre and the rest of the body was made of composite materials. A high roof allowed for a generous side glass area.

Particular attention was paid to the overall finish of the car, as the intention was to construct a sporting car of high performance allied to high quality finish and image.

Hyena

Artist Nani Tedeschi did some drawings for Andrea Zagato of a possible special two-seater coupé body that could utilize integrale underpinnings. Almost coincidentally. Paul Koot, a successful Dutch businessman and petrolhead Italophile, was thinking how sad it was that Lancia no longer sold Zagato-bodied versions of its sporting models.

The result was the Hyena, pronounced Heeaynar, and the classic drawings by Tedeschi depicting a Hyena animal morphing into the Hyena car were used as publicity.

This car was a sensational performer as its body was smaller, lighter and had considerably less frontal area than the integrale Evolution upon which it was based. Plans were drawn up to build a production run of seventy-five cars and Lancia's interest

The first prototype was photographed by Ing. Sergio Limone at the Paris show in 1992.

had been drawn by an IAD project based on the Dedra so they gave it its blessing.

Zagato built the first car with a steel superstructure on a Delta Evo 1 platform and built the body from aluminium using Kevlar for the doors, bumpers and much of the interior. The final result was exhibited at the 1992 Paris and 1993 Geneva shows receiving rave reviews. The price tag was high but much interest was generated.

As recounted in an earlier section of this book, management changes in Fiat started the beginning of the end of the integrale, so Lancia's interest simply evaporated.

Many a lesser person would have given up at that point, but instead, the project continued with the purchase of complete integrales, which were then stripped down for Hyena construction. This was obviously not only unsatisfactory and time-consuming but also added a substantial premium to the car's retail price. In the end only twenty-five examples, including the first prototype, were finished despite there being plans for roadster and spider versions.

The Hyena was born out of a great idea. It was a great car with great performance and handling and great looks. Its life was just cut tragically short by circumstance.

9 Buying and Driving: Happiness or Heartbreak?

Buying

The integrale has a pedigree second to none, because of that I would stick my neck out and say that in the future it will be the Lancia that most people remember. Phenomenally successful across the globe in premier league international motor sport, the car is somewhere near the top of virtually every enthusiast's wants list. One of the troubles though, is that they are also fairly high on the shopping list of car thieves so, if you do go ahead and purchase one, make sure that it is fitted with one of the best alarms you can buy, so you can keep it long enough to enjoy it. Your insurance company will insist anyway.

The first point to note is that there is no such thing as a cheap integrale. A service history is important but easy to falsify, so ensure that the bills are there to substantiate the car's story. I was shown a newly imported Evoluzione 1 from Italy that was considered to be in good condition. It looked immaculate and was generally very sound but still needed £1,500 (2002 prices) spent on it to replace bushes, brake discs, anti-roll bar drop-links and exhaust. None of these are substantial items in themselves, but all of them important.

Always go for the most expensive car you can afford. Low priced cars are just a waste of money. Even in good condition, a regularly used integrale will cost up to £2,000 a year in maintenance to keep on the road.

What are the problems to be looked for then?

Bodywork

With a performance car of this type, crash damage will always be a significant factor. Check for obvious signs such as the closing of the gap at the bottom of the A-pillar and for creases in the roof. Lift and check behind the windscreen rubber for evidence of a respray or rust. All cars gain stone chips on the A-pillars and bonnets, if there aren't any find out why. If there is a crack at the top, front corner of the driver's door aperture, it could be evidence of a front-end shunt and the same goes for signs of repair around the leading edge of the sunroof. Drain channels from the opening roof can block causing rust to start. At the rear, look above the top of the tailgate for evidence of any rust along the edge of the roof. This is the meeting point of three layers of metal and it is common on older cars for corrosion to set in along this edge. This can be very expensive to put right. The inner wings of 8v cars' are now beginning to become prone to rust.

Shut the doors and listen for the clunk. If there is a rattle it could mean that the door contains shattered glass left over from being broken into. Higher mileage/use cars will show wear on the seat bolsters and squabs. With the car stationary and the doors closed, get someone to turn the steering wheel from lock to lock and feel if the doors move. The bodyshell's rigidity is not great and reduces over time. A weak bodyshell can be felt by placing the heel of your hand just below the windscreen at the bottom of the A-pillar and feeling movement when the engine is revved.

It is important to ensure the shell is sound, as this is the whole basis of the car – other parts can always be replaced. Beware of uprated dampers as these can exacerbate body flexing.

Check the condition of the wheels; bad kerbing is always a sign that the car has not been well looked after. Wheels cost about £50 each for refurbishment.

Mechanicals

In general, all engines are robust. The 8v is almost bulletproof. All cars run happily on unleaded fuel. Richard Thorne's ran an 8v for 50,000 miles (80,045km) on 95 octane and found no problems whatsoever after a strip down. At that point the engine had covered a total of 133,000 miles (213,997km). Octane booster can be used and additives such as Millers VSP or Castrol Valvemaster, but they are not compulsory.

It is vital to use good synthetic oil and Barry Waterhouse recommends one with a cold start weight of a minimum of 10; the 16v uses oil through the turbo. Paul Baker advises that it is a good idea to check the oil level when cold, and then run the car for 1–2min before dipping it again. It is also a good idea to start the car up every day, whether it is to be driven or not, to ensure that oil is present in all parts of the engine. The lubricant drains down from the camshafts and, in some cases, bottom-end harshness can be experienced with the 16v due to the camshafts wearing and metal dropping into the sump and getting into the bearings. Under normal circumstances, oil consumption should be about 1ltr (0.22 gallons) every 600–700 miles (965–1,126km). In the case of a car that is driven hard, oil should be checked every time the petrol tank is filled. John Whalley has had cars in with no oil showing on the dipstick at all – 'must be a faulty dipstick!' is a remark he has hard more than once..

If you remove the bottom hose from the turbo to the inter-cooler and oil runs out, this could well be advance notice that the turbo is on its way out. Smoke from the exhaust usually indicates a turbo problem but beware of being sold a car with no oil in the turbo to stop it smoking. Check that the pick up pipe from the oil pump to the block has not been damaged, as in some cases these have been known to fracture leading to eventual engine failure.

Cambelts must be changed every 25,000–30,000 miles (40,225–48,270km) and Paul Baker recommends every 15,000–20,000 miles (21,135–32,180km) after that. Never leave the job until the handbook-recommended 36,000 miles (57,924km). Barry Waterhouse advises that over 50 per cent of cars he sees for the first time have belts that are over-tensioned, and it is common for the various plastic covers and plates to be missing. If the blue coolant temperature sensor fails, then this can result in the engine blowing out black smoke as the ECU tries to overcompensate on fuel delivery. Induction sensor failure in the distributor can cause the engine to die for no apparent reason. It is important that all connections from sensors are clean and good. The 8v relays, situated under the windscreen near the wiper motor, are subject to corrosion, so check if clean and making good contacts. If the engine revs go up and down at idle, the problem may only be a faulty idle control valve.

Beware, chipping is common. If done properly, with attention to all other ancillary parts, this may not be a problem, but it can cause serious engine difficulties otherwise. If the overboost solenoid has been disconnected, then the engine has probably been modified.

Transmission and Differentials

General opinion is that the diffs are robust and reasonably trouble-free. They definitely should not whine loudly – replacement could cost £1,800 each. Oil can leak from the output side of the front diff and the input end of the rear-pinion nuts may need restaking. Gearboxes can show weakness in third gear. If the box is rumbling it could be the bearings, which cost about £400–500 to fix.

Viewed from underneath: the Ferguson viscous coupling.

The only design problem on an Evoluzione: the anti-roll bar drop link.

A new clutch will set you back between £550 and £700, and it is a good idea to have the epicyclic torque converter checked at the same time, as this can become worn and need additional stakes applied. Clutches on 16v cars become heavy when they are worn; it is best to change both the master and slave cylinders when either require work.

A pinging sound as you drive away indicates the front prop-shaft joint has lost its grease and needs repacking. As always, use a synthetic grease.

Viewed from underneath: the Torsen rear differential.

A Torsen rear differential.

Suspension/Steering/Brakes

If any of the models have an inherent weakness or design fault, then the front anti-roll bar drop-links fitted to Evoluzione 1 and 2 cars are probably it. The rose-joints and links, as made at the factory, were of poor quality and need replacing every 5,000 miles (8,045km)at £80 each. If they have gone it is usually apparent from a tapping under the floor of the car when driving. Uprated parts are available and Barry Waterhouse reassembles them with grease. Barry has also known an Evo experience the anti-roll bar pulling away from the floor due to body flexing.

Suspension bushes, which can be heard clonking when worn, will probably need renewing (for about £300) on an annual basis on a frequently used car. Correct steering geometry is vital and the rear end should be set up first. If it is out, the front tyres wear on their inside edge but this could be caused only by the rear set up being out of alignment. Both front and rear dampers can leak and wear, especially at the top of the rears which can be enough to cause camber changes and lead to excessive tyre wear.

All integrales suffer from squeaky and noisy brakes, especially Evos. It is not possible to stop it. If the brakes are in good condition, a touch on the pedal should make the car slow down in a straight line. Rear brake calipers can seize up as they have less work to do than the fronts. Both TNI and Evo Engineering can rebuild them or supply rebuilt units. The front flexible hoses are prone to cracking. Check the rigid pipe from flexible to caliper for possible damage. Earlier model calipers can develop play, resulting in long pedal travel. The rear-brake compensator can cause trouble and, at worst, replacement may entail the removal of the petrol tank.

Anything else? Electrics are reasonably trouble-free, although the check panels on earlier cars often give false readings. If a car is not used much, the rear exhaust box will rust out at a cost of approximately £100 to replace.

If all of this sounds like a litany of disasters, I apologize. However, everyone I have spoken to, who has been involved with the integrale since it first appeared, has stressed many times that if you search for the right car, buy one sensibly and maintain it well, it will be one of the most rewarding purchases and driving experiences you will ever make. In good condition, these cars are icons, if you buy one you will own one of history's all time greats. Always remember to try to buy the very best you can afford. Top cars will always command top prices.

The trend today is towards buying the later Evoluzione cars as they are thought to be the very best of the bunch but some specialists consider a top condition 16v to be every bit the equal as far as driving satisfaction is concerned. It is now becoming extremely difficult to find very good original 16- and 8-valve cars, as accidents and modifications, such as after-market wheels and bonnet substitutions, become ever more common. These cars make excellent track-day cars, so altered examples are becoming more popular.

Driving

When the 16v was introduced, *Autocar* magazine had this to say:

> Once in a corner, the car's rear-biased torque-split is glaringly obvious. Gone is the old car's determined understeer on the limit.... A drifting front end can be eased back in line on the throttle, and even into oversteer if the corner is tight or the road slippery enough. Catching it with a twist of the steering and holding the integrale in a satisfying four-wheel drift soon becomes an experience that you seek out.... With 16 valves and all the chassis mods that go with them, the integrale gets serious, delivering more but demanding commitment. Work with it on a winding road, where every bend can conceal a different surface and the integrale 16v can satisfy like nothing else.

If you do decide to drive your four-wheel drive Delta to enjoy its considerable dynamic abilities and prodigious performance in this way, and there really would not be much point in having one otherwise, be warned, they WILL bite back under extreme provocation; it is a good idea to understand and experience these traits before it is too late. John Whalley, an accredited Lancia service agent from Bishop's Stortford, who has rallied integrales in the past, runs an occasional driving school to allow owners to experience and control the worst and enjoy the best of these cars.

John Whalley:

> Lower profile tyres give stiffer sidewalls and lower slip angles.... This gives better feel and response for a racetrack type performance, but it is also less forgiving of errors as the [slip] angles are smaller. This is not of benefit in a four-wheel drive car driven at the limit using that four-wheel drive ability as it limits the driver's options [due to the reduced margin of error much greater commitment and control are required to drive the car near the limit of grip]. It does, however, flatter to deceive if the car is driven within the tyres' limits in a conventional two wheel drive control manner.
>
> A tyre doesn't mind which direction it is working in as it will generate a specific amount of traction before it begins to slide across the road. Braking and accelerating whilst seeking

above *If you are going to do this…*

left and opposite top *…it is worth thinking about an integrale driving course.*

maximum cornering force will detract from the tyres' ability to deliver that maximum cornering force. The integrale allows us to take advantage of all this as it enables us to drive it using slightly different techniques to those normally accepted for other cars.

The driver of an integrale can influence the forces acting on the car's tyres in three ways: the traction forces of braking and accelerating, steering slip angles, weight distribution and thus grip available on each wheel. It is by varying these forces in combination that the integrale driver can make the car extract more from its tyres than many other cars, especially in adverse conditions.

The four-wheel drive integrale can display the attributes of both front and rear wheel drive cars. The trick is to be able to know when it will behave as one or the other and how to make it behave as one or the other. If you get the answer right the result is magic. If you get it wrong, the result will likely be more than confusing – it can be frightening. This is a condition that most integrale owners will have experienced at some time.

The message is clear. Treated with respect and understanding, the integrale will repay with staggering poise and agility; the alternative may well end in tears.

Appendix
Production Statistics

HF4WD, integrale,16v, New HF integrales

YEAR	NUMBER PRODUCED
1986	1566
1987	4339
1988	7509
1989	7967
1990	7054
1991	4646
1992	6992
1993	1996
1994	2227
TOTAL	44,296
HF4WD	5,298
8v	9,841
16v	12,860
CAT (8v)	2,700
Evo 1 and 2	13,597

Spot the difference: the full monty, a factory 16v evoluzione engine in the ex Dario Cerrato rally car (top) alongside a road car version in a Martini 6 special edition (bottom).

Further Reading

Abarth Catalogue Raisonne
Casucci, P. Lancia 037-S4-4WD-Integrale-16v Profili
d'Alessio, P. Martini Racing Story
Giugiaro Catalogue Raisonne
Holmes, M. Pirelli World rallying Titles
Klein, R. Rally Cars
Lancia Catalogue Raisonne
Ludvigsen, K. Classic Racing Engines
Mason, T. and Turner, S. Rallying
Oude Weernink, W. La Lancia
Philosophy of Innovation Lancia Various
Pininfarina Catalogue Raisonne
Robson, G. Fiat Sports Cars
Trow, N. Lancia Delta

Magazines
Autocar
Autosport
Car
Motor
Motor Sport

Dario Cerrato's workplace, now owned by Rodney Bennett.

Index

Whoosh, bang, whoosh, bang – or something like that! And there it was, gone.